Peterson's

MASTER THE
MILITARY FLIGHT
APTITUDE TESTS

7th Edition

Scott A. Ostrow
Lt. Col., USAF (Ret.)

PETERSON'S
A ⦿nelnet COMPANY

About Peterson's

To succeed on your lifelong educational journey, you will need accurate, dependable, and practical tools and resources. That is why Peterson's is everywhere education happens. Because whenever and however you need education content delivered, you can rely on Peterson's to provide the information, know-how, and guidance to help you reach your goals. Tools to match the right students with the right school. It's here. Personalized resources and expert guidance. It's here. Comprehensive and dependable education content—delivered whenever and however you need it. It's all here.

For more information, contact Peterson's, 2000 Lenox Drive, Lawrenceville, NJ 08648; 800-338-3282; or find us on the World Wide Web at www.petersons.com/about.

© 2009 Peterson's, a Nelnet company

Previous editions © 1989, 1994, 1997, 2000, 2002; © 2005 Solomon Wiener

Stephen Clemente, President; Bernadette Webster, Director of Publishing; Roger S. Williams, Sales and Marketing; Jill C. Schwartz, Editor; Ray Golaszewski, Manufacturing Manager; Linda M. Williams, Composition Manager

ISSN 1555-9793
ISBN 13: 978-0-7689-2793-1
ISBN 10: 0-7689-2793-5

Printed in the United States of America

10 9 8 7 6 5 4 3 2 1   11 10 09

Seventh Edition

By producing this book on recycled paper (40% post consumer waste) 213 trees were saved.

Petersons.com/publishing

Check out our Web site at www.petersons.com/publishing to see if there is any new information regarding the test and any revisions or corrections to the content of this book. We've made sure the information in this book is accurate and up-to-date; however, the test format or content may have changed since the time of publication.

Contents

PART III: QUESTIONS TYPES IN MILITARY FLIGHT APTITUDE TESTS

PART IV: THREE PRACTICE TESTS

Before You Begin

Congratulations! You have in your hands a powerful tool to ensure your best chances of getting a great score on one of the military flight aptitude tests. By taking time to work on the sample exercises in this book, studying the strategies and techniques for tackling each question type, and taking the full-length Practice Test and reviewing the answers and explanations, you will gain experience in answering real test questions and give yourself a significant advantage in achieving a top-notch score on your military flight aptitude test.

This book contains information on:

- careers in military aviation, including how to qualify, pay and benefits, and specific job descriptions
- flight training in the Air Force, Army, Navy, Marine Corps, and Coast Guard
- strategies for tackling multiple-choice test questions
- the Air Force Officer Qualifying Test (AFOQT) and its subtests
- the Army Flight Aptitude Selection Test (AFAST) and its subtests
- the Navy and Marine Corps Aviation Selection Test Battery (ASTB) and its subtests

HOW TO USE THIS BOOK

The book is designed as a self-training course, complete with test-taking tips and strategies, exercises, and three full-length Practice Tests. Every answer in the book comes with a detailed explanation. You learn immediately why a correct answer is correct and why a wrong answer is wrong. Studying the answer explanations for all the questions in your test—even those you answer correctly—will serve as a course in itself.

- **Part I** provides an overview of the opportunities and benefits available to military pilots, navigators, and flight officers. Officer rank structure, pay and benefits, and general commissioning requirements are covered in detail. You'll also find thorough information about how to get on the path to a career in military aviation, including available training and programs, for each branch of the Armed Forces.

- **Part II** explains three different military flight aptitude tests: the AFOQT, AFAST, and ASTB. You'll find comprehensive information about each subtest, including the number of questions you'll encounter and the length of every subtest, with special strategies for answering multiple-choice questions and top-notch tips on how to prepare for test day.

- **Part III** explains the kinds of questions you can expect on the AFOQT, AFAST, and ASTB. We include plenty of examples of every question type you are likely to encounter. This section also contains sample questions and practice exercises with detailed answer explanations.

- **Part IV** offers full-length AFOQT, AFAST, and ASTB Practice Tests. Each Practice Test is followed by an answer key with detailed explanations. For the AFOQT, you'll also find 110 sample Self-Description Inventory questions; we've provided sample questions for the Background Information and Self Description sections of the AFAST as well. To accurately measure your performance on these Practice Tests, be sure to adhere strictly to the stated time limits for each subtest.

SPECIAL STUDY FEATURES

Master the Military Flight Aptitude Tests is designed to be as user-friendly as it is complete. To this end, it includes these features to make your preparation more efficient.

Overview

Each chapter begins with a bulleted overview listing the topics covered in the chapter. This allows you to quickly target the areas in which you are most interested.

Summing It Up

Each chapter ends with a point-by-point summary that captures the most important points in the chapter. The summaries offer a convenient way to review key points.

YOU'RE WELL ON YOUR WAY TO SUCCESS

You've made the decision to seek a career in military aviation and have taken a very important step in the process. *Master the Military Flight Aptitude Tests* will help you get on the path you need to take to achieve your goal—from scoring high on your exam to becoming a military pilot, navigator, or flight officer in the U.S. Armed Forces.

GIVE US YOUR FEEDBACK

Peterson's publishes a full line of resources to help guide you through the career search process. Peterson's publications can be found at your local bookstore, library, and high school or college guidance office. You can also access us online at www.petersons.com.

We welcome any comments or suggestions you may have about this publication and invite you to complete our online survey at www.petersons.com/booksurvey. Or you can fill out the survey at the back of this book, tear it out, and mail it to us at:

Publishing Department
Peterson's, a Nelnet Company
2000 Lenox Drive
Lawrenceville, NJ 08648

Your feedback will help us make your education dreams possible.

PART I

MILITARY FLIGHT BASICS

CHAPTER 1 From Officer to Aviator: What
You Need to Know

From Officer to Aviator: What You Need to Know

OVERVIEW

- General information about military aviation
- So you want to become a commissioned officer
- Pay and benefits for military flight officers
- Officer rank structure
- General commissioning requirements
- The path to becoming an officer
- Summing it up

Thousands of the individuals who apply for commissioning programs in the U.S. military each year dream of a career in aviation. If you are reading this book, you are probably one of those hoping to join this elite group. This book will help you prepare for the various flight aptitude tests used by the military in part to determine your eligibility for a military flight training program. In addition to being a study guide, this book will also provide useful information to help you choose the commissioning path that's right for you.

As a commissioned officer, you will join the ranks of thousands who have come before you and will participate in a rich history and heritage that comes with serving your country.

GENERAL INFORMATION ABOUT MILITARY AVIATION

The U.S. military flies the most technologically advanced aircraft in the world. From supersonic fighters and bombers to giant cargo planes, from surveillance aircraft to weather-observation planes, from search-and-rescue helicopters to close-combat support planes and helicopters, U.S. military aircraft and the men and women who fly them serve in a wide variety of missions.

All military branches use airplanes and helicopters and therefore need pilots. With the exception of the Army, the military branches also need airplane navigators.

Airplane Pilots

In the movies, military airplane pilots simply hop into their aircraft and fly off. A real pilot's job begins long before he or she ever climbs into the aircraft cockpit. The day usually starts with planning the mission and developing flight plans,

3

routes, and timelines. Mission planning also includes checking weather conditions throughout the entire mission area.

Aircraft commanders are responsible for running through pre-flight checks to ensure that the aircraft used for the mission is flight-ready. Once in the air, pilots are responsible not only for flying the aircraft but also for continually monitoring its systems.

Pilots, especially those who fly fighter jets, may perform breathtaking maneuvers. These maneuvers require pilots in top physical form; they must also have 20/20 vision or better and excellent eye-hand coordination.

TRAINING FOR AIRPLANE PILOTS

As with any other military officer occupation, airplane pilots undergo extensive training and preparation—but pilot training is perhaps the longest and most intense instruction of all military officer training programs. Depending on the service branch and type of aircraft, pilot training can take two years or longer.

Initial training involves classroom instruction and flight simulator training and typically includes instruction on:

- Federal Aviation Administration (FAA) regulations
- Aircraft aerodynamics
- Aircraft propulsion (operation of aircraft engines)
- Aircraft navigation systems

Pilot training not only requires people who are intelligent and in excellent physical condition, but it also requires individuals who can perform several tasks at once, who can remain calm in extremely stressful situations, and—most important—who can master the "art" of flying. For these reasons, many individuals who begin their pilot training do not complete it. For those who do and who earn their pilot wings, the next step is advanced training. This prepares newly minted pilots to fly particular types of aircraft.

Helicopter Pilots

Just like airplane pilots, military helicopter pilots must meet demanding physical and mental requirements, and they must train to fly several models of helicopters, designed for different types of missions.

Like airplane pilots, helicopter pilots begin their days with mission planning, perform pre-flight checks, and, once in the air, continually monitor the status of their aircraft. Helicopter flight, however, tends to be more "up close and personal" than airplane flight. These pilots fly against enemy targets, transport military troops and cargo, and perform search-and-rescue missions.

They must take off and land in a range of situations and environments, many of which require them to maneuver safely in very close quarters. Helicopters are well-suited for reaching areas that are inaccessible to fixed-winged aircraft because they can move vertically and horizontally.

Except for the Army, which permits Warrant Officers to become helicopter pilots, every military branch requires its helicopter pilots to be commissioned officers. We will cover Army Warrant Officers in the next chapter.

TRAINING FOR HELICOPTER PILOTS

Depending on the type of aircraft one pilots, helicopter training may take up to two years, including classroom instruction and flight training. Flight training typically consists of learning:

- helicopter operation
- flying techniques
- emergency procedures
- combat skills and tactics

Airplane Navigators

It is an airplane navigator's responsibility to keep the aircraft on course and, depending on the aircraft type, to act as another set of eyes for the pilot during demanding flying missions. Airplane navigators may also perform bombing duties. To perform their jobs well, they rely on radar, radio, and a variety of other navigation equipment. Just like pilots, navigators must assist in planning missions, plotting courses, checking weather, and gathering target intelligence.

Navigators must be in top physical condition and are subjected to many of the same physical requirements as pilots. Although excellent vision is required, navigators are not required to have 20/20 vision, so individuals who have a strong desire to fly but do not meet the pilot vision standards often opt to apply for a position as an airplane navigator.

TRAINING FOR NAVIGATORS

Navigators spend many hours training in flight simulators and under actual flight conditions, as well as logging hours in the classroom. A typical course curriculum includes:

- Principles of navigation, including combat bombing procedures
- Operation of communication, weapon, and radar systems

Navigators in the Air Force, Navy, and Marine Corps undergo similar training and perform similar functions. Naval flight officers receive advanced training to take up specific positions such as radar intercept officers, bombardier/navigators, tactical coordinators, and airborne electronic warfare specialists. Marine Corps flight officers receive advanced training as radar intercept officers, tactical navigators, electronic countermeasure officers, and weapons and sensors officers.

SO YOU WANT TO BECOME A COMMISSIONED OFFICER

Serving as a commissioned officer in the U.S. military has many benefits, including:

- Competitive pay
- Life insurance coverage of $400,000 at a very low cost (as well as life insurance for one's family)
- Thirty days of vacation each year
- Retirement eligibility after twenty years
- Education benefits for earning an advanced degree
- Thrift savings plan (for additional retirement funds)
- Responsibility and leadership positions at an early age
- Tax-free shopping at base stores and commissaries

A career in the military is not without its drawbacks, however. Keep in mind that it comes with certain disadvantages, just like any other career:

- Inconsistent work hours
- Hazardous working conditions and locations
- Family separations due to assignments and/or deployments
- Frequent family moves
- Undesirable job locations

PAY AND BENEFITS FOR MILITARY FLIGHT OFFICERS

Military officers' pay once greatly lagged behind that of their civilian counterparts. Today, however, that is not the case. In addition to basic pay, officers may receive additional pay that is often tax-exempt—thereby increasing an officer's pay scale so that it surpasses that of comparable civilian positions. In addition to pay raises based on promotion, military members receive longevity pay raises based on the number of years they have served. They typically also receive annual cost-of-living pay increases.

Incentive Pay and Allowances

Military aviators receive monthly flight pay. The amount of flight pay varies, depending on several factors that include flight status and experience level.

Military officers receive some pay in the form of allowances, which are usually tax-exempt. For instance, officers living off-base receive a tax-exempt monthly housing allowance based on marital status, rank, and location. In 2008, monthly housing allowances for officers ranged from approximately $500 to $4,000. Officers also receive a monthly allowance for food, called Basic Allowance for Subsistence (BAS), which was $223.04 as of January 1, 2009.

Most military officers begin their careers as an 0–1 (Second Lieutenant in the Army, Air Force, and Marine Corps, and Ensign in the Navy and Coast Guard). For up-to-date and detailed information about military pay and allowances, visit the Defense Finance and Accounting Service (DFAS) Web site: www.dfas.mil. This site is an excellent tool, not only as you research military aviator opportunities, but also in the future for managing and keeping track of your pay and allowances.

Many other benefits are available to military officers in addition to base pay: retirement benefits, education benefits, and guaranteed home loans.

Retirement Benefits

Military members are eligible for retirement after serving twenty years. Active-duty retirees receive 50 percent of their base pay at the time of their retirement; National Guard and Reserve retirees receive a percentage of their base pay based on the number of "points" they have accumulated. They may not start receiving retirement pay (pension) until they have reached age 60 (although there are bills now being considered that would lower that age restriction). The major drawback of a military pension is that after a veteran dies, his or her pension cannot be passed on to surviving family members unless the veteran enrolled in an insurance program called the Survivors Benefit Plan.

Many military officers choose to remain in the service longer than twenty years. For these officers, active duty retirement pay is increased at 2.5 percent of their base pay for every year past twenty, usually up to a total of thirty years, depending on pay grade. Therefore, an active-duty member retiring after thirty years will receive a pension of 75 percent of his or her base pay. In recent years, many military members have begun participating in the Thrift Savings Plan. Previously available only to civil servants, this plan allows military members to contribute to their savings using pre-tax dollars.

Retirees from the military are also eligible for continuation of health-care benefits at no or little cost to them, depending on the level of insurance they selected. Base store and facilities privileges are continued as well.

Education Benefits

Numerous education benefits are available for military officers who wish to further their education, including the Montgomery GI Bill–Active Duty, the Montgomery GI Bill–Selected Reserve, the Post–9/11 GI Bill, the Tuition Assistance Program, and the Survivors' and Dependents' Educational Assistance Program (DEA).

MONTGOMERY GI BILL—ACTIVE DUTY

The Montgomery GI Bill–Active Duty (MGIB–AD) provides up to thirty-six months of education benefits to eligible veterans for:

- two-year or four-year college degree programs
- technical or vocational courses
- correspondence courses
- apprenticeship/job training
- flight training
- high-tech industry training
- licensing and certification tests

- entrepreneurship training
- certain entrance examinations

In general, to be eligible for the MGIB–AD (also known as Chapter 30), you must meet these requirements:

- entered active duty after June 30, 1985
- paid the $1,200 contribution (deducted from pay, with the option to add $600 for enhanced benefits)
- served on active duty for a period equal to or greater than the initial enlistment period

The monthly benefit is based on the type of training, length of your service, category, and whether the Department of Defense contributed extra money (called "kickers") in your MGIB Fund. You can use the MGIB–AD benefit while on active duty after you serve a minimum of twenty-four months or after you've completed your service duty. You usually have ten years to use your MGIB benefits, but this time limit can vary depending on individual circumstances. Currently, the Army is the only branch of the military that permits MGIB benefits to be transferred to dependents. Additional details about eligibility and benefits can be found at the Department of Veterans Affairs (VA) Web site: www.gibill.va.gov, or call 888-GI-BILL-1 (888-442-4551) toll-free.

MONTGOMERY GI BILL—SELECTED RESERVE

The Montgomery GI Bill–Selected Reserve (MGIB–SR) program may be available if you are a member of the Selected Reserve, which includes the Army, Navy, Air Force, Marine Corps, and Coast Guard Reserves and the Army and Air National Guards. You may be entitled to receive up to thirty-six months of education benefits for:

- degree and certificate programs
- flight training
- apprenticeship training
- on-the-job training
- correspondence courses
- remedial, deficiency, and refresher courses (approved in certain situations)

For eligibility requirements and benefit details, check out the VA's Web site at www.gibill.va.gov.

THE POST–9/11 GI BILL

In 2008, Congress approved the Post–9/11 Veteran's Educational Assistance Act, sometimes referred to as the New GI Bill. This program provides thirty-six months of education benefits to individuals who have served at least ninety days of active duty on or after September 11, 2001, or those discharged with a service-related disability after thirty days of service. This bill becomes effective for training on or after August 1, 2009.

For those who are eligible, the Post–9/11 GI Bill will pay:

- tuition and fees, not exceeding the maximum in-state costs at a public college or university
- a monthly housing allowance at the location of the school, based on the Basic Allowance for Housing for an E-5 with dependents
- an annual stipend of $1,000 for books and supplies, paid proportionately based on enrollment
- a one-time rural benefit payment for eligible individuals

Funded by the Department of Defense, the Post–9/11 GI Bill does not require service members to contribute to the program. Benefits must be used within fifteen years of service completion. In addition, learning must take place at a traditional educational institution, so service members who are enrolled solely in online training or are still in the military will not receive the housing allowance or the stipend for books and supplies. Unlike the MGIB, the benefits under the Post–9/11 GI Bill can be transferred to your spouse and children, as long as the request is approved by the Department of Defense.

For the most up-to-date information about the Post–9/11 GI Bill, visit the VA's GI Bill Web site: www.gibill.va.gov.

TUITION ASSISTANCE PROGRAM

Military members can take advantage of the Tuition Assistance (TA) program while serving on active duty or while in the National Guard or Reserve. The program defrays the cost of tuition; in return, the service member agrees to remain on active duty for two years after completing the TA-funded courses. The Tuition Assistance program funds 100 percent of:

- tuition costs for high school completion, up to a maximum of $4,500 per fiscal year
- institution charges for tuition
- instructional fees
- lab fees
- computer fees
- mandatory enrollment fees

Funding will not exceed $250 per semester hour equivalent and $4,500 per individual per fiscal year. TA funds do not cover the cost of books or costs for lower or lateral degrees, such as a second associate degree or bachelor's degree.

SURVIVORS' AND DEPENDENTS' EDUCATIONAL ASSISTANCE PROGRAM (DEA)

The Survivors' and Dependents' Educational Assistance Program provides education and training opportunities to eligible dependents of veterans who are permanently and totally disabled as the result of a service-related condition, or who died while on active duty or as a result of a service-related condition. The DEA program offers up to forty-five months of education benefits for:

- degree and certificate programs
- apprenticeships

on-the-job training

correspondence courses (for spouses)

remedial, deficiency, and refresher courses (approved under certain circumstances)

Guaranteed Home Loans

VA-guaranteed loans have been helping veterans realize their dreams of home ownership since the end of WWII. It does not provide mortgages, but it does offer a guarantee of payment to mortgage companies and banks on behalf of service members. This enables service members to obtain a mortgage with no down payment. A funding fee is charged, but it can be worked into the mortgage. Because of the guarantee from the VA, service members need not pay the Private Mortgage Insurance (PMI), which homebuyers with a down payment of less than 20 percent are usually required to pay.

OFFICER RANK STRUCTURE

When referring to military rank, the terms "pay grade" and "rank" are often used interchangeably. However, they have different definitions.

Pay grade refers to the number classification of an officer and is linked to how much that officer is paid. All officer pay grades begin with the letter "O," while enlisted members' pay grades begin with the letter "E." Officers in all branches of the military serve in pay grades of O-1 through O-10. The corresponding ranks linked to those number designators are called by different names depending on the branch of service. For instance an O-3 in the Navy is a lieutenant, but an O-3 in the Air Force is a captain. Therefore, a member of the Air Force who has the pay grade of O-3 and the rank of captain is equivalent in rank to a member of the Navy who has the pay grade of O-3 and the rank of Lieutenant.

Although most military officers start out as an O-1 and then progress through the ranks, very few make it to O-10. The charts on pages 11 and 12 illustrate the pay grades and their ranks for each military branch.

GENERAL COMMISSIONING REQUIREMENTS

Each branch of the military sets its own qualification standards for commissioned officers. The standards may exceed those set by the Department of Defense (DoD), but they may not be less stringent. On page 13, there is a "general" list of qualifications. For specific requirements, you should check out Peterson's *Master the Officer Candidate Tests*. Please note that requirements do change from time to time, so it is important to check with recruiting officials (or admissions counselors) for the most up-to-date information.

U.S. MILITARY OFFICER RANKS AND PAY GRADES

	ARMY	NAVY / COAST GUARD	MARINES	AIR FORCE
O1	Second Lieutenant (2LT)	Ensign (ENS)	Second Lieutenant (2nd Lt.)	Second Lieutenant (2nd Lt.)
O2	First Lieutenant (1LT)	Lieutenant Junior Grade (LTJG)	First Lieutenant (1st Lt.)	First Lieutenant (1st Lt.)
O3	Captain (CPT)	Lieutenant (LT)	Captain (Capt.)	Captain (Capt.)
O4	Major (MAJ)	Lieutenant Commander (LCDR)	Major (Maj.)	Major (Maj.)
O5	Lieutenant Colonel (LTC)	Commander (CDR)	Lieutenant Colonel (Lt. Col.)	Lieutenant Colonel (Lt. Col.)
O6	Colonel (COL)	Captain (CAPT)	Colonel (Col.)	Colonel (Col.)
O7	Brigadier General (BG)	Rear Admiral Lower Half (RDML)	Brigadier General (Brig. Gen.)	Brigadier General (Brig. Gen.)
O8	Major General (MG)	Rear Admiral Upper Half (RADM)	Major General (Maj. Gen.)	Major General (Maj. Gen.)
O9	Lieutenant General (LTG)	Vice Admiral (VADM)	Lieutenant General (Lt. Gen.)	Lieutenant General (Lt. Gen.)
O10	General (GEN): Army Chief of Staff	Admiral (ADM): Chief of Naval Operations and Commandant of the Coast Guard	General (Gen.): Commandant of the Marine Corps	General (Gen.): Air Force Chief of Staff
—	General of the Army (Reserved for wartime only)	Fleet Admiral (Reserved for wartime only)		General of the Air Force (Reserved for wartime only)

MONTHLY BASIC PAY TABLE

EFFECTIVE 1 JANUARY 2009

YEARS OF SERVICE

COMMISSIONED OFFICERS

PAY GRADE	<2	2	3	4	6	8	10	12	14	16	18	20	22	24	26	28	30	32	34	36	38	40
O-10	0.00	0.00	0.00	0.00	0.00	0.00	0.00	0.00	0.00	0.00	0.00	14688.60	14750.10	14750.10	14750.10	14750.10	14750.10	14750.10	14750.10	14750.10	14750.10	14750.10
O-9	0.00	0.00	0.00	0.00	0.00	0.00	0.00	0.00	0.00	0.00	0.00	12846.90	13032.00	13299.30	13765.80	13765.80	14454.60	14454.60	14750.10	14750.10	14750.10	14750.10
O-8	9090.00	9387.60	9585.30	9640.50	9887.10	10299.00	10395.00	10786.20	10898.10	11235.30	11722.20	12172.20	12472.50	12472.50	12472.50	12472.50	12784.50	12784.50	13104.30	13104.30	13104.30	13104.30
O-7	7553.10	7904.10	8066.40	8195.40	8429.10	8660.10	8926.80	9192.90	9460.20	10299.00	11007.30	11007.30	11007.30	11007.30	11063.10	11063.10	11284.50	11284.50	11284.50	11284.50	11284.50	11284.50
O-6	5598.30	6150.30	6553.80	6553.80	6578.70	6860.70	6897.90	6897.90	7290.00	7983.30	8390.10	8796.60	9027.90	9262.20	9716.70	9716.70	9910.80	9910.80	9910.80	9910.80	9910.80	9910.80
O-5	4666.80	5257.20	5621.40	5689.80	5916.60	6052.80	6351.60	6570.60	6853.80	7287.00	7493.40	7697.40	7928.70	7928.70	7928.70	7928.70	7928.70	7928.70	7928.70	7928.70	7928.70	7928.70
O-4	4026.90	4661.40	4972.20	5041.80	5330.40	5640.00	6025.20	6325.50	6534.30	6654.00	6723.30	6723.30	6723.30	6723.30	6723.30	6723.30	6723.30	6723.30	6723.30	6723.30	6723.30	6723.30
O-3	3540.30	4013.40	4332.00	4722.90	4948.80	5197.20	5358.00	5622.30	5759.70	5759.70	5759.70	5759.70	5759.70	5759.70	5759.70	5759.70	5759.70	5759.70	5759.70	5759.70	5759.70	5759.70
O-2	3058.80	3483.90	4012.50	4148.10	4233.30	4233.30	4233.30	4233.30	4233.30	4233.30	4233.30	4233.30	4233.30	4233.30	4233.30	4233.30	4233.30	4233.30	4233.30	4233.30	4233.30	4233.30
O-1	2655.30	2763.60	3340.50	3340.50	3340.50	3340.50	3340.50	3340.50	3340.50	3340.50	3340.50	3340.50	3340.50	3340.50	3340.50	3340.50	3340.50	3340.50	3340.50	3340.50	3340.50	3340.50

COMMISSIONED OFFICERS WITH OVER 4 YEARS ACTIVE DUTY SERVICE AS AN ENLISTED MEMBER OR WARRANT OFFICER

PAY GRADE	<2	2	3	4	6	8	10	12	14	16	18	20	22	24	26	28	30	32	34	36	38	40
O-3E	0.00	0.00	0.00	0.00	4948.80	5197.20	5358.00	5622.30	5844.90	5972.70	6146.70	6146.70	6146.70	6146.70	6146.70	6146.70	6146.70	6146.70	6146.70	6146.70	6146.70	6146.70
O-2E	0.00	0.00	0.00	4148.10	4233.30	4368.30	4595.70	4771.50	4902.30	4902.30	4902.30	4902.30	4902.30	4902.30	4902.30	4902.30	4902.30	4902.30	4902.30	4902.30	4902.30	4902.30
O-1E	0.00	0.00	0.00	3340.50	3567.60	3699.30	3834.30	3966.60	4148.10	4148.10	4148.10	4148.10	4148.10	4148.10	4148.10	4148.10	4148.10	4148.10	4148.10	4148.10	4148.10	4148.10

WARRANT OFFICERS

PAY GRADE	<2	2	3	4	6	8	10	12	14	16	18	20	22	24	26	28	30	32	34	36	38	40
W-5	0.00	0.00	0.00	0.00	0.00	0.00	0.00	0.00	0.00	0.00	0.00	6505.50	6835.60	7081.20	7353.60	7353.60	7721.40	7721.40	8107.50	8107.50	8513.10	8513.10
W-4	3658.50	3935.70	4048.80	4159.80	4351.20	4540.50	4732.20	5021.10	5274.00	5514.60	5711.40	5903.40	6185.70	6417.30	6681.90	6681.90	6815.40	6815.40	6815.40	6815.40	6815.40	6815.40
W-3	3340.80	3480.30	3622.80	3669.90	3819.60	4114.20	4420.80	4565.10	4731.90	4904.10	5213.10	5422.20	5547.30	5680.20	5860.80	5860.80	5860.80	5860.80	5860.80	5860.80	5860.80	5860.80
W-2	2956.50	3236.10	3322.20	3381.60	3573.30	3871.20	4018.80	4164.30	4341.90	4480.80	4606.80	4757.10	4856.40	4935.00	4935.00	4935.00	4935.00	4935.00	4935.00	4935.00	4935.00	4935.00
W-1	2595.30	2874.00	2949.60	3108.30	3296.10	3572.70	3701.70	3882.30	4059.90	4148.40	4328.10	4484.40	4484.40	4484.40	4484.40	4484.40	4484.40	4484.40	4484.40	4484.40	4484.40	4484.40

NOTE—BASIC PAY FOR 07-O10 IS LIMITED TO LEVEL II OF THE EXECUTIVE SCHEDULE ($14,750.10)

NOTE—BASIC PAY FOR O6 AND BELOW IS LIMITED TO LEVEL V OF THE EXECUTIVE SCHEDULE ($11,958.30)

FY2009, 3.9% Pay Raise Increase. Public Law No 110-417 National Defense Auth Act, signed into law on October 14, 2008.

Level II and Level V of the Executive Schedule increased by 2.8%.

GENERAL QUALIFICATION REQUIREMENTS
FOR BECOMING A COMMISSIONED OFFICER*

Age	Must be between 19 and 30 years for OCS/OTS; 17 and 21 years for ROTC; 17 and 22 years for the service academies.
Citizenship Status	Must be a U.S. citizen.
Physical Condition	Must meet minimum physical standards listed below. Some occupations have additional physical standards. Height (both males and females): Maximum—6'5" Minimum—4'10" Weight—There are minimum and maximum weights, according to age and height, for males and females. Vision: There are minimum vision standards. (For flight training vision requirements, see page 22.) Overall Health: Must be in good health and pass a medical exam. Certain diseases or conditions, such as diabetes, severe allergies, epilepsy, alcoholism, or drug addiction may exclude persons from enlistment.
Education	Must have a four-year college degree from an accredited institution. Some occupations require advanced degrees or four-year degrees in a particular field.
Aptitude	Must achieve the minimum entry score on an officer qualification test (or SAT, ACT, or ASVAB, depending on service).
Moral character	Must meet standards designed to screen out people unlikely to become successful officers. Standards cover court convictions, juvenile delinquency, arrests, and drug use.
Marital Status and Dependents	May be either single or married for ROTC, OCS/OTS, and direct appointment pathways. Must be single to enter and graduate from service academies. Number of allowable dependents varies by branch of service.
Waivers	On a case-by-case basis, exceptions (waivers) are granted by individual services for some of the above qualification requirements.

* Each service sets its own qualification requirements for officers.

THE PATH TO BECOMING AN OFFICER

Although there are four basic avenues available to becoming an officer, only three are available for those individuals desiring a career in aviation. The fourth avenue, "Direct Appointment," is reserved for health-care, legal, and religious professionals. The three available avenues for military aviators are:

- Reserve Officers' Training Corps (ROTC)
- Officer Candidate School (OCS) and Officer Training School (OTS)
- Service Academies

In the chart below, note that, by far, the greatest percentage of officers (approximately 40 percent) is commissioned through the ROTC.

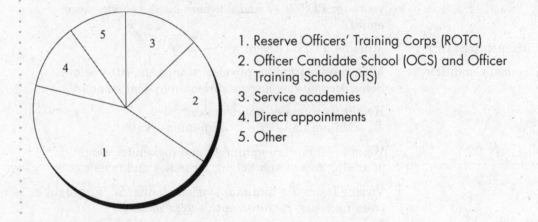

1. Reserve Officers' Training Corps (ROTC)
2. Officer Candidate School (OCS) and Officer Training School (OTS)
3. Service academies
4. Direct appointments
5. Other

Reserve Officers' Training Corps (ROTC)

Reserve Officers' Training Corps (ROTC) programs can be found at many public and private colleges and universities throughout the United States. Despite the name, the primary purpose of these programs is to educate and then commission individuals for active-duty service (although they receive what is called a Reserve commission). Although most graduates of ROTC programs go right to active duty, some individuals do go on to serve in the National Guard or Reserve.

ROTC is taken as an elective course with mandatory participation in additional activities, such as physical fitness training, in order to receive a commission upon graduation. Depending on the branch of service, students may participate in ROTC from two to four years in order to qualify for partial to full scholarships. Also, many colleges offer ROTC scholarship recipients additional scholarships and grants that may cover any tuition costs above the ROTC "cap," as well as room and board expenses. In addition, ROTC scholarship recipients also receive a monthly stipend (pay) as well as monies to help defray the cost of books. In return for receiving the ROTC scholarship, the student must agree to serve in the military upon graduation.

ROTC scholarships are competitive, and students must meet not only academic requirements but also moral and physical standards as well. Most ROTC scholarships are awarded to graduating high school seniors; however, scholarships are also awarded to current college students, as well as active-duty enlisted personnel.

For more information about ROTC scholarships, college students should contact the ROTC unit at their school. High school students may contact the ROTC program for the branch of their choice by visiting the following Web sites:

- Air Force: www.afrotc.com
- Army: www.armyrotc.com

- Navy: www.navy.com/careers/nrotc
- Marine Corps: www.officer.marines.com

Keep in mind that not all students taking ROTC classes are scholarship recipients; students may take ROTC as an elective with no scholarship and, therefore, no military commitment.

It is a good idea to apply to two or more services to maximize your options. Also, you've probably noticed that the Coast Guard does not offer the ROTC program, and although there is a Marine Corps option, Marine Corps ROTC students participate in the Naval ROTC program. If you are an active-duty enlisted member, contact your base/post education office for more information.

Officer Candidate School/Officer Training School (OCS/OTS)

The military offers programs for service members who already hold a bachelor's degree and want to earn a commission. They are referred to as either Officer Candidate School (OCS) or Officer Training School (OTS), depending on the branch of service.

Approximately 20 percent of all newly commissioned officers receive their commission through OCS/OTS each year. The competition for OCS/OTS slots is keen. You need to meet not only high academic and physical standards, but high moral standards as well.

OCS/OTS is, in essence, basic training for officers—but because the roles of junior officers differ from those of junior enlisted members, these programs place more emphasis on leadership training. Individuals attending OCS/OTS also learn military history and basic drill (marching), and they also participate in physical fitness training.

Many factors play a part in the selection process for OCS/OTS, including a potential candidate's college major and GPA and his or her officer candidate test scores. Each military branch has its own eligibility requirements, so contact the specific branch directly for more information and up-to-date requirements.

Service Academies

Undoubtedly the most competitive of all the pathways to earning a commission are the service academies. The academies of the Army, Navy, Coast Guard, and Air Force all offer high-quality, no-cost, four-year educations to highly qualified individuals.

To be accepted into one of the service academies, you must meet the following standards:

- Be a U.S. citizen
- Be at least 17 years old
- Be of good moral character
- Meet the service academy's minimum SAT/ACT scores
- Qualify physically and pass a physical fitness exam
- Meet minimum high school GPA requirements

- Obtain a Congressional nomination (not required for the Coast Guard Academy)
- Be single and remain unmarried for the duration of attendance

Remember, however, that even if you meet all of these requirements, there is no guarantee of acceptance.

In addition to the requirements listed above, the following qualifications, although not mandatory, increase an applicant's chances for acceptance:

- Be a member of at least one high school team sport
- Hold an office in student government
- Demonstrate a history of community service
- Show participation in an organization such as the Boy Scouts or Girl Scouts
- Be a member of an honor society (such as the National Honor Society)
- Complete a high school Junior Reserve Officer Training Corps (JROTC) program

Students in the Armed Forces service academies receive an education equal to that of the country's most competitive colleges and universities. In addition to high academic standards, service academy students live in a highly structured and disciplined environment, and they must participate in leadership courses, drill (marching), and a daily physical fitness regimen. Graduates of the service academies also incur a commitment to serve on active duty in the military.

Because not everyone has the opportunity to receive a high-quality high school education, three of the service academies also offer "preparatory schools" to prepare otherwise qualified individuals for entrance into a regular academy:

Air Force
U.S. Air Force Academy Preparatory School
Colorado Springs, CO
www.academyadmissions.com/admissions/prepschool/
800-443-9266 (toll-free)

Army
U.S. Military Academy Preparatory School
Fort Monmouth, NJ
www.usma.edu/USMAPS/
732-532-5307

Navy (also includes **Coast Guard** and **Merchant Marines**)
U.S. Naval Academy Preparatory School
Newport, RI
www.usna.edu/NAPS/
401-841-6966

Reserve and National Guard

The Reserve and National Guard offer another opportunity to earn a military commission. Although most positions are filled by fully qualified individuals who have separated from active duty, opportunities still exist for those in other situations to earn a commission. Contact a local Reserve and National Guard recruiter for more information, or check out the following Web sites:

Air Force
www.afreserve.com
800-257-1212 (toll-free)

Army
www.goarmy.com
800-272-2769 (toll-free)

Coast Guard
www.uscg.mil/reserve
877-669-8724 (toll-free)

Marine Corps
www.marforres.usmc.mil
800-627-4637 (toll-free)

Navy
www.navalreserve.com
800-872-8767 (toll-free)

Air National Guard
www.goang.com
800-864-6264 (toll-free)

Army National Guard
www.1800goguard.com
800-464-8273 (toll-free)

SUMMING IT UP

- Military pilot training is perhaps the longest and most intense of all military officer training programs. It can take up to two years to complete and consists of classroom instruction and flight training.

- Military helicopter pilots must meet the same demanding physical and mental requirements as military airplane pilots, and they must train to fly a variety of helicopters designed for different types of missions.

- Airplane navigators are responsible for keeping aircraft on course, acting as another set of eyes during demanding flying missions, and performing bombing duties as required. They rely on radar, radio, and a variety of other navigation equipment to perform their duties. In addition to classroom training, navigators spend many hours in flight simulators and under actual flight situations.

- Serving as a commissioned officer in the U.S. Armed Forces has numerous benefits, including incentive pay, allowances, educational support, guaranteed home loans, low-cost life insurance, and early retirement. Drawbacks include family separations and moves, unpredictable work hours, and hazardous working conditions.

- Pay grade refers to the number classification of an officer and is linked to how much that officer is paid. All officer pay grades begin with the letter "O," while enlisted members' pay grades begin with the letter "E." Officers in all branches of the military serve in the pay grades of O-1 through O-10. The corresponding ranks linked to those number designators may be referred to by different names, depending on the branch of service.

- Each branch of the military sets its own qualification standards for commissioned officers. The standards may exceed Department of Defense (DoD) standards, but they may not be less stringent.

- Although there are four basic avenues to becoming an officer, only three are available for those who seek a career in aviation: Reserve Officers' Training Corps (ROTC); Officer Candidate School (OCS) and Officer Training School (OTS); and the service academies of the Army, Navy, and Air Force.

PART II

MILITARY FLIGHT APTITUDE TESTS

Military Flight Training Programs

chapter 2

OVERVIEW

- General requirements for pilot training
- Flight training: it isn't for everyone!
- Air Force pilot and navigator training
- Army commissioned and warrant officer pilot training
- Navy pilot and navigator training
- Marine Corps flight training
- Coast Guard aviator training
- Summing it up

Regardless of which branch of service you choose, your career in aviation will start with flight training. As you can imagine, flight training is not accomplished in a short period. This chapter will acquaint you with the pilot and navigator training programs currently offered by all branches of the military. Because requirements do change from time to time, use this information as a guide, and be sure to get the most current information from a representative of the service branch in which you're interested.

GENERAL REQUIREMENTS FOR PILOT TRAINING

Candidates for pilot training must be commissioned officers (or warrant officers in some branches) to fly military airplanes. Although certain aircraft, such as bombers and cargo planes, do have enlisted crew members, only officers can pilot military aircraft. If you are reading this book, you have probably already checked out the requirements necessary for earning a commission or becoming a warrant officer. Earning a commission, however, is just one of the requirements for becoming a military pilot. Others include:

- Achieving minimum scores on the appropriate military flight aptitude test

- Meeting minimum physical requirements

- Meeting branch-specific age requirements (standards change depending on service needs, and few waivers are given)

- Meeting physical fitness requirements

Flight Physical Requirements

Physical requirements for flight training are much more stringent than those required to become a commissioned officer. An individual may pass a commissioning physical and be eligible to become a commissioned officer but still may not be eligible for pilot training.

VISION REQUIREMENTS

Service branches have differing vision requirements, but 20/20 uncorrected vision is the standard. In addition to visual acuity standards, individuals must also have normal depth perception and color vision. Vision correctable to 20/20 may be waived, depending on the amount of correction needed and the branch of service.

A word of caution is necessary here about corrective eye surgery. Certain types of corrective surgery may be waived; however, depending on the type and degree of eye surgery you have had, you may be ineligible not only for pilot training but also for commissioning. Be sure to obtain approval in writing from the specific branch in which you're interested before you have any corrective eye surgery—and remember that written approval does not guarantee that you will be granted a waiver. If you have already undergone corrective eye surgery, you must let your recruiter know this before scheduling your flight physical. Although the casual observer may not be able to detect your surgery, it will be detected during your flight physical and make you ineligible for pilot training under normal circumstances. Informing your recruiter beforehand will allow him or her to begin processing waiver paperwork to speed up the process.

HEIGHT, WEIGHT, AND OTHER REQUIREMENTS

Weight and height requirements also vary from among service branches, and they differ from commissioning requirements. Because of size constraints of certain aircraft cockpits, your weight and your standing and sitting heights may affect your chances of meeting flight physical requirements. In addition, individuals who have a history of motion sickness will have difficulty meeting flight physical standards.

FLIGHT TRAINING: IT ISN'T FOR EVERYONE!

Once you have met the general requirements we just reviewed and have either received your commission or have become a warrant officer, you will be cleared to start pilot training. Keep in mind that even though you have been tested mentally and physically for flight training, you may still find that you do not adapt well to a flight environment. The unfortunate truth is that not everyone has the fortitude or specific skills required for flying. Because of this, many individuals "wash out" or are eliminated from pilot training programs. Depending on the reason for being eliminated and the branch of service, these individuals may be offered another flight position, such as navigator, or an officer may suggest another non-flight military career field. In some cases, those who are eliminated from flight training programs may be offered discharge from the military. Of course, everyone who enters pilot training expects to complete the program—

but it's a good idea to be prepared for other outcomes. Consider asking about other possible options while you're still in the preliminary stage of training.

Pilot training programs vary with each branch of the military. Let's review what you will need to do to become a pilot for each of the five military branches.

AIR FORCE PILOT AND NAVIGATOR TRAINING

Pilot Training

Air Force pilot candidates begin with introductory flight training (IFT), during which civilian instructors provide 50 hours of flight instruction. Candidates must complete the requirements for a private pilot license. They will then attend either Euro-NATO joint jet pilot training (ENJJPT) or specialized undergraduate pilot training (SUPT).

ENJJPT is held at Sheppard Air Force Base (AFB), Texas. The entire course lasts about fifty-five weeks. Students learn with and are taught by U.S. Air Force officers along with officers from the air forces of U.S. NATO allies. Student pilots first fly the T-37 Tweet, mastering contact, instrument, low-level, and formation flying. They move on to a fighter-trainer, the T-38 Talon, on which they continue building the skills necessary to become fighter pilots.

T-37B

SUPT students attend primary training at one of these four AFBs or Naval Air Stations (NAS):

1. Columbus AFB, Mississippi

2. Laughlin AFB, Texas

3. Vance AFB, Oklahoma

4. NAS Whiting Field, Milton, Florida

During this phase, students learn the basic flight skills of all military pilots. Students who report to Laughlin AFB train in the T-6A Texan II; those who report to Columbus AFB fly the T-37; and students who go to Vance AFB fly either the T-6 or T-37. Whiting Field students fly the T-34C Turbomentor. Eventually, the Air Force and Navy will completely replace both the T-37 and T-34 with the T-6 as the primary trainer aircraft. Joint training is conducted at Vance and Whiting Field for Air Force and Navy students.

T-38

After primary training, student pilots are assigned to one of four advanced training tracks based on their class standing:

❶ Prospective airlift and tanker pilots are assigned to the airlift/tanker track and train in the T-1 Jayhawk at Columbus AFB, Laughlin AFB, or Vance AFB.

❷ Student pilots headed for bomber or fighter assignments are assigned to the bomber/fighter track and train in the T-38 Talon at Columbus, Laughlin, or Vance.

❸ Students assigned to the multiengine turboprop track fly the T-44 turboprop trainers at NAS Corpus Christi, Texas, and eventually pilot the C-130 Hercules.

❹ Those selected to fly helicopters are assigned to the helicopter track and fly the UH-1 Huey at Fort Rucker, Alabama.

Pilots assigned to fighter aircraft complete the introduction to fighter fundamentals course at Sheppard AFB or Moody AFB, Georgia, flying the AT-38B. These students then continue training either in the F-15 Eagle or F/A-22 Raptor at Tyndall AFB, Florida, or the F-16 Fighting Falcon at Luke AFB, Arizona. Altus AFB, Oklahoma, hosts training for pilots assigned to the C-5 Galaxy, C-141 Starlifter, KC-135 Strato-tanker, or C-17 Globemaster III aircraft.

KC-135 Stratotanker

Aircrews assigned to fly the C-130 train at Little Rock AFB, Arkansas, or Dobbins Air Reserve Base (ARB), Georgia. Pilots assigned to fly MC-130 Combat Talon, HC-130 aircraft, UH-1N, MH-53 Pave Low, HH-60 Pave Hawk helicopters, or CV-22 Osprey tilt-rotor receive their training at Kirtland AFB, New Mexico. Pilots for the C-21 aircraft are trained at Keesler AFB, Mississippi.

Navigator Training

Combat Systems Officer (CSO) training takes place at Randolph AFB, Texas, and NAS Pensacola, Florida. These courses provide training for Air Force and Navy student navigators. CSO training combines portions of navigator and electronic warfare training to produce aviators who are skilled in advanced navigation systems, electronic warfare, and weapons use. The new training flow, implemented in 2004, enables aviators to understand both the navigator and the electronic warfare positions on combat aircraft.

Students at Randolph are trained in one of two broad tracks:

1. Those completing the Advanced CSO Navigation track fly in the T-43A and move to follow-on assignments as navigators in the B-52 Stratofortress, KC/RC-135 Stratotanker, E-3 Sentry (AWACS), E-8C Joint Surveillance Target Attack Radar System (JSTARS), and all C-130 variants.

2. Students completing the Advanced CSO Electronic Warfare track complete training in the T-43A and move to follow-on assignments as Electronic Warfare Officers in the B-52, RC-135, and EC/MC/AC-130.

Students at NAS Pensacola complete primary and intermediate training in the T-6A and T-1 aircraft. These students then enter one of two tracks:

1. Strike track: These students serve as weapon systems officers (WSO) in the B-1B Lancer. WSOs assigned to the B-1B attend Electronic Warfare Upgrade training at Randolph.

2. Strike/fighter track: These students receive follow-on assignments to the F-15E Strike Eagle as WSOs and attend additional training in the Introduction to Fighter Fundamentals course.

ARMY COMMISSIONED AND WARRANT OFFICER PILOT TRAINING

Pilot Training for Commissioned Officers

Helicopter pilot training for commissioned Army officers takes place at Fort Rucker, Alabama. Initial training occurs in the five phases outlined below:

Phase One: Two weeks; instruction on aviation health hazards and applicable preventive measures.

Phase Two: Ten weeks; instruction on fundamentals of flight, first solo flight, basic maneuvers and eventually more complex maneuvers. The UH-1 Iroquois helicopter is used during this phase.

Phase Three: Eight weeks; basic instrument procedures, flight on federal airways, instrument qualification and helicopter instrument ratings upon graduation.

Phase Four: Fourteen to sixteen weeks; this phase is combat-mission oriented. Students are designated for training in the UH-1 or UH-60 as utility helicopter pilots, the OH-58 observation helicopter as aeroscout helicopter pilots, or the AH-1 as attack helicopter pilots.

Phase Five: Two weeks; professional development phase emphasizing basic leadership skills, graduates prepared for operational unit assignments.

Advanced flight training is offered to many graduates to provide them with additional skills, including those who are needed to fly specialty helicopters and fixed-wing aircraft.

UH-1B Iroquois (Huey)

UH-60 Black Hawk

Some of the helicopters flown in operational units include: AH-1 Cobra (attack helicopter); AH-64 Apache (attack helicopter); CH-47 Chinook (medium lift helicopter); OH-58 Kiowa (observation helicopter); UH-1 Huey (light helicopter); UH-60 Black Hawk (combat helicopter).

Some of the fixed-wing aircraft flown in operational units include the OV-1 Mohawk, U-21 Ute, and the C-12.

Pilot Training for Warrant Officers

Those who want to become Army aviation warrant officers must first attend the Warrant Officer Candidate School (WOCS), the Initial Entry Rotary Wing (IERW) Qualification Course, and the Warrant Officer Basic Course at Fort Rucker, Alabama.

After successful completion of these courses, warrant officers must complete the three-phase initial entry flight training program:

Phase One: Twelve weeks; academic and flight instruction in basic rotary wing maneuvers, first solo flight, progress to more complex maneuvers. The UH-1 helicopter is used in this phase.

AH-64 Apache

AH-1S Cobra

CH-47 Chinook

OV-1C Mohawk

Phase Two: Eight weeks; flying in various weather conditions and in darkness, relying solely on aircraft instruments. Students fly the UH-1 and are trained in the UH-1 flight simulator during this phase.

Phase Three: Fourteen weeks; advanced flight training in one of two aircraft: the UH-1 utility or the OH-58 scout. This combat skills phase concentrates on aircraft qualification and basic combat skills, including night flying.

NAVY PILOT AND NAVIGATOR TRAINING

All Navy flight training begins at NAS Pensacola, sometimes called the Cradle of Naval Aviation. Navy, Marine Corps, Air Force, and Coast Guard flight students spend about six weeks in Aviation Preflight Indoctrination (API) at NAS Pensacola's Naval Aviation Schools Command. Classes include engineering, aerodynamics, air navigation, aviation physiology, and water survival.

T-34C (Primary Trainer) Mentor

Pilot Training

Upon completion of API, student pilots, now called Student Naval Aviators (SNA), and student navigators, now called Student Naval Flight Officers (SNFO), proceed to separate primary training "pipelines." Primary SNA training occurs at three bases: NAS Whiting Field, NAS Corpus Christi, and Vance AFB. For SNAs reporting to the Navy bases, primary training takes approximately twenty-two weeks. It includes ground-based academics, simulators, and flight training either in the T-34 Turbomentor or the T-6A Texan II. Primary training consists of six stages:

1. Familiarization (FAM)
2. Basic Instruments
3. Precision Aerobatics
4. Formation
5. Night FAM
6. Radio Instruments

Following primary training, students are assigned to different aircraft types based on the current and projected needs of the services and each student's performance and preferences. SNAs are selected for the following assignments:

- Maritime (multiengine propeller)
- E-2/C-2, Rotary (helicopters)
- Strike (jets)
- E-6 TACAMO (Take Charge and Move Out communications)

MARITIME TRAINING

Maritime students complete their advanced training at NAS Corpus Christi flying the twin engine T-44 Pegasus or TC-12 Huron. Particular emphasis is placed on single-engine flight in varying conditions. After they complete this training and receive their wings, Navy pilots report to the P-3 Fleet Replacement Squadron (FRS), and Marine pilots report to the C-130 FRS.

E-2/C-2 TRAINING

SNAs selected for E-2/C-2 training must complete multiengine training and receive carrier landing qualification. After primary training, students report to VT-31 at NAS Corpus Christi to complete 44 hours of flight training during approximately seventeen weeks in the T-44. After intermediate training, E-2/C-2 students report to NAS Kingsville, Texas, for advanced training in the T-45. Students earn their wings in about twenty-seven weeks and receive carrier landing qualification.

T-44A (Multiengine) King Air

TH-57 (Primary Helo) Sea Ranger

E-2C (Electronic Warfare) Hawkeye

Student pilots selected for helicopter training report to NAS Whiting Field and complete advanced training in the TH-57 Sea Ranger. Students learn the unique characteristics and tactics of rotary-wing aviation, and are introduced to shipboard landing on the Helo (helicopter) Landing Trainer, the Navy's only ship dedicated to teaching helicopter pilots how to land onboard a moving vessel. Once they receive their wings, Navy helicopter pilots report to their respective FRS for SH-60, CH-46, or CH-53 training. Marine helicopter pilots report to an AH-1, CH-46, MH-53, or UH-1

FRS for training. The Navy also trains helicopter pilots for the Coast Guard and for the armed forces of several allied nations.

CH-46 Sea Knight

CH-53 Sea Stallion

STRIKE TRAINING

SNAs who enter the Strike pipeline complete their training either at NAS Kingsville in the T-45A or at NAS Meridian, Mississippi, in the T-45C. During Strike training, pilots learn strike tactics, weapons delivery, and air combat maneuvering, and they receive carrier landing qualification. After earning their wings, Strike pilots report to an F-14, F/A-18, S-3, or EA-6B FRS and eventually report to their first Fleet squadron.

EA-6B (Electronic Warfare) Prowler

E-2C (Electronic Warfare) Hawkeye

F-14 Tomcat

T-45 Goshawk

E-6 TACAMO TRAINING

Navy TACAMO pilots complete advanced training in the T-1A Jayhawk, a militarized business jet with digital cockpit displays. This training takes place at the Air Force's 32nd FTS at Vance AFB.

T-1A

Navigator (Naval Flight Officer) Training

Student Naval Flight Officers (SNFOs) report to VT-10 or VT-4 at NAS Pensacola for primary NFO training. SNFOs fly the T-6 Texan II in an abridged primary training syllabus. Students are selected for specific aircraft at the end of the primary, intermediate, and Strike core phases of training.

SNFOs selected to fly as navigators in large, multiengine aircraft report to P-3C Orion, EP-3 Aries II, or E-6 Mercury FRS. Intermediate training for Tactical Jet SNFOs is conducted in the T-6, T-39 Sabreliner, and T-1 Jayhawk. Upon completion of the intermediate training, students receive advanced training in the VT-86.

F/A-18 (Fighter-Attack) Hornet

SNFOs selected for Strike train to become Electronic Countermeasures Officers (ECMO) for the EA-6B. SNFO Strike training is conducted in the T-39 and the T-45. Students in the Strike/Fighter program train to become Navy or Marine F/A-18 Weapons Systems Officers (WSO). Strike/Fighter training uses the T-39 and T-45. After receiving their wings, Navy and Marine SNFOs report to their respective FRS and then to a Fleet squadron.

E-2C SNFOs report directly to the FRS after intermediate training to learn the Aviation Tactical Data System (ATDS).

MARINE CORPS FLIGHT TRAINING

All Marine Corps flight training begins at NAS Pensacola. Marine Corps flight students spend about six weeks in Aviation Preflight Indoctrination (API) at the Naval Aviation Schools Command, where they are challenged academically and physically. Classes include engineering, aerodynamics, air navigation, aviation physiology, and water survival.

Pilot Training

Upon completion of API, student pilots train at one of three bases: NAS Whiting Field, NAS Corpus Christi, or Vance AFB. For students reporting to the Navy bases, primary training runs approximately twenty-two weeks and includes ground-based academics, simulator training, and flight training either in the T-34 Turbomentor or the T-6A Texan II. Primary training consists of six stages:

1. Familiarization (FAM)
2. Basic Instruments
3. Precision Aerobatics
4. Formation
5. Night FAM
6. Radio Instruments

AH-1J Cobra

UH-1 Huey

After they complete primary training, students are assigned to an aircraft type based on the current and projected needs of the Marine Corps and each student's performance and preferences. Students are selected for the following assignments:

- Maritime (multiengine prop)

- E-2/C-2

- Rotary (helicopters)

- Strike (jet)

- E-6 TACAMO

Students complete their advanced training at NAS Corpus Christi flying the twin engine T-44 Pegasus or TC-12 Huron. Particular emphasis is placed on single-engine flight in varying conditions. After receiving their wings, Marine pilots report to the C-130 FRS.

E-2/C-2 TRAINING

Students selected for E-2/C-2 training must complete multiengine training and earn carrier landing qualification. After primary training, students report to VT-31 at NAS Corpus Christi to complete 44 hours of flight training in approximately seventeen weeks in the T-44. After intermediate training, E-2/C-2 students report to NAS Kingsville for advanced training in the T-45. Students earn their wings in approximately twenty-seven weeks and receive carrier landing qualification.

Student pilots selected for helicopter training report to NAS Whiting Field and complete advanced training in the TH-57 Sea Ranger. Here they learn the unique characteristics and tactics of rotary-wing aviation and are introduced to shipboard landing on the Helo Landing Trainer. After they receive their wings, Marine helicopter pilots report to an AH-1, CH-46, MH-53, or UH-1 FRS for training.

STRIKE TRAINING

Students who enter the Strike pipeline complete their training either at NAS Kingsville in the T-45A or at NAS Meridian in the T-45C. Strike training instruction includes strike tactics, weapons delivery, and air combat maneuvering. Students must also earn carrier landing qualification. After receiving their wings, Strike pilots report to an F-14, F/A-18, S-3, or EA-6B FRS, and they eventually report to their first Fleet squadron.

COAST GUARD AVIATOR TRAINING

Coast Guard aviators are commissioned officers who have graduated from the Coast Guard Academy or the Coast Guard Officer Candidate School, or they are selectees of the Coast Guard's Direct Commission Aviation Program.

Coast Guard aviator selection is highly competitive. It is based on job performance, flight aptitude, and strict medical requirements. Each year, depending on service need, 60 to 80 junior officers are selected to attend eighteen to twenty-four months of training at the Navy's Flight Training Command in Pensacola. After earning their wings, successful graduates fly aircraft at one of the Coast Guard air stations in the United States or Puerto Rico.

Coast Guard pilots must be accomplished all-weather pilots, because they fly in some of the most challenging weather situations. These pilots fly propeller-driven fixed-wing aircraft, high-speed jet aircraft, and several models of helicopters on Coast Guard missions, which include search and rescue, law enforcement, environmental response, ice operations, and air interdiction.

Coast Guard aircraft operate from flight-deck–equipped cutters, air stations, and air facilities. They include these fixed-wing and rotary-wing aircraft:

- H-65 Dolphin
- HH-60 Jayhawk
- MH-68A Stingray
- HC-130 Hercules
- HU-25 Guardian
- HC-144 Ocean Sentry

Pilot Training

Coast Guard pilot training begins with flight school, which lasts eighteen to twenty-four months and covers basic ground school subjects, aircraft systems, academics, sea-and-land survival, and a series of primary and intermediate levels of flight training. The advanced flight training phase involves additional ground school courses; helicopter,

HU-25 Guardian   HH-65A Dolphin

HH-60J Jayhawk

C-130 Hercules

single engine, and multiengine fixed-wing training; and flight-transitional training. Coast Guard pilots are trained on the HH-65 Dolphin, the HH-60 Jayhawk, the HU-25 Guardian, and HC-144 Ocean Sentry.

The Coast Guard Aviation Training Center (ATC) in Mobile, Alabama, is a multi-mission unit that acts both as the Coast Guard's aviation and capabilities development center and an operational air station. All pilots initially trained at ATC return annually for a one-week proficiency course in their designated airframe. The ATC Mobile evaluation center is responsible for ensuring that Coast Guard aviation forces are using the best equipment and tactics to successfully complete all required missions. The Operations Division, whose pilots fly the HU-25, is the part of the ATC command that conducts traditional Coast Guard air station missions, including search and rescue, Homeland Security, and environmental protection.

SUMMING IT UP

- To fly military aircraft, one must either be a commissioned officer or a warrant officer (in some branches). Requirements include meeting minimum scores on the appropriate military flight aptitude test, minimum flight physical requirements, physical fitness requirements, and branch-specific age requirements.

- Air Force pilot candidates begin with introductory flight training, in which civilian instructors provide 50 hours of flight instruction. After completing requirements for a private pilot license, pilot candidates attend either ENJJPT or SUPT. Following the primary phase of specialized training, student pilots are assigned to one of four advanced training tracks based on class standing.

- Combat Systems Officer (CSO) training combines portions of navigator and electronic warfare training to produce aviators skilled in advanced navigation systems, electronic warfare, and weapons employment.

- Helicopter pilot training for commissioned Army officers occurs in five phases over approximately thirty-eight weeks. Advanced flight training is offered to many graduates to provide them with additional skills, including those needed to fly specialty helicopters and fixed-wing aircraft (airplanes).

- Those seeking to become Army aviation warrant officers must attend the WOCS, the IERW Qualification Course, and the Warrant Officer Basic Course before completing a three-phase initial entry flight training program of approximately thirty-four weeks.

- Navy, Marine Corps, Air Force, and Coast Guard flight students spend about six weeks in Aviation Preflight Indoctrination (API) at the Naval Aviation Schools Command. Classes include engineering, aerodynamics, air navigation, aviation physiology, and water survival. Students are assigned to different aircraft types after completing primary training.

- Marine Corps flight students spend about six weeks in API at the Naval Aviation Schools Command. Classes include engineering, aerodynamics, air navigation, aviation physiology, and water survival. Upon completion, student pilots train at one of three bases for approximately twenty-two weeks. They are assigned to an aircraft type after completion of primary training.

- Coast Guard aviators are commissioned officers who have graduated from the Coast Guard Academy or the Coast Guard Officer Candidate School, or they are selectees of the Coast Guard's Direct Commission Aviation Program. Select officers attend eighteen to twenty-four months of training at the Navy's Flight Training Command in Pensacola; after graduation they are sent to one of the Coast Guard air stations throughout the United States or in Puerto Rico.

Introduction to Military Flight Aptitude Tests

OVERVIEW

- Air Force Officer Qualifying Test (AFOQT)
- Alternate Flight Aptitude Selection Test (AFAST)
- Aviation Selection Test Battery (ASTB)
- Summing it up

This chapter will introduce you to the military flight aptitude tests currently in use. Although the tests vary somewhat depending on the branch of service, all military flight aptitude tests consist of multiple-choice questions.

Just as the SAT or ACT exam may determine your suitability to enter a particular college or university, a standardized test helps the military to judge, in part, your suitability for training as a military aviator. No matter what test you are studying for, this book will help you raise your scores and be better prepared to take the test. Of course, no book will be of any assistance if you don't actually use it. So, don't let this book sit around gathering dust!

In this chapter, we'll review the various tests used by military branches to help select pilot candidates. Although this information was accurate when this book was published, be sure to check with your recruiter or admissions officer to be sure it is still current before you commit time to studying.

AIR FORCE OFFICER QUALIFYING TEST (AFOQT)

The Air Force uses one exam, the Air Force Officer Qualifying Test (AFOQT), for all officer candidates, whether or not they are applying for a flying position. The AFOQT is used to select applicants for specific training programs such as pilot and navigator training, as well as officer commissioning programs such as Officer Training School (OTS) and Air Force Reserve Officer Training Corps (ROTC). Taking the AFOQT is required for all cadets and students on scholarship or in the Professional Officer Course.

Because this book deals with military flight aptitude tests, the section on the AFOQT focuses only on the parts of the test that pertain to Air Force pilot and navigator applicants.

chapter 3

The AFOQT takes approximately 3½ hours and contains 250 test questions and 220 Self Description questions. The test is divided into the twelve subtests outlined in the chart below, including sections for pilot and navigator aptitude testing.

SUBTEST	NO. OF QUESTIONS	TIME ALLOWED (minutes)	MEASURES
Verbal Analogies	25	8	Ability to reason and see relationships between words
Arithmetic Reasoning	25	29	Ability to use arithmetic to solve problems
Word Knowledge	25	5	Knowledge of basic word definitions (synonyms)
Math Knowledge	25	22	Knowledge of mathematical terms and principles
Instrument Comprehension	20	6	Ability to determine position of an airplane from reading instruments
Block Counting	20	3	Ability to look at a 3-dimensional stack of blocks and determine how many pieces are touched by certain numbered blocks
Table Reading	40	7	Ability to read tables quickly and accurately
Aviation Information	20	8	Knowledge of general aviation concepts and terminology
General Science	20	10	Knowledge of high school science
Rotated Blocks	15	13	Ability to visualize and manipulate objects
Hidden Figures	15	8	Ability to see a simple figure in a complex drawing, also known as template matching
Self-Description Inventory	220	40	"Inventory" of personal traits and attitudes. (There are no "right" or "wrong" answers.)

Your Scores and What They Mean

The AFOQT is a standardized multiple-choice test similar to the SAT, with additional sections for pilot and navigator aptitude testing. It takes about 3½ hours to complete the test.

It's scored in five areas. You will receive a score based on a percentile for each area (0–99). The AFOQT is scored in these five areas:

❶ Pilot: If you are a pilot candidate, you must have a minimum Pilot score of 25; if you are a navigator candidate, you must have a minimum Pilot score of 10.

❷ Navigator: If you are a pilot candidate, you must have a minimum Pilot score of 10; if you are a navigator candidate, you must have a minimum Pilot score of 25.

❸ Academic Aptitude: No minimum score requirement.

❹ Verbal: All candidates must achieve a minimum score of 15.

❺ Quantitative (Math): All candidates must achieve a minimum score of 10.

In addition to these scores, all pilot and navigator candidates must have a Combined Pilot and Navigator score minimum of 50.

Every test taker receives a score for each of these five areas; all are based on percentile (0–99) but they are not combined. These are the only reported scores. Each commissioning source determines how high these scores must be for the test taker to be selected or considered for its program.

Retest Policy

The AFOQT may be taken only twice. Waivers may be granted, but an exception is not guaranteed. Examinees must wait 180 days between tests, and the most recent AFOQT test score is counted. AFOQT scores never expire.

ALTERNATE FLIGHT APTITUDE SELECTION TEST (AFAST)

The AFAST is not an intelligence test. It measures special aptitudes and personality/background characteristics that are commonly predictive of success in Army helicopter flight training. The AFAST consists of 200 questions in seven subtests. Each subtest has a separate set of directions and time limit.

Your Scores and What They Mean

To become an Army aviator, one must be highly motivated, have good coordination, and have exceptional leadership skills. He or she must also be in excellent physical condition. Because flight training is so expensive and because only a limited number of openings are available for new students, the Army screens applicants to ensure that only those highly likely to succeed in flight school are accepted for training. Experience shows that applicants who score high on the test tend to be more successful in flight training than those who score lower.

The AFAST is divided into the seven subtests outlined in the chart below.

SUBTEST	NO. OF QUESTIONS	TIME ALLOWED (minutes)	MEASURES
Background Information Form	25	10	Not an assessment; items are questions about test taker's background
Instrument Comprehension	15	5	Ability to determine the position of an airplane in flight, the amount of climb or dive, the degree of bank to left or right, and the heading
Complex Movements	30	5	Ability to judge distance and visualize motion
Helicopter Knowledge	20	10	General understanding of the principles of helicopter flight
Cyclic Orientation	15	5	Ability to recognize simple changes in helicopter position and to indicate the corresponding cyclic (stick) movement
Mechanical Functions	20	10	Understanding of general mechanical principles
Self-Description Form	75	25	Items are questions about test taker's interests, likes, and dislikes

What to Expect on Test Day

When you arrive at the testing center, your test administrator provides you with a test booklet, a separate answer sheet, and two soft-lead pencils. You also receive complete instructions for each test section, and you are instructed on how to mark your answers.

In some subtests, answering every question may help raise your score. In other subtests, however, your wrong answer choices are counted against your correct ones. In both cases, make the best choice you can, unless your answer would be a pure guess; if you can't make an educated guess to answer a question in a subtest in which wrong answers carry penalties, it's best not to answer that question at all.

Retest Policy

Your application for flight training will be considered only if your AFAST score is equal to or greater than the established "cut" or qualifying score (currently 90). If you meet the cut score, you may not retest—so it's to your advantage to score as high as you can. Should you fail to achieve a qualifying score, you must wait six months before retesting. If you fail to achieve a qualifying score on the retest, you are not permitted to take the test again.

AVIATION SELECTION TEST BATTERY (ASTB)

The ASTB is administered by the Navy, Marine Corps, and Coast Guard to help determine suitability for aviation officer candidates. The Navy and Coast Guard also use portions of the ASTB to select candidates for their Officer Candidate School (OCS) programs. Applicants who do not wish to be considered for pilot training may choose to take only the Officer Aptitude Rating (OAR) portion of the exam, which includes the Math Skills, Reading Skills, and Mechanical Comprehension subtests.

The ASTB takes approximately 2½ hours and consists of the six subtests outlined in the chart below.

SUBTEST	NO. OF QUESTIONS	TIME ALLOWED (minutes)	MEASURES
Math Skills Test (MST)	30	25	Math skills, including arithmetic, algebra, and some geometry
Reading Skills Test (RST)	27	25	Ability to extract information from text passages
Mechanical Comprehension Test (MCT)	30	15	Knowledge of information commonly covered in an introductory high school physics course
Spatial Apperception Test (SAT)	25	10	Ability to match external and internal views of an aircraft regarding its direction and orientation relative to the ground
Aviation and Nautical Information Test (ANIT)	30	15	Knowledge of aviation history, nautical terminology, aircraft components, aerodynamic principles, and flight rules and regulations
Aviation Supplemental Test (AST)	34 *(number of items varies)*	25	Contains a variety of items similar to those found in the other subtests

Math Skills Test

- Designed to assess test taker's ability to perform basic arithmetic operations; solve for variables; work with fractions, roots, and exponents; and calculate angles, area, and perimeters of geometric shapes

- Includes equations and word problems—some require solving for variables, others are time and distance problems, and some require estimating simple probabilities

Reading Skills Test

- Requires test takers to extract meaning from several text passages and to determine which answer choice can correctly be inferred from the passage itself

- Some incorrect response options may appear to be true, but only one answer to each item can be derived solely from the information in the passage

Mechanical Comprehension Test

- Covers principles typically learned in an introductory high school physics course; test taker is asked to apply these principles in a variety of situations

- Topics include gases and liquids and their behavior related to pressure, volume, and velocity; components and performance of engines; principles of electricity; gears; weight distribution; and the operation of simple machines such as pulleys and fulcrums

Spatial Apperception Test

- Evaluates ability to match external and internal views of an aircraft based on visual cues about its direction and orientation relative to the ground

- Each item consists of a view from inside the cockpit that the test taker must match to one of five external views, evaluating test taker's ability to visualize the orientation of objects in three-dimensional space

Aviation and Nautical Information Test

- Measures familiarity with aviation history, nautical terminology and procedures, and aviation-related concepts such as aircraft components, aerodynamic principles, and flight rules and regulations

- Includes a variety of item types similar in format and content to those in the other ASTB subtests

Aviation Supplemental Test

- Typically contains a variety of items that are similar in format and content to items in preceding subtests

Your Scores and What They Mean

- **Academic Qualifications Rating (AQR):** This is used to predict academic performance in aviation preflight instruction (API) and primary-phase ground school. The AQR score is based on your performance on all subtests, but the Math Skills Test (MST) is weighted most heavily in this rating.

- **Pilot Flight Aptitude Rating (PFAR):** This score is used to predict primary flight performance for Student Naval Aviators (SNAs). The PFAR score is based on your performance on all subtests, but most heavily weighted subtests are the ANIT and SAT.

- **Flight Officer Flight Aptitude Rating (FOFAR):** This score is used to predict primary flight performance for Student Naval Flight Officers (SNFOs). It is based on your performance on all subtests, but the MST score is weighted most heavily.

- **Officer Aptitude Rating (OAR):** This score is used by the Navy to predict academic performance in OCS. It is based on your performance on the MST, RST, and MCT.

Retest Policy

Examinees who wish to improve their scores on the ASTB must wait thirty days following their initial attempt before taking a different version (or form) of the test. For example, an individual who first takes Form 3 must take Form 4 or Form 5 as a retest. A third and final attempt at Form 3, 4, or 5 can only be authorized ninety days after the second test. These test interval requirements cannot be waived, so if you choose to take a retest, it is important to be aware of the form you took during previous administrations and the amount of time since the test.

A July 2004 regulation established a three-test lifetime limit for taking the ASTB. Every examinee may take each version of the test (Form 3, Form 4, or Form 5) only once. This means that you may only take the ASTB three times. Although examinees must be administered a different form for each retest, the forms can be taken in any order.

This limit applies only to Forms 3, 4, and 5. If an individual took a previous version, such as Forms 1 or 2 that are no longer in use, that test does not count toward the lifetime limit.

Illegal Testing

An examinee who retests too early or who retests using a form that he or she has already been administered will generate an illegal test. This disqualifies the test taker from receiving valid scores for that particular administration—and the illegal test will be counted against the individual's lifetime limit.

SUMMING IT UP

- All military flight aptitude tests use multiple-choice questions.

- The Air Force uses the AFOQT as the single exam for all officer candidates, whether or not they apply for a flying position. The AFOQT takes approximately 3½ hours and contains 250 test questions and 220 self-description questions. It is divided into twelve subtests: Verbal Analogies, Arithmetic Reasoning, Word Knowledge, Math Knowledge, Instrument Comprehension, Block Counting, Table Reading, Aviation Information, General Science, Rotated Blocks, Hidden Figures, and the Self-Description Inventory.

- The AFAST is meant to help predict the test taker's success in Army helicopter flight training. It contains 200 questions in seven subtests: Background Information, Instrument Comprehension, Complex Movements, Helicopter Knowledge, Cyclic Orientation, Mechanical Functions, and the Self-Description Form.

- The ASTB is administered by the Navy, Marine Corps, and Coast Guard to help determine suitability of aviation officer candidates. Portions of the test are also used by the Navy and Coast Guard to select candidates for their OCS programs. The ASTB has a three-test lifetime limit; each examinee may take each version of the test (Form 3, Form 4, or Form 5) only once.

PART III

QUESTIONS TYPES IN MILITARY FLIGHT APTITUDE TESTS

Preparing to Take a Military Flight Aptitude Test

chapter 4

OVERVIEW

- **About multiple-choice tests**
- **Tips for taking computer-adaptive tests**
- **Seven strategies for taking a military flight aptitude test**
- **Preparing for test day**
- **Summing it up**

Chances are if you are reading this book, you have already begun the application process for a commissioning program. If you haven't done so already, now would be a good time to contact a recruiter or admissions counselor. It is important that you understand the requirements of the service and commissioning program for which you wish to apply. Also make sure that you know the test requirements, so you do not waste time studying material that will not be on your test.

Following the instructions of your recruiter or admissions counselor will help you ensure that everything goes smoothly on the test day. You may be required to produce identifying documents, such as your Social Security card, a copy of your birth certificate, your driver's license, and so on.

ABOUT MULTIPLE-CHOICE TESTS

Millions of people take multiple-choice exams every year. You have probably taken at least one, such as the SAT or ACT. Educational institutions, government agencies, industry, and the military all use multiple-choice exams to measure candidate aptitude, achievement, specific knowledge, and essential skills. Test scores are used to determine eligibility for school exams and admissions, scholarships, employment in public and private sectors, and suitability for military service.

Multiple-choice tests are used widely throughout the U.S. military. These tests are extremely versatile and can be easily and reliably scored, and test results are highly suitable for statistical analysis, research, and development. Most multiple-choice tests administered by the military contain four or five options per question, although some may include fewer options. Examples of two-option test items are true/false, right/wrong, agree/disagree, like/dislike, or yes/no questions. This type is commonly used to determine characteristics or traits, such as opinions or preferences.

The following is an example of a typical multiple-choice question with four options:

The U.S. President's place of residence in Washington, DC, is called

(A) the President's Mansion.
(B) the House of Representatives.
(C) the Washington Monument.
(D) the White House.

The Stem of a test item either asks a question or states a problem. In the above example, the stem is the phrase "The U.S. President's place of residence in Washington, DC, is called."

The Choices (options) represent all available answer choices or solutions to a question. In the example above, answers (A), (B), (C), and (D) are all answer choices.

Distracters (foils) are incorrect answer choices. Often they are worded in such a way as to make you think that they may be the correct answer, even if you know that another one is correct. Can you find the distracters in the above example?

The Key (correct answer) is, obviously, the only correct answer to the stem. In this example, the key is (D). That means that the distracters—the answer choices that are incorrect—are (A), (B), and (C).

TIPS FOR TAKING COMPUTER-ADAPTIVE TESTS

A computer-adaptive test format tailors questions to the ability level of each test taker. For example, the first test question is in the middle ability range—not too difficult and not too easy. If you answer it correctly, the next question will be more difficult. If you answer it incorrectly, the next question is less difficult. The CAT continues this way until your proficiency level is determined. You will answer questions that are appropriate for your ability level, so you will not waste time answering questions that are too easy or too difficult for you. However, you will not be able to skip a question or go back to check your answers, as you might on a paper-and-pencil test.

Advantages of Computer-Adaptive Tests:

- Test session is shorter

- Test can be scored immediately

- Scoring errors are reduced and score accuracy is higher than standard (non-adaptive) exams

- Test security is higher than with non-adaptive exams

- Periodic review and refinement of test items is readily and easily conducted

Disadvantages of Computer-Adaptive Tests:

- Test takers cannot skip a part or go back to an earlier section of the exam to change or check an answer

- Test takers cannot review answers at the end of the test

- Unlike the paper-and-pencil subtest raw scores, computer-adaptive subtest raw scores usually are not equal to the total number of correct answers. Computer-adaptive test scores are calculated using formulas that take into account the difficulty of each test item and the correctness of the answer. Both paper-and-pencil raw scores and computer-adaptive raw scores are calculated so that they are equivalent to one another

- It is up to you to decide which version of the exam you want to take. Be sure that you choose the one you feel more comfortable with, so you can increase your chances of scoring high on test day

SEVEN STRATEGIES FOR TAKING A MILITARY FLIGHT APTITUDE TEST

Let's review some general strategies for taking a military flight aptitude test. Even if you've read these elsewhere or they seem like common sense to you, it's a good idea to review again and reinforce them in your mind.

❶ **Know your optimal pace and stay at it.** Time is definitely a factor in multiple-choice exams. On certain sections, you may find that to complete all the questions, you need to work at a quicker pace than is comfortable for you. Check your pace after every few questions and adjust it accordingly so that you have time to at least consider every question. The best way to avoid the time squeeze is to practice under timed conditions before you take the actual exam. This will give you a sense of what your optimal pace should be.

❷ **If you're not sure about an answer, don't dwell on it—move on.** This follows logically from the first tip. You might find yourself reluctant to leave a question until you're sure your answer is correct. While this is admirable, doing this under the time conditions of the test will only defeat you. Remember: You can miss *some* questions and still earn a high score.

❸ **Make educated guesses—but avoid random guesswork if possible.** Some multiple-choice exams levy penalty points or fractions of points on questions you answer incorrectly. In those cases, guessing at an answer could hurt your overall score. The military flight aptitude tests do not assess penalty points. For the Air Force Qualifying Test (AFOQT) and the Navy and Marine Corps Aviation Selection Test Battery (ASTB), there is no penalty for incorrect answers—test scores are determined by the number of correct answers. For some subtests of the Alternate Flight Aptitude Test Selection (AFAST), a portion of wrong answers is counted against the right answers; however, for all other sections, you should try to answer every question. It makes sense to make an educated guess rather than leaving the question unanswered. This means that you should always try to eliminate obvious wrong-answer choices first; then go with your hunch. On multiple-choice questions, eliminating even one possible answer improves your odds of answering correctly. If you're out of time and haven't answered every available question, though, there's no advantage to making random guesses.

4 **Read each question in its entirety.** Beware: Some multiple-choice questions offer wrong-answer choices that may seem correct if you haven't read the entire question and all the answer choices thoroughly. Unless you're running out of time, make sure you read every question from start to finish, and never confirm an answer unless you've first compared it with all the other answer choices for that question.

5 **Maintain an active mindset.** When taking an exam such as the military flight aptitude tests, it's easy to fall into a "passive" mode in which you scan answer choices and hope that the correct answer "jumps out" at you as you do so. Fight this tendency by keeping your mind engaged while reading each question. Remember, each question on the test is designed to measure a specific ability or skill. Try to adopt an active, investigative approach to answering the questions. Ask yourself: What skill is the question measuring? What is the most direct thought process for determining the correct response? How might I be tripped up on this type of question if I'm not careful?

6 **Use your pencil and scratch paper.** Scratch work helps keep your mind in active mode. Make brief notes, draw simple diagrams and flow charts, and scribble equations and geometry figures. All of this will help you think clearly.

7 **Know the test directions thoroughly.** It bears repeating: *Always* read directions for each test section completely and thoroughly before answering any questions in that section.

PREPARING FOR TEST DAY

The Night Before the Test

- Get plenty of sleep.

- Avoid alcohol, caffeine, or any substance that may prevent your getting a good night's sleep.

On Test Day

- Eat a light breakfast if testing is in the morning or a light lunch if testing is in the afternoon.

- Make sure you know exactly where to report for the test and how you will get there. If the area is unfamiliar to you, you may want to consider taking a "dry run" a few days before test day.

- Leave home in plenty of time to arrive at least 15 minutes before you're scheduled to report to the test center. Remember to take into account traffic delays and/or problems with your vehicle or other transportation.

- Be sure to bring everything you need for the exam: Number 2 pencils (with good erasers), proof of identification, a watch, and anything else you were instructed to bring to the test. (Usually, pencils and scratch paper are provided at the test center.)

- If you do not feel well on the day of the test, try to reschedule if possible. You want to do your best, so you should be feeling your best.

- Drink sparingly; you do not want the distraction of having to use the restroom during the test. You may lose your momentum, and this may adversely affect your score.

- Try to prepare for the unexpected. For example, if you wear contact lenses, bring a backup pair of eyeglasses.

- If you are given a choice of where you can sit in the testing room, find a seat where you will be most comfortable and least distracted. If you are left-handed and taking a paper-and-pencil exam, for example, seek a desk or table with a left return or ask whether any are available.

- Dress in layers so that you can adjust to the room temperature and stay comfortable.

- Keep track of the time—but don't spend too much time looking at your watch or the clock.

- Listen carefully to all instructions given by the test proctor. If you don't understand something, don't be embarrassed to ask for clarification.

- If you're taking a paper-and-pencil exam, go back and check your answers if you have time, and make sure you have not skipped any questions. Be aware, however, that your first response is generally your best, so only change your answer if you're absolutely sure that you answered incorrectly the first time. If you are only second-guessing, chances are you're better off leaving your answer choice as it is.

- Use all the time allotted for each section. If you finish a section early (on paper-and-pencil exams), review all of your answers in that section.

- Try to relax. If you've prepared properly, you will do well—so don't stress out.

SUMMING IT UP

- If you've already begun the application process for a commissioning program, make sure to contact a recruiter or admissions counselor to confirm the requirements of the service and commissioning program in which you're interested. Find out what your test requirements are to avoid wasting time studying material that will not be on the test.

- Multiple-choice tests are widely used throughout U.S. military branches. Most multiple-choice tests administered by the military contain four or five options per question, although some may include two or three options. Two-option test items are usually true/false, right/wrong, agree/disagree, like/dislike, or yes/no questions.

- A typical multiple-choice question includes a stem, which asks a question or states a problem; the choices, which represent all available answer choices or solutions to the question; distracters, which are incorrect answer choices; and the key, which is the only correct answer to the stem.

- Computer-adaptive tests tailor questions to the ability level of each test taker. The length of the test session is reduced; the test can be scored immediately; scoring errors are reduced and score accuracy is increased; test security is higher; and periodic review and refinement of test items is readily and easily conducted. However, test takers cannot skip parts or return to an earlier part of the exam to change or check an answer, and test takers cannot review answers at the end of the test.

- Follow the commonsense strategies listed in this chapter for taking military flight aptitude tests.

- To be at your best on test day, follow the tips in this chapter, such as planning your route to the test center ahead of time and getting plenty of sleep the night before the test.

The Kind of Questions
You Can Expect

chapter 5

OVERVIEW

- Synonyms
- Verbal Analogies
- Reading/Paragraph Comprehension
- Arithmetic Reasoning
- Math Knowledge
- Mechanical Comprehension
- Instrument Comprehension
- Block Counting
- Table Reading
- Aviation Information
- Nautical Information
- Rotated Blocks
- General Science
- Hidden Figures
- Complex Movements
- Cyclic Orientation
- Spatial Apperception
- Background Information Questions and Self-Description subtests
- Summing it up

SYNONYMS

Synonym test items appear as five-option questions (with answer choices A–E) in the Word Knowledge subtest of the AFOQT. This subtest is not used in the Pilot or Navigator-Technical composite scores. Synonym questions also appear as four-option questions (with answer choices A–D) in the Word Knowledge subtest of the ASVAB, which is part of the General Technical (GT) score used in screening active-duty enlisted service members of any branch of the Armed Forces who want to enter the Army Warrant Officer Flight Training Program.

Synonym test items measure breadth of vocabulary or word knowledge. For each word supplied, you must select from the available options the answer choice that is the same or most nearly the same in meaning. The usual dictionary definition is required only if the word is presented alone; if it appears in a sentence, you are asked to choose the contextual meaning of the word.

Consider all options before answering a synonym test question. Although several options may have some connection with the key word, the word that is *closest* in meaning to the key word is always the correct answer.

SUCCUMB means most nearly to

(A) aid

(B) be discouraged

(C) check

(D) oppose

(E) yield

The correct answer is (E). To *succumb* means "to cease to resist before a superior strength or overpowering desire or force." Choice (D) indicates the stage prior to succumbing. Choices (A) and (C) are unrelated in meaning. Choice (B) is only remotely related in the sense that one who succumbs may be discouraged. Choice (E) is the only one that means almost the same as *succumb*.

SUBSUME means most nearly to

(A) belong

(B) cover

(C) include

(D) obliterate

(E) understate

The correct answer is (C). To *subsume* is "to include within a larger class or category." Choices (A), (B), and (D) are somewhat related since an element included within a larger class or category may be said to belong to it, to be covered by it, or to be obliterated by it. Choice (E) is completely unrelated in meaning. Of all the choices given, choice (C) is closest in meaning to *subsume*.

> **Directions:** Each of the following five questions consists of a word in capital letters followed by five suggested meanings of the word. For each question, select the word or phrase that most nearly means the same as the word in capital letters. Answers are on page 139.

1. ANOMALOUS:

   (A) disgraceful
   (B) formless
   (C) irregular
   (D) threatening
   (E) unknown

2. CREDENCE:

   (A) belief
   (B) claim
   (C) payment
   (D) surprise
   (E) understanding

3. FORTUITOUS:

   (A) accidental
   (B) conclusive
   (C) courageous
   (D) prosperous
   (E) severe

4. MALIGN:

   (A) disturb
   (B) mislead
   (C) praise
   (D) provoke
   (E) slander

5. PERMEABLE:

   (A) flexible
   (B) penetrable
   (C) soluble
   (D) variable
   (E) volatile

> **Directions:** Each of the following five questions has an underlined word. You are to decide which one of the five choices most nearly means the same as the underlined word.

6. The packages were kept in a <u>secure</u> place.

   (A) distant
   (B) safe
   (C) convenient
   (D) secret
   (E) obscure

7. The benefits of the plan are likely to be <u>transitory</u>.

   (A) significant
   (B) obvious
   (C) temporary
   (D) cumulative
   (E) encouraging

8. It is my <u>conviction</u> that you are wrong.

   (A) guilt
   (B) imagination
   (C) firm belief
   (D) fault
   (E) vague recollection

9. The hikers found several <u>crevices</u> in the rocks.

   (A) plants
   (B) minerals
   (C) uneven spots
   (D) puddles
   (E) cracks

10. The parent <u>consoled</u> the child.

   (A) found
   (B) scolded
   (C) carried home
   (D) comforted
   (E) bathed

VERBAL ANALOGIES

Verbal analogy test items appear as five-option questions in the Verbal Analogies subtest of the AFOQT. This AFOQT score is part of the Pilot composite score.

Verbal analogy questions test not only your knowledge of word meanings and your vocabulary level, but they also test your ability to reason; that is, to see the relationships between words and the ideas they represent. To determine such relationships, you must know the meaning of each word in the first given pair and determine the precise relationship between the two words. You complete the analogy by selecting the pair of words that best expresses a relationship similar to that expressed by the first two paired words.

Two forms of verbal analogy questions are in general use:

1. You are given the first pair of words and the first word of the second pair. Of the given options, only one best expresses a relationship to the third word that is similar to that expressed between the first two words.

   MAN is to BOY as WOMAN is to

   (A) BABY
   (B) BRIDE
   (C) CHILD
   (D) GIRL
   (E) LAD

2. Only the first pair of words is provided. Each answer choice consists of a pair of words.

   MAN is to BOY as

   (A) ADULT is to GIRL
   (B) BRIDE is to GROOM
   (C) LASS is to CHILD
   (D) WOMAN is to YOUTH
   (E) WOMAN is to GIRL

Let's analyze the first analogy form.

What is the relationship of the first two paired words?

   MAN: member of the human race, male, mature

   BOY: member of the human race, male, young

Both are male members of the human race. MAN is mature; BOY is young.

What is the meaning of the word WOMAN and each of the words appearing in the options?

WOMAN: member of the human race, female, mature

BABY: member of the human race, either male or female, very young

BRIDE: member of the human race, female, about to be married or newly married

CHILD: member of the human race, either male or female, young

GIRL: member of the human race, female, young

LAD: member of the human race, male, young

To complete the analogy with WOMAN as the first word, we need a term denoting a young, female member of the human race.

Choice (A) is incorrect because BABY may be male or female and is very young. Choice (B) is incorrect because BRIDE is a special kind of female—one about to be married or newly married. If GROOM had been substituted for BOY in the first half of the analogy, then BRIDE would have been the proper choice. Choice (C) is incorrect because CHILD may be male or female. Choice (E) is incorrect because LAD is a male.

Choice (D) is the correct choice because GIRL denotes a young, female member of the human race.

Here's a list of relationships commonly encountered in the Verbal Analogies subtests.

Relationship	Example
synonyms	ask : inquire
antonyms	long : short
homonyms	mail : male
location	Phoenix : Arizona
measurement (time, distance, weight, volume, etc.)	distance : mile
cause : effect	negligence : accident
whole : part	chapter : paragraph
object : purpose or function	keyboard : type
object : user	camera : photographer
creator : creation	artist : painting
early stage : later stage	infant : adult
raw material: finished product	wood : bench
female : male	cow : bull
general : specific	vegetable : broccoli
larger : smaller	lake : pond
more : less (degree)	arid : dry
singular noun : plural noun	child : children
singular pronoun : plural pronoun	he : they
normative pronoun : objective pronoun	she : her
first-person pronoun : third-person pronoun	we : they
verb tense : verb tense	run : ran
comparative adjective : comparative adjective	good : better

adjective : superlative adjective	bad : worst
noun : adjective	texture : coarse
verb : adjective	expand : large

Pay careful attention when answering this type of question. The order of the two words in the answer choice must be in the same sequence as the order of words in the question stem. If the sequence of the second pair of words is reversed, the relationship between the two word pairs is not analogous. Here's an example of when the word pairs are not analogous.

> 2 is to 5 as 4 is to 10 (correct)
> 2 is to 5 as 10 is to 4 (incorrect)
> MAN is to BOY as WOMAN is to GIRL (correct)
> MAN is to BOY as GIRL is to WOMAN (incorrect)

Directions: Each of the following five questions consists of an incomplete analogy. Select the answer that best completes the analogy presented in the first two words of each question. Answers are on page 139.

1. BOTANY is to PLANTS as ENTO-MOLOGY is to

   (A) ANIMALS
   (B) CLIMATE
   (C) DISEASES
   (D) LANGUAGES
   (E) INSECTS

2. EPILOGUE is to PROLOGUE as

   (A) APPENDIX is to INDEX
   (B) APPENDIX is to PREFACE
   (C) PREFACE is to FOOTNOTE
   (D) PREFACE is to TABLE OF CONTENTS
   (E) TABLE OF CONTENTS is to INDEX

3. OCTAGON is to SQUARE as HEXAGON is to

   (A) CUBE
   (B) MILITARY
   (C) PYRAMID
   (D) RECTANGLE
   (E) TRIANGLE

4. GLOW is to BLAZE as

   (A) COMPACT is to SPRAWLING
   (B) EAGER is to RELUCTANT
   (C) GLANCE is to STARE
   (D) HINT is to CLUE
   (E) WICKED is to NAUGHTY

5. WATER is to THIRST as FOOD is to

   (A) FAMINE
   (B) GRIEF
   (C) HUNGER
   (D) INDIGESTION
   (E) SCARCITY

READING/PARAGRAPH COMPREHENSION

The Reading Comprehension subtest is no longer a part of the AFOQT, but reading comprehension questions appear as four-option test items in the Paragraph Comprehension subtest of the ASVAB. This subtest score is used to calculate the General Technical (GT) score used in screening active-duty enlisted service members of any branch of the Armed Forces who want to enter the Army Warrant Officer Flight Training Program. In addition, Sentence Comprehension questions appear in the Reading Skills test of the Navy and Marine Corps Aviation Selection Test Battery (ASTB).

The ability to read and understand written or printed material is an important skill. Reading comprehension tests present passages that vary in length from one sentence to several paragraphs, followed by one or more questions about the content of each passage. The reading selections are usually samples of the type of material that you would be required to read on the job or at school.

Here are six examples of common types of reading comprehension items.

❶ **Finding specific information or directly stated detail in the passage.**

Although this type is commonly found in elementary-level tests, it is also found in intermediate-level tests such as the Armed Services Vocational Aptitude Battery. At the intermediate level, the vocabulary is more difficult, the reading passages are of greater complexity, and the questions posed are much more complicated. Here are some examples:

Helping to prevent accidents is the responsibility of _____.

The principal reason for issuing traffic summonses is to _____.

The reason for maintaining ongoing safety education is that _____.

❷ **Recognizing the central theme, the main idea, or concept expressed in the passage.**

Although questions of this type may be phrased differently, they generally require that you summarize or otherwise ascertain the main purpose or idea expressed in the reading passage. In addition to reading and understanding, the ability to analyze and interpret written material is essential. Some questions require the ability to combine separate ideas or concepts found in the reading passage to get the correct answer. Other questions merely require reaching a conclusion that is equivalent to a restatement of the main idea or concept expressed in the passage. Let's review some examples.

The most appropriate title for the above passage is _____.

The best title for this paragraph would be _____.

This paragraph is mainly about _____.

The passage best supports the statement that _____.

The passage means most nearly that _____.

③ Determining the meaning of certain words as used in context.

The particular meaning of a word as used in the passage requires an understanding of the central or main theme of the reading passage, as well as the idea being conveyed by the sentence containing the word.

The word ...... as used in this passage means _____.

The expression ...... as used in the passage means _____.

④ Finding implications or drawing inferences from a stated idea.

This type of item requires the ability to understand the stated idea and then to reason by logical thinking to the implied or inferred idea. *Implied* means not exactly stated but simply suggested; *inferred* means derived by reasoning. Although the terms are somewhat similar in meaning, *inferred* implies being further removed from the stated idea. Much greater reasoning ability is required to arrive at the proper inference.

Which of the following is implied by the above passage?

Of the following, the most valid implication of the above paragraph is _____.

The author probably believes that _____.

It can be inferred from the above passage that _____.

The best of the following inferences that can be made is that _____.

⑤ Sentence completion items.

Sentence completion items are considered both vocabulary items and reading comprehension items. They are vocabulary items because they test the ability to understand and use words. However, they also measure an important aspect of reading comprehension: the ability to understand the implications of a sentence or a paragraph.

Sentence completion items consist of a sentence or paragraph in which one or two words are missing. The omissions are indicated by a blank underlined space: _____. You must read and understand the sentence or paragraph as given and then choose the option that best completes the idea in the reading passage. Your choice must also be consistent in style and logic with other elements in the sentence.

⑥ Word substitution items.

Word substitution items are very similar to sentence completion items and are also considered both vocabulary and reading comprehension items. These items consist of a sentence or paragraph in which a key word has been changed. The changed word is incorrect, and it is not in keeping with the meaning that the sentence is intended to convey. Determine which word is used incorrectly. Then select from the choices the word that, when substituted for the incorrectly used word, would best convey the meaning of the sentence or paragraph.

Eight General Suggestions for Answering Reading/Paragraph Comprehension Questions:

1 Scan the passage to determine the general intent of the reading selection.

2 Read the passage carefully to understand the main idea and any related ideas. If necessary for comprehension, read the passage again.

3 Read each question carefully and base your answer only on the material in the reading passage. Be careful to base your answer on what is stated, implied, or inferred. Do not be influenced by your opinions, personal feelings, or any information not expressed or implied in the reading passage.

4 Options that are partly true and partly false are incorrect.

5 Be very observant for such words as *least, greatest, first, not,* and so on, appearing in the preamble of the question.

6 Be suspicious of options containing words such as *all, always, every, forever, never, none, wholly,* and so on.

7 Be sure to consider all answer choices before selecting the one you believe is correct.

8 Speed is an important consideration in answering reading comprehension questions. Try to proceed as rapidly as you can without sacrificing careful thinking or reasoning.

Directions: For each of the following questions, select the choice that best completes the statement or answers the question.

1. The rates of vibration perceived by the ears as musical tones lie between fairly well-defined limits. In the ear, as in the eye, there are individual variations. However, variations are more marked in the ear, since its range of perception is greater.

   The paragraph best supports the statement that the ear

   (A) is limited by the nature of its variations.
   (B) is the most sensitive of the auditory organs.
   (C) differs from the eye in its broader range of perception.
   (D) is sensitive to a great range of musical tones.
   (E) depends for its sense on the rate of vibration of a limited range of sound waves.

   The correct answer is (C). The passage makes the point that individual differences in auditory range are greater than individual differences in visual range because the total range of auditory perception is greater. Although the statements made by choices (D) and (E) are both correct, neither expresses the main point of the reading passage.

2. The propaganda of a nation at war is designed to stimulate the energy of its citizens and their will to win, and to imbue them with an overwhelming sense of the justice of their cause. Directed abroad, its purpose is to create precisely contrary effects among citizens of enemy nations and to assure to nationals of allied or subjugated countries full and unwavering assistance.

   The title that best expresses the ideas of this passage is

   (A) "Propaganda's Failure."
   (B) "Designs for Waging War."
   (C) "Influencing Opinion in Wartime."
   (D) "The Propaganda of Other Nations."
   (E) "Citizens of Enemy Nations and Their Allies."

   The correct answer is (C). The theme of this passage is influencing opinion in wartime, both at home and abroad.

Directions: Answer the following two questions on the basis of the information contained in the passage below:

I have heard it suggested that the "upper class" English accent has been of value in maintaining the British Empire and Commonwealth. The argument runs that all manner of folk in distant places, understanding the English language, will catch in this accent the notes of tradition, pride, and authority and so will be suitably impressed. This might have been the case some nine or ten decades ago but it is certainly not true now. The accent is more likely to be a liability than an asset.

3. The title below that best expresses the ideas of this passage is

   (A) "Changed Effects of a 'British Accent'."
   (B) "Prevention of the Spread of Cockney."
   (C) "The Affected Language of Royalty."
   (D) "The Decline of the British Empire."
   (E) "The 'King's English'."

   The correct answer is (A). The last two sentences of the reading passage indicate that folks in distant places might have been suitably impressed decades ago, but they're not now.

4. According to the author, the "upper class" English accent

   (A) has been imitated all over the world.
   (B) has been inspired by British royalty.
   (C) has brought about the destruction of the British Commonwealth.
   (D) may have caused arguments among the folk in distant corners of the Empire.
   (E) may have helped to perpetuate the British Empire before 1900.

   The correct answer is (E). The "upper class" English accent might have been of value in maintaining the British Empire nine or ten decades ago (or before 1900).

Directions: For each of the following questions, select the choice that best completes the statement or answers the question.

5. The view is widely held that butter is more digestible and better absorbed than other fats because of its low melting point. There is little scientific authority for such a view. As margarine is made today, its melting point is close to that of butter, and tests show only the slightest degree of difference in digestibility of fats of equally low melting points.

The paragraph best supports the statement that

(A) butter is more easily digested than margarine.

(B) the concept that butter has a lower melting point than other fats is a common misconception, disproved by scientists.

(C) there is not much difference in the digestibility of butter and margarine.

(D) most people prefer butter to margarine.

The correct answer is (C). The passage states that the melting points of butter and margarine are similar and that, therefore, they are about equally digestible.

Directions: Answer the following two questions on the basis of the information contained in the passage below:

Science made its first great contribution to war with gunpowder. But since gunpowder can be used effectively only in suitable firearms, science also had to develop the iron and steel that were required to manufacture muskets and cannons on a huge scale. To this day, metallurgy receives much inspiration from war. Bessemer steel was the direct outcome of the deficiencies of artillery as they were revealed by the Crimean War. Concern with the expansion and pressure of gases in guns and combustibility of powder aroused interest in the laws of gases and other matters that seemingly have no relation whatever to war.

6. The title below that best expresses the ideas of this passage is

(A) "Gunpowder, the First Great Invention."

(B) "How War Stimulates Science."

(C) "Improvement of Artillery."

(D) "The Crimean War and Science."

The correct answer is (B). The basic theme of the reading passage is that science contributes to the war effort and that war stimulates science research.

7. An outcome of the Crimean War was the

(A) invention of gunpowder.

(B) origin of metallurgy.

(C) study of the laws of gases.

(D) use of muskets and cannons.

The correct answer is (C). The last sentence in the reading passage indicates that interest in the laws of gases arose as a direct outcome of artillery deficiencies revealed by the Crimean War.

8. We find many instances in early science of "a priori" scientific reasoning. Scientists thought it proper to carry generalizations from one field to another. It was assumed that the planets revolved in circles because of the geometrical simplicity of the circle. Even Newton assumed that there must be seven primary colors corresponding to the seven tones of the musical scale.

The paragraph best supports the statement that

(A) Newton sometimes used the "a priori" method of investigation.

(B) scientists no longer consider it proper to uncritically carry over generalizations from one field to another.

(C) the planets revolve about the earth in ellipses rather than in circles.

(D) even great men like Newton sometimes make mistakes.

The correct answer is (B). The tone of the passage and the choice of illustrations showing the fallacy of "a priori" reasoning make it evident that scientists no longer carry generalizations automatically from one field to another. Choices (A) and (D) are true statements, but they are only illustrative points. Choice (B) carries the real message of the passage.

Directions: Questions 9 and 10 consist of sentences containing a blank space indicating that a word has been omitted. Beneath each sentence are four or five choices. Select the choice that, when inserted in the sentence, best fits in with the meaning of the sentence as a whole.

9. If the weather report forecasts fog and smoke, we can anticipate having _____.

(A) rain
(B) sleet
(C) smog
(D) snow
(E) thunder

The correct answer is (C). A mixture of fog and smoke is called smog.

10. Although her argument was logical, her conclusion was _____.

(A) illegible
(B) natural
(C) positive
(D) unreasonable

The correct answer is (D). When a subordinate clause begins with *although,* the thought expressed in the main clause will not be consistent with that contained in the subordinate clause. Since the argument was *logical,* the conclusion would have to be illogical. Of the options given, *unreasonable* is the only opposite to logical.

Directions: Questions 11 and 12 consist of sentences with two blank spaces. Each blank indicates that a word has been omitted. Beneath the sentence are four or five lettered sets of words. Choose the set of words that, when inserted in the sentence, best fits in with the meaning of the sentence as a whole.

11. Although the publicity has been _____, the film itself is intelligent, well acted, handsomely produced, and altogether _____.

    (A) extensive . . arbitrary
    (B) tasteless . . respectable
    (C) sophisticated . . amateurish
    (D) risqué . . crude
    (E) perfect . . spectacular

    The correct answer is (B). The correct answer should involve two words that are more or less opposite in meaning, because the word *although* suggests that the publicity was not representative of the film. Another clue to the correct answer is that the second word should have the same connotation as the words *intelligent, well acted, handsomely produced*. Choices (A), (D), and (E) are not opposites. Choice (C) cannot be the correct answer even though the words in it are nearly opposites, because if the film is intelligent, well acted, and handsomely produced, it is not amateurish. Only choice (B), when inserted in the sentence, produces a logical statement.

12. The desire for peace should not be equated with _____, for _____ peace can be maintained only by brave people.

    (A) intelligence . . ignoble
    (B) bravery . . stable
    (C) cowardice . . lasting
    (D) neutrality . . apathetic

    The correct answer is (C). The word *not* indicates a shift in meaning between two parts of the sentence: If peace can be maintained only by the brave, the desire for peace cannot be equated with *cowardice*.

Directions: Questions 13 and 14 consist of quotations that contain one word that is incorrectly used and is not in keeping with the meaning that the quotation intends to convey. Determine which word is incorrectly used. Then select from the lettered options the word that, when substituted for the incorrectly used word, would best convey the intended meaning of the quotation.

13. "College placement officials have frequently noted the contradiction that exists between the public statements of the company president who questions the value of a liberal arts background in the business world and the practice of his recruiters who seek specialized training for particular jobs."

    (A) admissions
    (B) praises
    (C) reject
    (D) science
    (E) technical

    The correct answer is (B). A careful reading of the passage shows no inconsistency until the word *questions*. If a contradiction exists and the recruiters seek specialized training, the company president would accept, endorse, or praise, rather than question the value of a liberal arts background. Choice (B) appears to be the choice that would best convey the intended meaning of the quotation. *Contradiction* is used properly; none of the options can be substituted for it. Although *reject* may appear to be an appropriate substitution for *seek*, it does not help convey the intended meaning of the quotation.

14. "In manufacturing a fabric-measuring device, it is advisable to use a type of cloth whose length is highly susceptible to changes of temperature, tension, etc."

    (A) decreases
    (B) increases
    (C) instrument
    (D) not

    The correct answer is (D). A careful reading of the passage shows no inconsistency until the word *highly* is reached. To give a true measure, the device's length should not change with temperature or tension but should be constant.

Directions: For question 15, select the option that best completes the statement or answers the question.

15. "Look before you leap."

    This quotation means most nearly that you should

    (A) always be alert.
    (B) always be carefree.
    (C) move quickly but carefully.
    (D) proceed rapidly when directed.

    The correct answer is (C). The quotation does not state or imply that you should *always* be alert or carefree or that you should proceed rapidly when directed. It says you should move quickly but carefully.

Directions: For each question, select the choice that best completes the statement or answers the question. Answers are on pages 139–140.

1. The mental attitude of the employee toward safety is exceedingly important in preventing accidents. All efforts designed to keep safety on the employee's mind and to keep accident prevention a live subject in the office will help substantially in a safety program. Although it may seem strange, it is common for people to be careless. Therefore, safety education is a continuous process.

   The reason given in the above passage for maintaining ongoing safety education is that

   (A) employees must be told to stay alert at all times.
   (B) office tasks are often dangerous.
   (C) people are often careless.
   (D) safety rules change frequently.
   (E) safety rules change infrequently.

2. One goal of law enforcement is the reduction of stress between one population group and another. When no stress exists between population groups, law enforcement can deal with other tensions or simply perform traditional police functions. However, when stress between population groups does exist, law enforcement, in its efforts to prevent disruptive behavior, becomes committed to reduce that stress.

   According to the above passage, during times of stress between population groups in the community, it is necessary for law enforcement to attempt to

   (A) continue traditional police functions.
   (B) eliminate tension resulting from social change.
   (C) punish disruptive behavior.
   (D) reduce intergroup stress.
   (E) warn disruptive individuals.

Directions: Answer questions 3–5 on the basis of the information contained in the following passage:

Microwave ovens use a principle of heating different from that employed by ordinary ovens. The key part of a microwave oven is its magnetron, which generates the microwaves that then go into the oven. Some of these energy waves hit the food directly, while others bounce around the oven until they find their way into the food. Sometimes the microwaves intersect, strengthening their effect. Sometimes they cancel each other out. Parts of the food may be heavily saturated with energy, while other parts may receive very little. In conventional cooking, you select the oven temperature. In microwave cooking, you select the power level. The walls of the microwave oven are made of metal, which helps the microwaves bounce off them. However, this turns to a disadvantage for the cook who uses metal cookware.

3. Based on the information contained in this passage, it is easy to see some advantages and disadvantages of microwave ovens. The greatest disadvantage would probably be

   (A) overcooked food.
   (B) radioactive food.
   (C) unevenly cooked food.
   (D) the high cost of preparing food.
   (E) cold food.

4. In a conventional oven, the temperature selection would be based upon degrees. In a microwave oven, the power selection would probably be based upon

   (A) wattage.

   (B) voltage.

   (C) lumens.

   (D) solar units.

   (E) ohms.

5. The source of the microwaves in the oven is

   (A) reflected energy.

   (B) convection currents.

   (C) the magnetron.

   (D) short waves and bursts of energy.

   (E) the food itself.

Directions: Read the paragraph(s) and select the one lettered choice that best completes the statement or answers the question.

6. Few drivers realize that steel is used to keep the road surface flat in spite of the weight of buses and trucks. Steel bars, deeply embedded in the concrete, are sinews to take the stresses so that the stresses cannot crack the slab or make it wavy.

   The passage best supports the statement that a concrete road

   (A) is expensive to build.

   (B) usually cracks under heavy weights.

   (C) looks like any other road.

   (D) is reinforced with other material.

7. Blood pressure, the force that the blood exerts against the walls of the vessels through which it flows, is commonly meant to be the pressure in the arteries. The pressure in the arteries varies with contraction (work period) and relaxation (rest period) of the heart. When the heart contracts, the blood in the arteries is at its greatest, or systolic, pressure. When the heart relaxes, the blood in the arteries is at its lowest, or diastolic, pressure. The difference between the two pressures is called the pulse pressure.

   According to the passage, which one of the following statements is most accurate?

   (A) The blood in the arteries is at its greatest pressure during contraction.

   (B) Systolic pressure measures the blood in the arteries when the heart is relaxed.

   (C) The difference between systolic and diastolic pressure determines the blood pressure.

   (D) Pulse pressure is the same as blood pressure.

Questions 8–10 are based on the passage below.

Arsonists are people who set fires deliberately. They don't look like criminals, but they cost the nation millions of dollars in property loss and sometimes loss of life. Arsonists set fires for many different reasons. Sometimes a shopkeeper sees no way out of losing his business and sets fire to it to collect the insurance. Another type of arsonist wants revenge and sets fire to the home or shop of someone he feels has treated him unfairly. Some arsonists just like the excitement of seeing the fire burn and watching the firefighters at work; arsonists of this type have been known to help fight the fire.

8. According to the passage above, an arsonist is a person who

   (A) intentionally sets a fire.
   (B) enjoys watching fires.
   (C) wants revenge.
   (D) needs money.

9. Arsonists have been known to help fight fires because they

   (A) felt guilty.
   (B) enjoyed the excitement.
   (C) wanted to earn money.
   (D) didn't want anyone hurt.

10. According to the passage above, we may conclude that arsonists

   (A) would make good firefighters.
   (B) are not criminals.
   (C) are mentally ill.
   (D) are not all alike.

Directions: Questions 11–14 each consist of a sentence in which one word is omitted. Select the lettered choice that best completes the thought expressed in each sentence.

11. The explanation by the teacher was so _____ that the students solved the problem with ease.

   (A) complicated
   (B) explicit
   (C) protracted
   (D) vague

12. A(n) _____ listener can distinguish fact from fiction.

   (A) astute
   (B) ingenuous
   (C) prejudiced
   (D) reluctant

13. Since corn is _____ to the region, it is not expensive.

   (A) alien
   (B) exotic
   (C) indigenous
   (D) indigent

14. Our colleague was so _____ that we could not convince him that he was wrong.

   (A) capitulating
   (B) complaisant
   (C) light-hearted
   (D) obdurate

Directions: Questions 15–17 each consist of a sentence with two blank spaces, each blank indicating that a word or figure has been omitted. Select one of the lettered choices that, when inserted in the sentence, best completes the thought expressed in the sentence as a whole.

15. He is rather _____ and, therefore, easily _____.

   (A) caustic..hurt
   (B) dangerous..noticed
   (C) immature..deceived
   (D) worldly..misunderstood

16. _____ education was instituted for the purpose of preventing _____ of young children, and guaranteeing them a minimum of education.

   (A) Compulsory..exploitation
   (B) Free..abuse
   (C) Kindergarten..ignorance
   (D) Secondary..delinquency

17. Any person who is in _____ while awaiting trial is considered _____ until he or she has been declared guilty.

   (A) custody..innocent
   (B) jail..suspect
   (C) jeopardy..suspicious
   (D) prison..rehabilitated

Directions: Questions 18–20 each consist of a quotation that contains one word that is incorrectly used; the word is not in keeping with the meaning that the quotation is evidently intended to convey. Determine which word is incorrectly used. Then select from the lettered choices the word that, when substituted for the incorrectly used word, would best help to convey the intended meaning of the quotation.

18. "Under a good personnel policy, the number of employee complaints and grievances will tend to be a number that is sufficiently greater to keep the supervisory force on its toes and yet large enough to leave time for other phases of supervision."

   (A) complete
   (B) definite
   (C) limit
   (D) small

19. "One of the important assets of a democracy is an active, energetic local government, meeting local needs and giving an immediate opportunity to legislators to participate in their own public affairs."

   (A) citizens
   (B) convenient
   (C) local
   (D) officials

20. "The cost of wholesale food distribution in large urban centers is related to the cost of food to ultimate consumers, because they cannot pay for any added distribution costs."

(A) eventually

(B) sales

(C) some

(D) unrelated

ARITHMETIC REASONING

Arithmetic reasoning test items appear as five-option questions in the Arithmetic Reasoning subtest of the AFOQT and are used in calculating the Pilot, Navigator-Technical, Academic Aptitude, and Quantitative composite scores. Arithmetic reasoning questions also appear in the Math Skills Test of the Navy and Marine Corps ASTB.

In addition, arithmetic reasoning questions appear in the subtest of the ASVAB, which contributes to the General Technical (GT) score for screening active-duty enlisted service members of any branch of the Armed Forces who want to enter the Army Warrant Officer Flight Training Program.

1. An airplane flying a distance of 875 miles used 70 gallons of gasoline. Under the same conditions, how many gallons will this plane need to travel 3,000 miles?

(A) 108

(B) 120

(C) 144

(D) 188

(E) 240

The correct answer is (E). $\frac{875}{70} = \frac{3,000}{x}$; $875x = 210,000$; $x = 240$ gallons.

2. A mechanic repairs 16 cars per 8-hour work day. Another mechanic in the same shop repairs $1\frac{1}{2}$ times this number in the same period. Theoretically, how long will it take these mechanics, working together, to repair 12 cars in the shop?

(A) 2 hours

(B) $2\frac{2}{5}$ hours

(C) $2\frac{4}{5}$ hours

(D) $3\frac{1}{5}$ hours

(E) $3\frac{3}{5}$ hours

The correct answer is (B). The second mechanic repairs $1\frac{1}{2} \times 16$, or 24 cars per 8-hour day. On an hourly rate, the first mechanic repairs 2 cars/hour; the second mechanic repairs 3 cars/hour. Adding both outputs, they repair 5 cars/hour. To determine the time required to repair 12 cars, divide the 12 cars by the 5 cars/hour. The answer is $2\frac{2}{5}$ hours, or choice (B).

3. On a scaled drawing of a warehouse, 1 inch represents 10 feet of actual floor dimension. A floor that is actually 15 yards long and 10 yards wide would have which of the following dimensions on the scaled drawing?

   (A) $1\frac{1}{2}$ inches long and 1 inch wide

   (B) 3 inches long and 2 inches wide

   (C) $4\frac{1}{2}$ inches long and 3 inches wide

   (D) 6 inches long and 4 inches wide

   (E) None of the above

   The correct answer is (C). First convert actual floor dimensions to feet: 15 yards = 45 feet; 10 yards = 30 feet.

   If 1 inch represents 10 feet, $4\frac{1}{2}$ inches represents 45 feet (length).

   If 1 inch represents 10 feet, 3 inches represents 30 feet (width).

4. An empty can weighs 10 pounds. When filled with water, it weighs 85 pounds. If one gallon of water weighs 8.32 pounds, the capacity of the can is approximately

   (A) 8 gallons.

   (B) $8\frac{1}{2}$ gallons.

   (C) 9 gallons.

   (D) $9\frac{1}{2}$ gallons.

   (E) 10 gallons.

   The correct answer is (C). The weight of the filled can (85 pounds) minus the weight of the empty can (10 pounds) equals the weight of the water that can fill the can (85 − 10 = 75 pounds). The number of gallons that will fill the can equals $\frac{75}{8.32}$, which equals 9.01, or choice (C).

5. If there are red, green, and yellow marbles in a jar and 60 percent of these marbles are either red or green, what are the chances of blindly picking a yellow marble out of the jar?

   (A) 2 out of 3

   (B) 3 out of 4

   (C) 2 out of 5

   (D) 3 out of 5

   (E) 4 out of 5

   The correct answer is (C). If 60 percent of the marbles are either red or green, 40 percent of the marbles are yellow. With 40 percent of the marbles being yellow, the probability of selecting a yellow marble is 4 out of 10, or 2 out of 5.

Directions: Each of the following five questions consists of an arithmetic problem. Solve each problem and choose the correct answer choice. Answers are on page 141.

1. A rectangular bin 4 feet long, 2 feet wide, and $1\frac{1}{2}$ feet high is solidly packed with bricks whose dimensions are 8 inches, 4 inches, and 2 inches. The number of bricks in the bin is

   (A) 162
   (B) 243
   (C) 324
   (D) 486
   (E) 648

2. On a house plan on which 2 inches represents 5 feet, the length of a room measures 7 inches. The actual length of the room is

   (A) $14\frac{1}{2}$ feet.
   (B) $15\frac{1}{2}$ feet.
   (C) $16\frac{1}{2}$ feet.
   (D) $17\frac{1}{2}$ feet.
   (E) $18\frac{1}{2}$ feet.

3. A person travels 24 miles at 6 mph, 20 miles at 10 mph, and 20 miles at 5 mph. What is the person's average rate for the complete distance?

   (A) 6.4 mph
   (B) 6.9 mph
   (C) 7.4 mph
   (D) 7.9 mph
   (E) 8.4 mph

4. A fax machine was listed at $240 and was bought at $192. What was the rate of discount?

   (A) 18 percent
   (B) 20 percent
   (C) 22 percent
   (D) 24 percent
   (E) 25 percent

5. If shipping charges to a certain point are 82 cents for the first 5 ounces and 9 cents for each additional ounce, the weight of the package for which the charges are $2.35 is

   (A) 1 pound, 1 ounce.
   (B) 1 pound, 2 ounces.
   (C) 1 pound, 3 ounces.
   (D) 1 pound, 5 ounces.
   (E) 1 pound, 6 ounces.

MATH KNOWLEDGE

Test items on math knowledge appear as five-option questions in the Math Knowledge subtest of the AFOQT. This score is used to calculate the Pilot, Navigator-Technical, Academic Aptitude, and Quantitative composite scores. Math knowledge test items also appear in the Math Skills Test of the Navy and Marine Corps ASTB.

Math knowledge—the ability to use basic mathematical relationships learned in basic courses in mathematics—is one of the important skills for which the military tests. Most of these concepts are included in elementary courses in algebra and geometry. Here are some examples.

1. The reciprocal of 2 is

   (A) 0.02
   (B) 0.25
   (C) 0.50
   (D) 0.80
   (E) 1.20

   The correct answer is (C). If the product of two numbers is 1, either number is called the reciprocal of the other. For example, for $2 \times \frac{1}{2}$, 2 is the reciprocal of $\frac{1}{2}$, and $\frac{1}{2}$ is the reciprocal of 2. $\frac{1}{2}$ is equivalent to 0.50.

2. If a pole 12 feet high casts a shadow 5 feet long, how long a shadow will be cast by a 6-foot person standing next to the pole?

   (A) $1\frac{1}{2}$ feet
   (B) 2 feet
   (C) $2\frac{1}{2}$ feet
   (D) 3 feet
   (E) $3\frac{1}{2}$ feet

   The correct answer is (C). Let x = length of shadow cast by 6-foot person. Use a simple proportion: $12:5 = 6:x$; $12x = 30$; $x = \frac{30}{12} = 2\frac{1}{2}$.

3. The numerical value of 4! is

   (A) 8
   (B) 12
   (C) 16
   (D) 20
   (E) 24

   The correct answer is (E). The factorial of a natural number is the product of that number and all the natural numbers less than it. $4! = 4 \times 3 \times 2 \times 1 = 24$.

4. In the following series of numbers arranged in a logical order, ascertain the pattern or rule for the arrangement and then select the appropriate choice to complete the series.

   2 3 5 8 12 ___

   (A) 14
   (B) 15
   (C) 16
   (D) 17
   (E) 18

   The correct answer is (D). A study of the series of numbers shows a pattern of +1, +2, +3, +4, etc. Inserting 17 in the blank space will conform with this pattern, as 12 + 5 = 17.

5. The square root of 998.56 is

   (A) 30.4
   (B) 30.6
   (C) 31.4
   (D) 31.6
   (E) 32.4

The correct answer is (D). Starting from the decimal point, separate the number in groups of two going in both directions and then solve with a modified form of long division as shown in the following calculation:

$$
\begin{array}{r}
3 \quad 1. \; 6 \\
\sqrt{9 \; 98.56}
\end{array}
$$

$$
\begin{array}{r}
9 \\
61)\overline{0\ 98}
\end{array}
$$

$$
\begin{array}{r}
61 \\
626)\overline{37\ 56} \\
\underline{37\ 56} \\
00\ 00
\end{array}
$$

Directions: Each of the following questions is a mathematical problem. Solve each problem and indicate which of the five choices is the correct answer. Answers are on page 141.

1. $\dfrac{2}{3} \times \dfrac{3}{4} \times \dfrac{4}{5} \times \dfrac{5}{6} \times \dfrac{6}{7} \times \dfrac{7}{8} =$

   (A) $\dfrac{1}{16}$

   (B) $\dfrac{1}{8}$

   (C) $\dfrac{1}{4}$

   (D) $\dfrac{1}{2}$

   (E) None of the above

2. Of the following, the pair that is NOT a set of equivalents is

   (A) 0.15%, 0.0015

   (B) $\dfrac{1}{4}$%, 0.0025

   (C) 1.5%, $\dfrac{3}{200}$

   (D) 15%, $\dfrac{15}{100}$

   (E) 115%, 0.115

3. $10^4 \times 10^3 \times 10^2 =$

   (A) 10^9

   (B) 10^{12}

   (C) 10^{15}

   (D) 10^{24}

   (E) None of the above

4. The hypotenuse of a right triangle whose legs are 3 feet and 4 feet is

   (A) $3\dfrac{1}{2}$ feet.

   (B) 5 feet.

   (C) $5\dfrac{1}{2}$ feet.

   (D) 6 feet.

   (E) 7 feet.

5. If $a = 4b$, then $\dfrac{3}{4}a =$

   (A) $\dfrac{3}{3}b$

   (B) $\dfrac{4}{3}b$

   (C) $3b$

   (D) $\dfrac{b}{3}$

   (E) $\dfrac{b}{4}$

MECHANICAL COMPREHENSION

Test items on mechanical comprehension are widely used by the military. They appear in the Mechanical Functions subtest of the Alternate Flight Aptitude Selection Test (AFAST) and in the Mechanical Comprehension Test of the Navy and Marine Corps ASTB, where they are used in calculating the Pilot Flight Aptitude Rating (PFAR) and the Flight Officer Flight Aptitude Rating (FOFAR).

Mechanical comprehension items utilize drawings and diagrams about which brief questions are to be answered. This requires an understanding of mechanical principles that comes from observing the physical world, working with or operating mechanical devices, or reading and studying.

Tests	Test Time (in minutes)	Number of Questions	Options/ Questions
AFAST	10	20	2
ASTB	15	30	3

Directions: For each of the following questions, study the diagram carefully and select the choice that best answers the question or completes the statement.

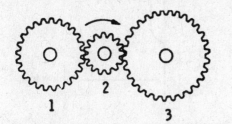

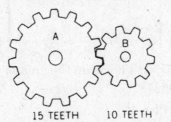

15 TEETH   10 TEETH

1. Which of the other gears is moving in the same direction as gear 2?

   (A) Gear 1

   (B) Gear 3

   (C) Neither of the gears

   (D) Both of the gears

   (E) It cannot be determined.

   The correct answer is (C). The arrow indicates gear 2 is moving clockwise. This would cause both gear 1 and gear 3 to move counterclockwise.

2. In the illustration above, if gear A makes 30 revolutions, gear B will make

   (A) 20 revolutions.

   (B) 30 revolutions.

   (C) 35 revolutions.

   (D) 40 revolutions.

   (E) 45 revolutions.

   The correct answer is (E). For every revolution made by gear A, gear B will make $1\frac{1}{2}$ times as many. If gear A makes 30 revolutions, gear B will make 45.

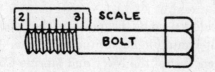

3. The number of threads per inch on the bolt is

(A) 7
(B) 8
(C) 10
(D) 14
(E) 16

The correct answer is (B). The bolt thread makes one revolution per eighth of an inch. Accordingly, it has 8 threads in 1 inch.

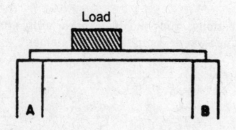

4. Which post holds up the greater part of the load?

(A) Post A
(B) Post B
(C) Both equal

The correct answer is (A). The weight of the load is not centered but is closer to A. The distance from the center of the load to A is less than the distance from the center of the load to B. Therefore, post A would support the greater part of the load.

5. The convenience outlet that is known as a polarized outlet is number

(A) 1
(B) 2
(C) 3

The correct answer is (A). The plug can go into the outlet in only one way in a polarized outlet. In the other outlets, the plug can be reversed.

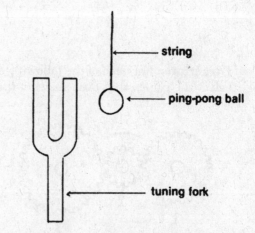

6. When the tuning fork is struck, the Ping-Pong ball will

(A) remain stationary.
(B) bounce up and down.
(C) swing away from the tuning fork.

The correct answer is (C). When a tuning fork vibrates, it moves currents of air. This vibrating air would cause the Ping-Pong ball to be pushed away.

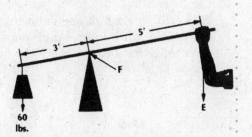

7. In the figure shown here, the pulley system consists of a fixed block and a movable block. The theoretical mechanical advantage is

(A) 2

(B) 3

(C) 4

The correct answer is (A). The number of parts of the rope going to and from the movable block indicates the mechanical advantage. In this case, it is 2.

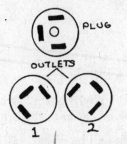

8. The outlet that will accept the plug is

(A) 1

(B) 2

(C) None of the above

The correct answer is (B). Note that the openings in outlet 2 and the prongs of the plug match exactly. The two parallel openings in outlet 1 are too close to the third opening to accept the prongs of the plug.

9. What effort must be exerted to lift a 60-pound weight in the figure of a first-class lever shown above (disregard weight of lever)?

(A) 36 pounds

(B) 45 pounds

(C) 48 pounds

The correct answer is (A).

Let x = effort that must be exerted.

$$x \cdot 5 = 60 \cdot 3$$
$$5x = 180$$
$$x = \frac{180}{5} = 36$$

Directions: Each of the following questions contains a diagram followed by a question or an incomplete statement. Study each diagram carefully and select the choice that best answers the question or completes the statement. Answers are on page 142.

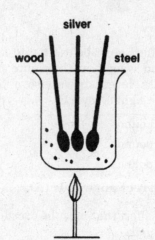

1. Which spoon handle is hottest?

   (A) Wood

   (B) Silver

   (C) Steel

   (D) Silver and steel are equally hot.

   (E) Wood, silver, and steel are all equally hot.

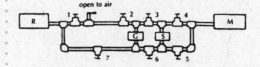

2. In the figure shown above, assume that all valves are closed. For air flow from R through G and then through S to M, open valves

   (A) 7, 6, and 5.

   (B) 7, 3, and 4.

   (C) 7, 6, and 4.

   (D) 7, 3, and 5.

   (E) 7, 4, and 5.

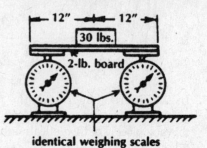

identical weighing scales

3. In the figure shown above, the weight held by the board and placed on the two identical scales will cause each scale to read

   (A) 8 pounds.

   (B) 15 pounds.

   (C) 16 pounds.

   (D) 30 pounds.

   (E) 32 pounds.

4. If the block on which the lever is resting is moved closer to the brick,

   (A) the brick will be easier to lift and will be lifted higher.

   (B) the brick will be harder to lift and will be lifted higher.

   (C) the brick will be easier to lift but will not be lifted as high.

   (D) the brick will be harder to lift and will not be lifted as high.

   (E) the same effort will be required to lift the brick to the same height.

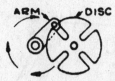

5. The figure above shows a slotted disc turned by a pin on a rotating arm. One revolution of the arm turns the disc

    (A) $\frac{1}{8}$ turn.

    (B) $\frac{1}{4}$ turn.

    (C) $\frac{1}{2}$ turn.

    (D) $\frac{3}{4}$ turn.

    (E) one complete turn.

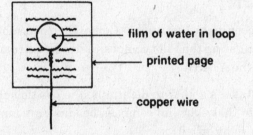

film of water in loop

printed page

copper wire

6. The print looked at through the film of water will

    (A) be enlarged.

    (B) appear smaller.

    (C) look the same as the surrounding print.

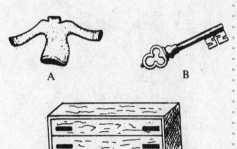

A   B

C

7. If all of these are at the same temperature, and your temperature is higher than the items' temperature, which one will feel the coldest?

    (A) A

    (B) B

    (C) C

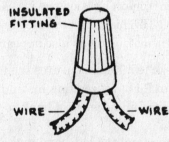

INSULATED FITTING

WIRE — — WIRE

8. Wires are often spliced by the use of a fitting like the one shown above. The use of this fitting does away with the need for

    (A) skinning.

    (B) soldering.

    (C) twisting.

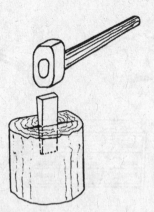

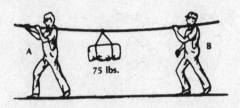

9. The simple machine pictured above is a form of

(A) inclined plane.

(B) torque.

(C) pulley.

10. The weight is being carried entirely on the shoulders of the two people shown above. Which person bears more weight on the shoulders?

(A) A

(B) B

(C) Both are carrying the same weight.

INSTRUMENT COMPREHENSION

Instrument comprehension test items appear in the Instrument Comprehension subtest of the AFOQT. This subtest is used in calculating the Pilot composite score. Instrument comprehension questions also appear in the AFAST.

This type of test item measures the test taker's ability to determine the position of an airplane in flight by reading instruments that show its compass heading, amount of climb or dive, and degree of bank to the right or left.

In each question, the left-hand dial is labeled ARTIFICIAL HORIZON. On the face of this dial the small aircraft silhouette remains stationary, while the positions of the heavy black line and the black pointer vary with changes in the position of the airplane in which the instrument is located.

The heavy black line represents the HORIZON LINE, and the black pointer shows the degree of BANK to right or left. If the airplane has no bank, the black pointer is at zero. It should be noted that each 3 to the left and right of zero is equivalent to 30 degrees of bank and that each 6 to the left and right of zero is equivalent to 60 degrees of bank. The small marks on either side of the centerline are equivalent to 10 degrees of bank.

The illustrations on page 84 show how to read the artificial horizon dial.

If the airplane is neither climbing nor diving, the horizon line is directly on the silhouette's fuselage, as in dials 1, 2, and 3.

If the airplane is climbing, the fuselage silhouette is seen between the horizon line and the pointer, as in dials 4, 5, and 6. The greater the amount of climb, the greater the distance between the horizon line and the fuselage silhouette.

If the airplane is diving, the horizon line is seen between the fuselage silhouette and the pointer, as in dials 7, 8, and 9. The greater the amount of dive, the greater the distance between the horizon line and the fuselage silhouette.

The HORIZON LINE tilts as the aircraft is banked and is always at right angles to the pointer. Refer to the illustration on page 84.

Dial 1 shows an airplane neither climbing nor diving, but banked 90 degrees to the pilot's left.

Dial 2 shows an airplane neither climbing nor diving, with no bank.

Dial 3 shows an airplane neither climbing nor diving, but banked 60 degrees to the pilot's right.

Dial 4 shows an airplane climbing and banking 30 degrees to the pilot's left.

Dial 5 shows an airplane climbing, with no bank.

Dial 6 shows an airplane climbing and banking 45 degrees to the pilot's right.

Dial 7 shows an airplane diving and banking 45 degrees to the pilot's left.

Dial 8 shows an airplane diving, with no bank.

Dial 9 shows an airplane diving and banking 30 degrees to the pilot's right.

In each question, the right-hand dial is labeled COMPASS. On this dial, the arrow shows the compass direction in which the airplane is headed at the moment.

Compasses (see page 85) are graduated in degrees clockwise from north. The cardinal points are:

North 0° or 360°
East 90°
South 180°
West 270°

The intercardinal points are:

Northeast 45°
Southeast 135°
Southwest 225°
Northwest 315°

How to Read the Artificial Horizon Dial

ARTIFICIAL
HORIZON

Dial 1

If the airplane is banked to the pilot's left, the pointer is seen to the right of zero, as in dial 1, above.

ARTIFICIAL
HORIZON

Dial 2

If the airplane has no bank, the black pointer is seen at zero, as in dial 2, above.

ARTIFICIAL
HORIZON

Dial 3

If the airplane is banked to the pilot's right, the pointer is seen to the left of zero, as in dial 3, above.

ARTIFICIAL
HORIZON

Dial 4

If the airplane is banked to the pilot's left, the pointer is seen to the right of zero, as in dial 4, above.

ARTIFICIAL
HORIZON

Dial 5

If the airplane has no bank, the black pointer is seen at zero, as in dial 5, above.

ARTIFICIAL
HORIZON

Dial 6

If the airplane is banked to the pilot's right, the pointer is seen to the left of zero, as in dial 6, above.

ARTIFICIAL
HORIZON

Dial 7

If the airplane is banked to the pilot's left, the pointer is seen to the right of zero, as in dial 7, above.

ARTIFICIAL
HORIZON

Dial 8

If the airplane has no bank, the black pointer is seen at zero, as in dial 8, above.

ARTIFICIAL
HORIZON

Dial 9

If the airplane is banked to the pilot's right, the pointer is seen to the left of zero, as in dial 9, above.

The compass card below shows degrees, cardinal points, and intercardinal points.

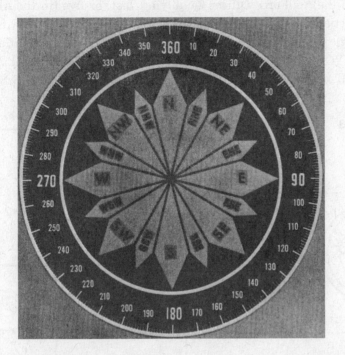

The combination points midway between the cardinal and intercardinal points are:

$$\text{NNE } 22\tfrac{1}{2}°$$ $$\text{SSW } 202\tfrac{1}{2}°$$

$$\text{ENE } 67\tfrac{1}{2}°$$ $$\text{WSW } 247\tfrac{1}{2}°$$

$$\text{ESE } 112\tfrac{1}{2}°$$ $$\text{WNW } 292\tfrac{1}{2}°$$

$$\text{SSE } 157\tfrac{1}{2}°$$ $$\text{NNW } 337\tfrac{1}{2}°$$

Examples of the compass dial are shown below:

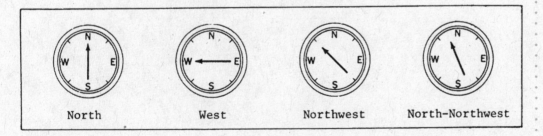

North   West   Northwest   North-Northwest

Each question on instrument comprehension in these tests consists of two dials and either four (in the Air Force Officer Qualifying Test) or five (in the Alternate Flight Aptitude Selection Test) silhouettes of airplanes in flight. Your task is to determine which one of the four or five airplanes is MOST NEARLY in the position indicated by the two dials. YOU ARE ALWAYS LOOKING NORTH AT THE SAME ALTITUDE AS EACH OF THE PLANES. EAST IS ALWAYS TO YOUR RIGHT AS YOU LOOK AT THE PAGE.

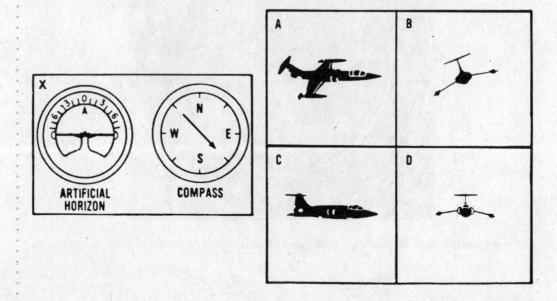

Item X is a sample from the Air Force Officer Qualifying Test. In item X, the dial labeled ARTIFICIAL HORIZON shows that the airplane is NOT banked, and is neither climbing nor diving. The COMPASS shows that it is headed southeast. The only one of the four airplane silhouettes that meets these specifications is in the box lettered C, so the answer to X is C. Note that B is a rear view, while D is a front view. Note also that A is banked to the right and that B is banked to the left.

Item Y is a sample from the Alternate Flight Aptitude Selection Test. In item Y, the dial labeled ARTIFICIAL HORIZON shows that the airplane is NOT banked, and is climbing to a slight èxtent. The COMPASS shows that it is headed southeast. The only one of the five airplane silhouettes that meets these specifications is in the box labeled C, so the answer to Y is C. Note that A is diving and is headed southeast; B is neither diving nor climbing, and is banking to the pilot's right; D is in a slight dive, headed southeast; and E is in a slight dive, headed southwest.

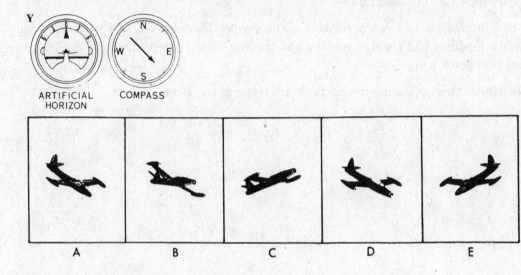

The airplane silhouettes appearing in the Air Force Officer Qualifying Test and those shown in this book are those of the F-104 Starfighter.

The Starfighter was built by Lockheed Aircraft Corporation. It served as a tactical fighter with the Air Force Tactical Air Command and as a day-night interceptor with the Air Defense Command. The Starfighter had a long, sleek body with short, stubby, razor-sharp wings.

    Span: 21'11"
    Length: 54'9"
    Height: 13'6"
    Speed: 1,400 mph
    Ceiling: Above 58,000'
    Range: Beyond 1,450 miles
    Armament: "Sidewinder" missiles and M-61 20mm cannon

F-104 Starfighters underwent many revisions. These were lettered A–G. The F-104C featured a removable boom for aerial refueling on the left side of the fuselage, which extended the plane's range to intercontinental distances.

The airplane silhouettes appearing in the Alternate Flight Aptitude Selection Test (AFAST) booklets and those shown in this book are those of the F-84 Thunderjet.

The Thunderjet was built by Republic Aviation Corporation. It was a low-mid-wing monoplane powered by a single turbo-jet engine mounted in a round fuselage with the air intake in the nose. The jet outlet in the tail extended slightly beyond the rudder's trailing edge.

Removable 230-gallon aluminum fuel tanks were fitted to the wing tips.

> Span: 36′5″
> Length: 37′2″
> Speed: 521 knots/sea level
> Range: 1,360 nautical miles

F-84 Thunderjets had many revisions. These were lettered A–G. All were designed with wings that had tapered leading and trailing edges, except for the F-84F, which had sweptback wings.

The silhouettes appearing in this book are those of the F-84G.

Directions: Each of the following questions consists of two dials and four silhouettes of airplanes in flight. Determine which one of the four airplanes is MOST NEARLY in the position indicated by the two dials. YOU ARE ALWAYS LOOKING NORTH AT THE SAME ALTITUDE AS EACH OF THE PLANES. EAST IS ALWAYS TO YOUR RIGHT AS YOU LOOK AT THE PAGE.

Questions 6–10 are similar to those in the Alternate Flight Aptitude Selection Test. Each question consists of two dials and five silhouettes of airplanes in flight. Determine which one of the five airplanes is MOST NEARLY in the position indicated by the two dials. YOU ARE ALWAYS LOOKING NORTH AT THE SAME ALTITUDE AS EACH OF THE PLANES. EAST IS ALWAYS TO YOUR RIGHT AS YOU LOOK AT THE PAGE. Answers are on page 143.

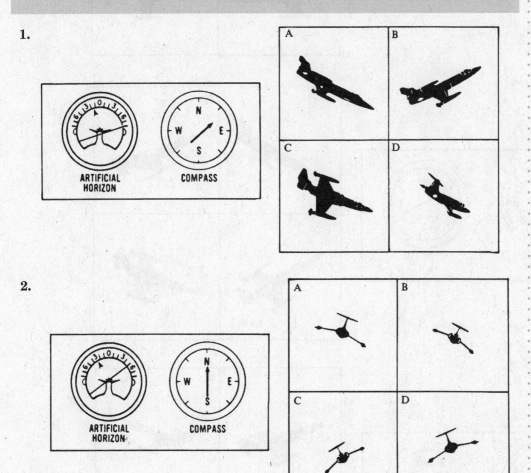

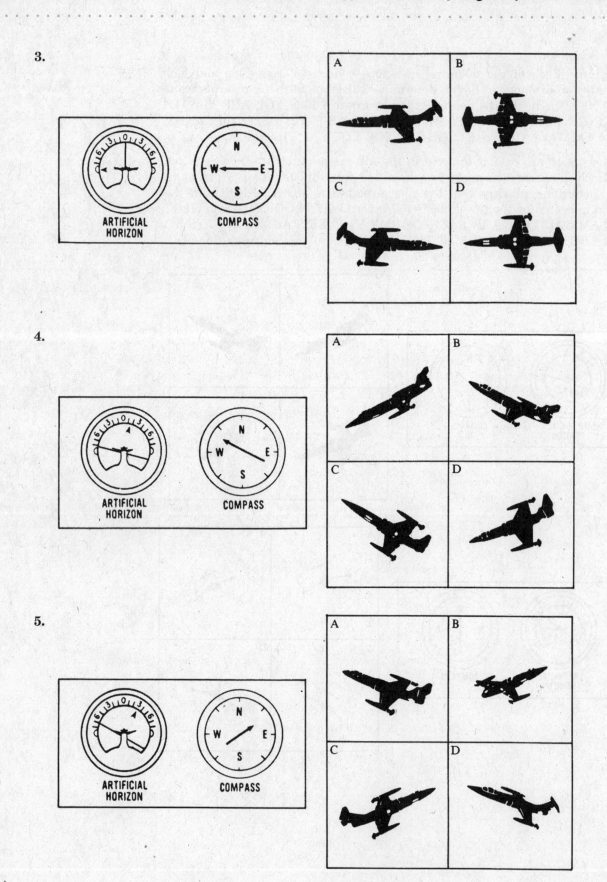

6.

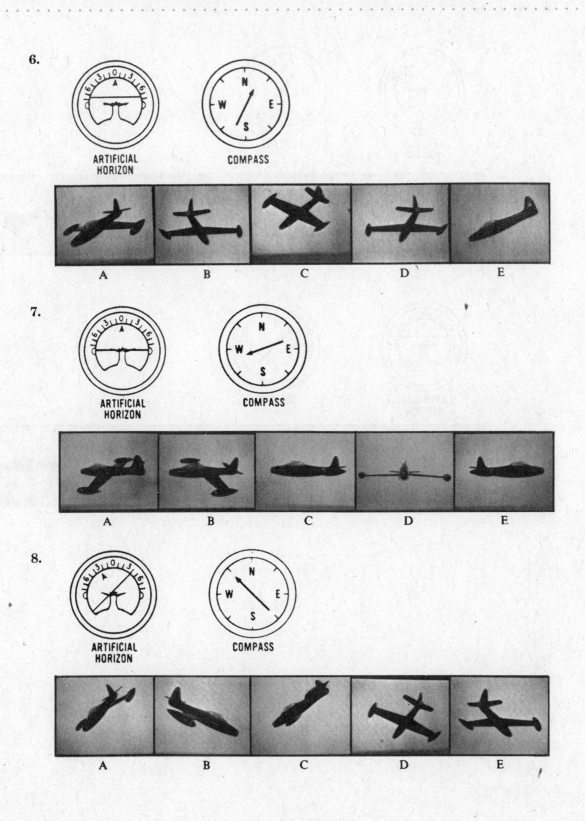

ARTIFICIAL HORIZON   COMPASS

A   B   C   D   E

7.

ARTIFICIAL HORIZON   COMPASS

A   B   C   D   E

8.

ARTIFICIAL HORIZON   COMPASS

A   B   C   D   E

9.

ARTIFICIAL HORIZON

COMPASS

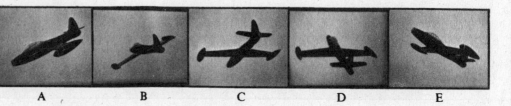

A   B   C   D   E

10.

ARTIFICIAL HORIZON

COMPASS

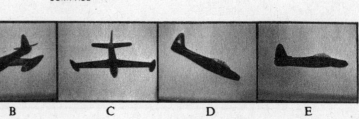

A   B   C   D   E

BLOCK COUNTING

Block Counting test items constitute a subtest of the AFOQT and are used in calculating the Navigator-Technical composite score. They are designed to assess the test taker's ability to "see into" a three-dimensional stack of blocks. These questions help determine one's sense of spatial relations. Questions of this type are also used frequently in exams for vocational fields such as architecture, computer technology, design, drafting, engineering, and many military occupational specialties.

Let's review some sample questions that illustrate the kinds of block counting questions you are likely to encounter. You should assume that all of the blocks in each pile are the same size and shape.

1.

How many boxes are in the diagram shown above?

(A) 23

(B) 24

(C) 25

(D) 26

(E) 27

The correct answer is (C). There are 12 boxes in the front row and 13 in the back row, or a total of 25 boxes.

2.

How many cubes are in the diagram shown above?

(A) 12

(B) 13

(C) 14

(D) 15

(E) 16

The correct answer is (E). There are 9 cubes in the bottom tier, 5 in the middle tier, and 2 in the top tier, or a total of 16 cubes.

3.

What is the total number of boxes that touch the top box in the stack shown above?

(A) 2

(B) 3

(C) 4

(D) 5

(E) 6

The correct answer is (B). The boxes in the stack that are touching the top box are shaded. A total of 3 boxes touch the top box.

Answer sample items 4 and 5 on the basis of the pile of boxes shown below:

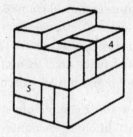

4. What is the total number of boxes that touch box number 4?

(A) 2

(B) 3

(C) 4

(D) 5

(E) 6

The correct answer is (B). Box 4 is touched by the box below it, the box alongside it, and the box on top, or a total of 3 boxes.

5. What is the total number of boxes that touch box number 5?

(A) 3

(B) 4

(C) 5

(D) 6

(E) 7

The correct answer is (C). Box 5 is touched by the box below it, the box alongside it, and 3 boxes on top, or a total of 5 boxes.

Directions: Each of the following five questions contains a diagram of a three-dimensional pile of blocks. You are to ascertain the number of blocks in each pile. All of the blocks in each pile are the same size and shape. Answers are on pages 143–144.

1.

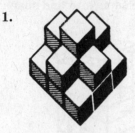

What is the total number of blocks in the pile shown above?

(A) 11
(B) 12
(C) 13
(D) 14
(E) 15

2.

How many blocks are in the above diagram?

(A) 23
(B) 24
(C) 25
(D) 26
(E) 27

3.

How many blocks are in the diagram shown above?

(A) 40
(B) 41
(C) 42
(D) 43
(E) 44

4.

What is the total number of blocks in the above diagram?

(A) 54
(B) 56
(C) 58
(D) 60
(E) 62

5.

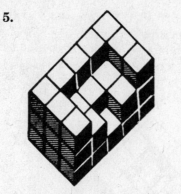

Each of the following 5 questions numbered 6–10 are based on the three-dimensional pile of blocks shown below. Determine how many pieces are touched by each numbered block. All of the blocks in the pile are the same size and shape.

What is the number of blocks in the pile shown above?

(A) 34

(B) 35

(C) 36

(D) 37

(E) 38

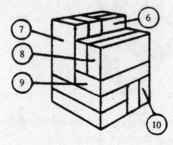

Choices					
Block	**A**	**B**	**C**	**D**	**E**
6	3	4	5	6	7
7	4	5	6	7	8
8	1	2	3	4	5
9	4	5	6	7	8
10	4	5	6	7	8

TABLE READING

Table Reading test items constitute a subtest of the AFOQT. They are used in calculating the Pilot and Navigator-Technical composite scores and are designed to measure a test taker's ability to read and comprehend tabular material quickly and accurately.

Directions: Answer questions 1–3 on the basis of the data in the following table:

RECORD OF EMPLOYEES

| Name of Employee | Where Assigned | Number of Days Absent | | Yearly Salary |
		Vacation	Sick Leave	
Carty	Laundry	18	4	$19,300
Hart	Laboratory	24	8	17,860
Intersoll	Buildings	20	17	18,580
King	Supply	12	10	17,860
Lopez	Laboratory	17	8	17,500
Martin	Buildings	13	12	17,500
Page	Buildings	5	7	17,500
Quinn	Supply	19	0	17,380
Sage	Buildings	23	10	18,940
Vetter	Laundry	21	2	18,300

1. The only employee who was not absent because of illness is

   (A) Hart.
   (B) Lopez.
   (C) Page.
   (D) Quinn.
   (E) Vetter.

   The correct answer is (D). Look down the sick leave column and note that only Quinn had not used any sick leave.

2. The employee with the lowest salary was absent on vacation for

   (A) seventeen days.
   (B) eighteen days.
   (C) nineteen days.
   (D) twenty days.
   (E) twenty-one days.

   The correct answer is (C). Look down the yearly salary column and note that the lowest salary is $17,380. This is the salary received by Quinn who was absent on vacation for nineteen days.

3. Which one of the following was absent on vacation for more than twenty days?

   (A) Carty
   (B) Ingersoll
   (C) Lopez
   (D) Quinn
   (E) Vetter

   The correct answer is (E). Note that there are three employees who were absent on vacation for more than twenty days. However, the only one of the three such employees listed in the choices is Vetter.

Directions: Answer questions 1–5 on the basis of the table below. Notice that the X-values are shown at the top of the table and the Y-values are shown on the left of the table. Find the entry that occurs at the intersection of the row and column corresponding to the values given. Answers are on page 144.

X-VALUE

		−3	−2	−1	0	+1	+2	+3
	+3	22	23	25	27	28	29	30
	+2	23	25	27	29	30	31	32
	+1	24	26	28	30	32	33	34
Y-VALUE	0	26	27	29	31	33	34	35
	−1	27	29	30	32	34	35	37
	−2	28	30	31	33	35	36	38
	−3	29	31	32	34	36	37	39

	X	Y	A	B	C	D	E
1.	−1	0	29	33	32	35	34
2.	−2	−2	22	29	23	31	30
3.	+2	−1	25	31	35	30	27
4.	0	+3	22	24	25	27	29
5.	+1	−2	36	33	39	35	32

AVIATION INFORMATION

Test items about Aviation Information constitute a subtest of the AFOQT and are used in calculating the Pilot composite score. Aviation Information questions also appear in the Aviation Nautical Information Test (ANIT) of the Navy and Marine Corps ASTB, which is used in calculating the Pilot Flight Aptitude Rating and the Flight Officer Flight Aptitude Rating. The Helicopter Knowledge subtest of the AFAST tests your general understanding of the principles of helicopter flight.

For further preparation for this subtest, you may want to consult one or more of the many basic books on aviation that have been published. Your local library or bookstore should stock at least a few. You might also check the U.S. Government Printing Office for manuals or booklets on aviation. The office's Web site is www.gpo.gov.

Questions 1–8 are based on the following diagram of an airplane:

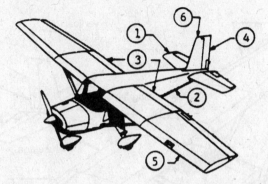

1. The part of the airplane numbered 1 is the

   (A) horizontal stabilizer.
   (B) left aileron.
   (C) left wing.
   (D) right aileron.
   (E) right wing.

2. The part of the airplane numbered 2 is the

   (A) empennage.
   (B) flight control and control surfaces.
   (C) fuselage.
   (D) landing gear.
   (E) wing assembly.

3. The parts of the airplane numbered 3 are the

   (A) ailerons.
   (B) horizontal stabilizers.
   (C) landing flaps.
   (D) landing wheels.
   (E) trim tabs.

4. The part of the airplane numbered 4 is the

   (A) elevator.
   (B) fuselage.
   (C) landing flap.
   (D) rudder.
   (E) vertical fin.

5. The part of the airplane numbered 5 is the

   (A) horizontal stabilizer.
   (B) leading edge, left wing.
   (C) leading edge, right wing.
   (D) trailing edge, left wing.
   (E) trailing edge, right wing.

6. The part of the airplane numbered 6 is part of the

   (A) vertical fin.
   (B) flight control and control surfaces.
   (C) fuselage.
   (D) landing gear.
   (E) wings.

Answers for questions 1–6 can be found in the diagram below.

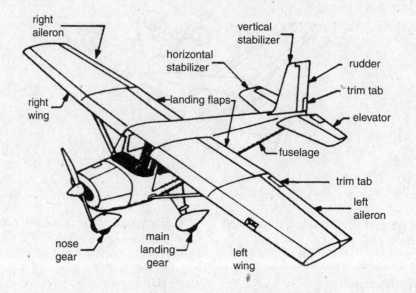

7. The airplane in the diagram above may best be described as

   (A) high wing—externally braced; conventional type landing gear.
   (B) high wing—externally braced; tricycle type landing gear.
   (C) high wing—full cantilever; conventional type landing gear.
   (D) high wing—full cantilever; tricycle type landing gear.
   (E) mid wing—semi cantilever; tricycle type landing gear.

   The correct answer is (B). Note the high wings and external braces, as well as the two main wheels and a steerable nose wheel—the tricycle type.

8. The landing gear on the airplane in the diagram above has a

   (A) nose skid.
   (B) nose wheel.
   (C) tail skid.
   (D) tail wheel.
   (E) set of parallel skids.

   The correct answer is (B). Note the nose wheel. There are no skids.

9. The small hinged section on the elevator of most airplanes is called the

   (A) flap.
   (B) aileron.
   (C) stringer.
   (D) trim tab.
   (E) vertical fin.

   The correct answer is (D). The small hinged section on the elevator is called the trim tab. It helps prevent pilot fatigue by relieving control pressure at any desired flight altitude.

10. The wing shape shown below is best described as

   (A) double tapered.
   (B) straight leading and trailing edges.
   (C) straight leading edge, tapered trailing edge.
   (D) tapered leading and trailing edges.
   (E) tapered leading edge, straight trailing edge.

The correct answer is (E). Note the tapered leading or forward edge of the wing and the straight trailing or rear edge of the wing.

11. Movement about the longitudinal axis of the aircraft is termed

    (A) bank.
    (B) pitch.
    (C) skid.
    (D) slip.
    (E) yaw.

The correct answer is (A). In aviation terminology, to *bank* is to roll about the longitudinal axis of the aircraft.

12. Which one of the following does NOT affect density altitude?

    (A) Altitude
    (B) Atmospheric pressure
    (C) Moisture content of air
    (D) Temperature
    (E) Wind velocity

The correct answer is (E). Density altitude pertains to a theoretical air density that exists under standard conditions at a given altitude. The four factors that affect density altitude are altitude, atmospheric pressure, temperature, and moisture content of the air.

13. The lifting power for dirigibles is now provided by

    (A) helium.
    (B) hot air.
    (C) hydrogen.
    (D) nitrogen.
    (E) oxygen.

The correct answer is (A). The dirigible, or zeppelin, is lifted by helium. Hydrogen is highly flammable and is no longer used for lifting. Hot air is used to lift balloons.

14. The name Sikorsky is generally associated with the development of

    (A) lighter-than-air aircraft.
    (B) rotary wing aircraft.
    (C) supersonic aircraft.
    (D) turbojets.
    (E) turboprops.

The correct answer is (B). Igor Sikorsky designed and produced the first practical helicopter. Versatile rotary wing aircraft are now produced in various military and civilian versions.

15. The maneuver in which the helicopter is maintained in nearly motionless flight over a reference point at a constant altitude and a constant heading is termed

    (A) autorotation.
    (B) feathering action.
    (C) hovering.
    (D) free wheeling.
    (E) torque.

The correct answer is (C). Hovering is the term applied when a helicopter maintains a constant position at a selected point, usually several feet above the ground.

Directions: Each of the following 25 questions or incomplete statements is followed by five answer choices. Decide which one best answers the question or completes the statement. Answers are on pages 144–146.

1. Most airplanes are designed so that the outer tips of the wing are higher than the wing roots attached to the fuselage in order to

   (A) increase the maximum permissible payload.

   (B) provide lateral stability.

   (C) provide longitudinal stability.

   (D) reduce fuel consumption.

   (E) streamline the fuselage.

2. If an airfoil moves forward and upward, the relative wind moves

   (A) backward and downward.

   (B) backward and upward.

   (C) forward and downward.

   (D) forward and upward.

   (E) forward horizontally.

3. Many factors influence lift and drag. If the wing area is doubled,

   (A) the lift will be doubled, but the drag will be halved.

   (B) the lift will be halved, but the drag will be doubled.

   (C) the lift and drag will be doubled.

   (D) the lift and drag will be halved.

   (E) there is no effect on lift or drag.

4. Tetraethyl lead (TEL) is used principally as an additive that

   (A) absorbs moisture in gasoline.

   (B) decreases viscosity of gasoline.

   (C) has a low antiknock quality.

   (D) increases gasoline antiknock quality.

   (E) increases volatility of gasoline.

5. Standard weights have been established for numerous items used in weight and balance computations. The standard weight for gasoline used in an airplane is

   (A) 6 lbs./U.S. gal.

   (B) 7.5 lbs./U.S. gal.

   (C) 8.35 lbs./U.S. gal.

   (D) 10 lbs./U.S. gal.

   (E) 15 lbs./U.S. gal.

6. The internal pressure of a fluid decreases at points where the speed of the fluid increases. This statement, which partially explains how an airplane wing produces lift, is called

   (A) Archimedes' Principle.

   (B) Bernocilli's Principle.

   (C) Kepler's Law.

   (D) Newton's Law.

   (E) Pascal's Principle.

7. The rearward force acting on an airplane during flight is termed

   (A) drag.

   (B) gravity.

   (C) lift.

   (D) thrust.

   (E) weight.

8. The acute angle between the chord line of the wing and the direction of the relative wind is the

   (A) angle of attack.

   (B) angle of incidence.

   (C) axis of rotation.

   (D) lift vector.

   (E) pitch angle.

9. Which of the following statements is true regarding lift and drag?

   (A) As the air density increases, lift and drag decrease.

   (B) As the air density increases, lift increases but drag decreases.

   (C) As the air density increases, lift decreases but drag increases.

   (D) As the air density increases, lift and drag increase.

   (E) Lift varies inversely with the density of air.

10. The aft end of the airfoil where the airflow over the upper surface meets the airflow from the lower surface is called the

    (A) camber.

    (B) chord.

    (C) leading edge.

    (D) relative wind.

    (E) trailing edge.

11. The empennage of an airplane is the

    (A) fuselage.

    (B) landing gear.

    (C) power plant.

    (D) tail section.

    (E) wing assembly.

12. The primary use of the ailerons is to

    (A) bank the airplane.

    (B) control the direction of yaw.

    (C) control the pitch attitude.

    (D) permit a lower landing speed.

    (E) provide a steeper climb path.

13. The pitot is an important component in measuring

    (A) airspeed.

    (B) altitude.

    (C) direction.

    (D) fuel pressure.

    (E) oil pressure.

14. Applying forward pressure on the control causes the elevator surfaces to move downward. This

    (A) pushes the airplane's tail downward and the nose downward.

    (B) pushes the airplane's tail downward and the nose upward.

    (C) pushes the airplane's tail upward and the nose downward.

    (D) pushes the airplane's tail upward and the nose upward.

    (E) yaws the nose in the desired direction.

15. Runways are assigned numbers that are determined by the magnetic direction of the runway. The runway's magnetic direction is rounded off to the closest 10 degrees and the last 0 is omitted. If a runway is numbered 3 at one end of the runway strip, what would it be numbered at the other end?

    (A) 3

    (B) 12

    (C) 15

    (D) 21

    (E) 33

16. At a controlled airport, the light signal used by the tower to warn an aircraft in flight that the airport is unsafe and not to land is a(n)

    (A) alternating red and green.

    (B) flashing green.

    (C) flashing red.

    (D) steady green.

    (E) steady red.

17. Airport runway lights used to illuminate the runway are

    (A) blue.

    (B) green.

    (C) red.

    (D) white.

    (E) yellow.

18. The illustration shown below is a ground view of a weathervane, looking up from the street below. The wind is coming from the

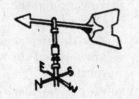

(A) NE

(B) SE

(C) SW

(D) NW

(E) SSE

19. The time 2:00 p.m. is expressed in the 24-hour system as

(A) zero two zero zero.

(B) zero four zero zero.

(C) one four.

(D) one four zero zero.

(E) two zero zero.

20. In the figure below, the pilot has banked the airplane

(A) 30 degrees to the right.

(B) 45 degrees to the right.

(C) 60 degrees to the right.

(D) 45 degrees to the left.

(E) 30 degrees to the left.

Questions 21–25 pertain to helicopter operations.

21. Which of the following is used by the helicopter pilot to increase or decrease tail-rotor thrust, as needed, to counteract torque effect?

(A) Clutch

(B) Collective

(C) Throttle control

(D) Pedals

(E) Free wheeling unit

22. Limiting airspeeds are shown on an airspeed indicator by a color coding. The radial line placed on the airspeed indicator to show the airspeed limit beyond that operation is dangerous is colored

(A) blue.

(B) brown.

(C) green.

(D) red.

(E) yellow.

23. If engine failure is experienced while hovering below 10 feet, the pilot should cushion the landing by applying the

(A) clutch.

(B) collective.

(C) cyclic.

(D) pedals.

(E) throttle.

24. Weight and balance limitations must be met before takeoff. Which of the following is NOT part of the useful load (payload)?

(A) Baggage

(B) Oil

(C) Passengers

(D) Pilot

(E) Usable fuel

25. A basic principle of helicopter performance states that for any given gross weight,

(A) the higher the density altitude, the lesser the rate of climb.

(B) the higher the density altitude, the greater the rate of climb.

(C) the lower the density altitude, the lesser the rate of climb.

(D) the density altitude and rate of climb are directly proportional.

(E) There is no relationship between density altitude and rate of climb.

NAUTICAL INFORMATION

Questions on nautical information appear in the Aviation/Nautical Information Test of the Navy and Marine Corps Aviation Selection Test Battery. The Aviation/Nautical Information Test is used in constructing the Pilot Flight Aptitude Rating and the Flight Officer Flight Aptitude Rating.

1. To go in the direction of the ship's bow is to go

(A) aft.

(B) below.

(C) forward.

(D) outboard.

(E) topside.

The correct answer is (C). The bow is the forward part of a ship. To go in that direction is to go forward.

2. In marine navigation, speed is measured in

(A) knots.

(B) miles.

(C) nautical miles.

(D) range.

(E) standard miles.

The correct answer is (A). Speed is measured in knots, a term meaning nautical miles per hour.

3. The ratio of the international nautical mile to the statute mile is most nearly

(A) $\frac{3}{4}$

(B) $\frac{7}{8}$

(C) $\frac{1}{1}$

(D) $\frac{8}{7}$

(E) $\frac{4}{3}$

The correct answer is (D). The international nautical mile is most nearly 6,078 feet; the statute mile is 5,280 feet. The ratio is approximately $\frac{8}{7}$.

4. On the compass, which is used to determine direction, EAST is indicated at a reading of

(A) 000 degrees.

(B) 090 degrees.

(C) 180 degrees.

(D) 270 degrees.

(E) 360 degrees.

The correct answer is (B). All directions are measured from north on a 360-degree system. East is 090 degrees; south is 180 degrees; west is 270 degrees; north is 000 or 360 degrees.

5. Compass north is generally not the same as magnetic north because of

(A) diurnal change.

(B) gyrocompass error.

(C) parallax.

(D) the influence of local magnetic forces.

(E) vessel speed, heading, and latitude.

The correct answer is (D). The influence of local magnetic forces, such as iron, near the compass causes deviation from magnetic north.

6. Using the 24-hour basis in navigation, 8:45 a.m. would be written as

(A) 845

(B) 0845

(C) 08.45

(D) 2045

(E) 20.45

The correct answer is (B). The 24-hour clock uses four digits. Hours and minutes less than 10 are preceded by a zero.

7. Delicate, feather-like, white clouds occurring at very high altitude are termed

(A) altostratus clouds.

(B) cirrocumulus clouds.

(C) cirrus clouds.

(D) cumulus clouds.

(E) nimbostratus clouds.

The correct answer is (C). Cirrus clouds are high-altitude delicate white clouds with little shading.

8. The formation of fog may be predicted by determining the

(A) atmospheric pressure.

(B) changes in atmospheric pressure.

(C) color of the sky.

(D) difference between the wet-and-dry bulb temperatures.

(E) wind speed.

The correct answer is (D). The formation of fog may be predicted by using the wet-and-dry bulb. Fog usually forms when the wet-bulb depression is less than 4 degrees.

9. Icebreakers are operated by the

(A) U.S. Army.

(B) U.S. Coast Guard.

(C) U.S. Department of Commerce.

(D) U.S. Department of the Interior.

(E) U.S. Navy.

The correct answer is (B). The U.S. Coast Guard is responsible for national icebreaking missions.

10. A ship, at a latitude of 35°N and a longitude of 30°E, is in the

(A) Bering Sea.

(B) Caribbean Sea.

(C) Mediterranean Sea.

(D) North Sea.

(E) Sea of Japan.

The correct answer is (C). The coordinates given indicate a position in the Mediterranean Sea.

Directions: Each of the following 25 questions or incomplete statements is followed by five answer choices. Decide which one best answers the question or completes the statement. Answers are on pages 146–148.

1. "Zulu Time" used in ship communication is

   (A) Daylight Savings Time.
   (B) Local Mean Time.
   (C) Greenwich Mean Time.
   (D) Standard Time.
   (E) Zone Time.

2. Which of the following is a common type of visual communication used shipboard?

   (A) Facsimile
   (B) Foghorn
   (C) Radiotelegraph
   (D) Satellite
   (E) Semiphore

3. The plane perpendicular to the earth's axis and midway between the two poles divides the earth into the

   (A) eastern and western hemispheres.
   (B) north and south poles.
   (C) northern and southern hemispheres.
   (D) parallels and meridians.
   (E) upper meridian and lower meridian.

4. Which of the following types of rope is strongest?

   (A) Cotton
   (B) Hemp
   (C) Manila
   (D) Nylon
   (E) Sisal

5. Greenwich, at prime meridian, is at a latitude of approximately 50°N. Which of the following cities is closest to Greenwich?

   (A) Amsterdam—52°22′N 4°53′E
   (B) Athens—37°58′N 23°43′E
   (C) Copenhagen—55°40′N 12°54′E
   (D) Oslo—50°57′N 10°42′E
   (E) Stockholm—59°17′N 18°3′E

6. A latitude of 21°N and longitude of 159°W is in the vicinity of

   (A) Cuba.
   (B) the Falkland Islands.
   (C) Hawaii.
   (D) the Philippines.
   (E) Samoa.

7. An unlighted buoy, used to mark the left side of a channel when facing inland, is called a

   (A) bell buoy.
   (B) can buoy.
   (C) nun buoy.
   (D) spar buoy.
   (E) whistle buoy.

8. If the clock shows the time to be 1400 aboard a ship sailing in time zone +3, what would be the time in the Greenwich zone?

   (A) 0800
   (B) 1100
   (C) 1400
   (D) 1700
   (E) 2000

9. The navigation light associated with "port" is colored

   (A) green.
   (B) red.
   (C) white.
   (D) yellow.
   (E) None of the above

10. To go in the direction of the ship's stern is to go

   (A) aft.
   (B) below.
   (C) forward.
   (D) inboard.
   (E) topside.

11. The vertical distance from the waterline to the lowest part of the ship's bottom is the

   (A) draft.
   (B) freeboard.
   (C) list.
   (D) sounding.
   (E) trim.

12. The forward part of the main deck of a ship is generally called the

   (A) fantail.
   (B) forecastle.
   (C) quarterdeck.
   (D) superstructure.
   (E) topside.

13. The International Date Line is located at

   (A) the 0 meridian.
   (B) the 180th meridian.
   (C) the celestial meridian.
   (D) Greenwich, England.
   (E) the prime meridian.

14. Compass error in a magnetic compass caused by change in the magnetic field of the earth from place to place is termed

   (A) bearing.
   (B) deviation.
   (C) reckoning.
   (D) sighting.
   (E) variation.

15. The lubber's line used in ascertaining the ship's heading indicates

   (A) compass error.
   (B) the direction of the ship's bow.
   (C) the ship's heading.
   (D) magnetic north.
   (E) true north.

16. A tide falling after high tide is

   (A) breaking.
   (B) bulging.
   (C) ebbing.
   (D) flooding.
   (E) slacking.

17. Low even clouds that form just above the earth and give the sky a hazy appearance are termed

   (A) altocumulus clouds.
   (B) altostratus clouds.
   (C) cirrocumulus clouds.
   (D) cirrus clouds.
   (E) stratus clouds.

18. The Beaufort scale is generally used at sea in estimating

   (A) wind direction.
   (B) wind speed.
   (C) atmospheric pressure.
   (D) relative humidity.
   (E) water depth.

19. The instrument used in celestial navigation to measure angles in degrees, minutes, and seconds is called a(n)

    (A) azimuth.
    (B) compass.
    (C) protractor.
    (D) sextant.
    (E) transit.

20. When a person is reported overboard, the action to take first is to

    (A) bring the ship to a halt.
    (B) track the person with a pair of binoculars.
    (C) throw life buoys over at once.
    (D) turn the ship around 180 degrees.
    (E) reduce the ship's speed.

21. A fathometer is generally used to

    (A) determine direction.
    (B) determine Greenwich mean time.
    (C) make deep-sea soundings.
    (D) make shallow water soundings.
    (E) measure distance in nautical miles.

22. 6:00 p.m. is written in the 24-hour system as

    (A) 0600
    (B) 0900
    (C) 1200
    (D) 1500
    (E) 1800

23. In marine navigation, which of the following is NOT a method of determining position?

    (A) Celestial navigation
    (B) Dead reckoning
    (C) Electronic navigation
    (D) Piloting
    (E) Ranging

24. The intersection of the ship's main deck with the side plating is termed the

    (A) bilge.
    (B) fantail.
    (C) gunwale.
    (D) platform.
    (E) stanchion.

25. The docking structure built at right angles to the shore is called a(n)

    (A) abutment.
    (B) mooring.
    (C) pier.
    (D) slip.
    (E) wharf.

Questions 26–30 deal with boat rudder operations on a single-screw boat with a right-hand propeller. These questions are 3-choice items.

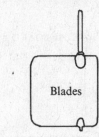

Blades

26. A balanced rudder (shown above) has about $\frac{1}{5}$ of the total rudder area projecting ahead of the rudder stock. An unbalanced rudder has the rudder stock attached to the edge of the blade. Which one of the following statements is characteristic of the balanced rudder but NOT of the unbalanced rudder?

    (A) It makes steering easier.
    (B) It makes steering more difficult.
    (C) It exerts considerable effect in increasing the strain on the steering gear.

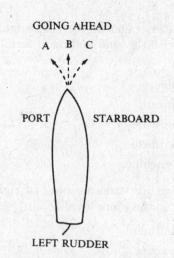

27. The figure above shows a boat that has left rudder and is going ahead. The bow of the boat would proceed in direction

   (A) A
   (B) B
   (C) C

29. In the figure above, for the boat to swing from position 1 to position 2, she should proceed with

   (A) left rudder.
   (B) right rudder.
   (C) rudder amidship.

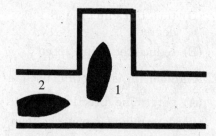

28. The figure above shows a boat that has left rudder and is going astern. The stem of the boat would proceed in direction

   (A) A
   (B) B
   (C) C

30. In the figure above, for the boat to back out from position 1 in a slip to position 2 into the channel, she should back out with

   (A) left rudder.
   (B) right rudder.
   (C) rudder amidship.

ROTATED BLOCKS

Test items on the Rotated Blocks subtest of the AFOQT are designed to test your ability to visualize and manipulate objects in space.

In each question, you are shown a picture of a block. To the right of the pictured block are five choices, each showing a different block. You are required to select the choice containing a block that is just like the pictured block at the left although turned in a different position. In order to arrive at the correct answer, you may have to mentally turn blocks over, turn them around, or turn them both over and around.

Look at the two blocks below. Although viewed from different angles, the blocks are just alike.

Look at the two blocks below. They are not alike. They can never be turned so that they will be alike.

Now look at each sample item below. Which of the five choices is just like the first block?

SAMPLE ITEMS

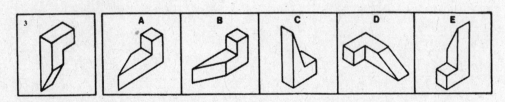

The correct answer for 1 is D.

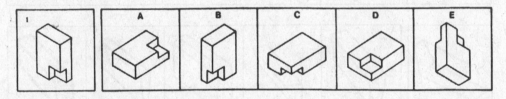

The correct answer for 2 is C.

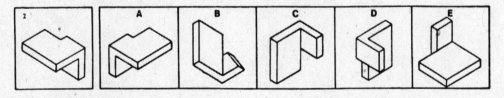

The correct answer for 3 is A.

Directions: Each of the following five questions is followed by five choices. Decide which one of the choices is the best answer. Answers are on page 148.

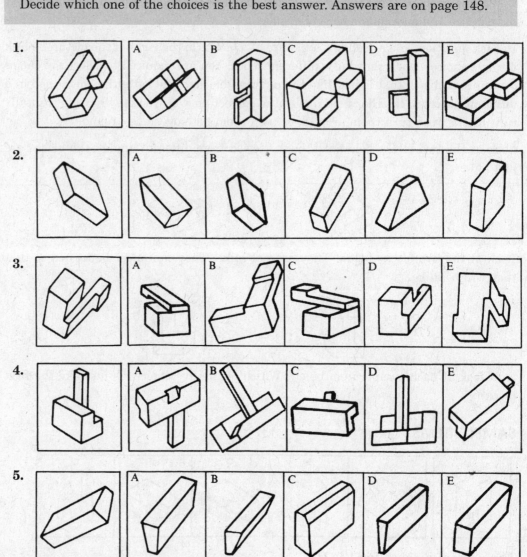

GENERAL SCIENCE

Test items in the General Science subtest of the AFOQT are five-option questions; they are used in calculating the Navigator-Technical composite score. The questions assess the test taker's familiarity with life science, physical science, and earth science.

Life science items cover basic biology, human nutrition, and health. Physical science items pertain to elementary chemistry and physics. Fundamentals of geology, meteorology, and astronomy are included in the earth science section.

1. What temperature is shown on a Fahrenheit thermometer when the centigrade thermometer reads 0°?

   (A) −40°
   (B) −32°
   (C) 0°
   (D) +32°
   (E) +40°

   The correct answer is (D). Water freezes at 0° on the centigrade or Celsius thermometer. Water freezes at 32° Fahrenheit.

2. Saliva contains an enzyme that acts on

   (A) carbohydrates.
   (B) fats.
   (C) minerals.
   (D) proteins.
   (E) vitamins.

   The correct answer is (A). The salivary glands secrete the enzyme ptyalin that acts on carbohydrates.

3. In 4 hours, the earth rotates

   (A) 20 degrees.
   (B) 30 degrees.
   (C) 40 degrees.
   (D) 60 degrees.
   (E) 90 degrees.

   The correct answer is (D). The earth rotates 360 degrees in 24 hours. Four hours is $\frac{1}{6}$ of 24 hours; $\frac{1}{6}$ of 360° is 60°.

4. The moon is a

   (A) meteor.
   (B) planet.
   (C) planetoid.
   (D) satellite.
   (E) star.

   The correct answer is (D). The moon is a satellite of Earth.

5. The vitamin manufactured by the skin with the help of the sun is

   (A) A
   (B) B6
   (C) B12
   (D) C
   (E) D

   The correct answer is (E). Vitamin D can be found in fish liver oils and egg yolks. It can also be manufactured within the skin that is exposed to sunlight.

Directions: Each of the following five questions or incomplete statements is followed by five answer choices. Decide which one of the choices best answers the question or completes the statement. Answers are on page 148.

1. "Shooting stars" are

   (A) exploding stars.
   (B) cosmic rays.
   (C) meteors.
   (D) planetoids.
   (E) X-rays.

2. Organisms that sustain their life cycles by feeding off other living organisms are known as

   (A) bacteria.
   (B) molds.
   (C) parasites.
   (D) saprophytes.
   (E) viruses.

3. When two or more elements combine to form a substance that has properties different from those of the component elements, the new substance is known as a(n)

   (A) alloy.
   (B) compound.
   (C) mixture.
   (D) solution.
   (E) suspension.

4. If a $33\frac{1}{3}$ rpm phonograph record is played at a speed of 45 rpm, it will

   (A) give no sound.
   (B) play louder.
   (C) play softer.
   (D) sound higher-pitched.
   (E) sound lower-pitched.

5. Which one of the following gases is necessary for burning?

   (A) Argon
   (B) Carbon dioxide
   (C) Hydrogen
   (D) Nitrogen
   (E) Oxygen

HIDDEN FIGURES

Questions on hidden figures appear in the Hidden Figures subtest of the Air Force Officer Qualifying Test, and are used in constructing the Navigator-Technical composite. They are designed to measure your ability to see simple figures in complex drawings. Although these figures are fairly well camouflaged, proper visualization should enable you to discern them without too much difficulty.

At the top of each section of this subtest are five figures lettered A, B, C, D, and E. Below these on each page are several numbered drawings. You must determine which lettered figure is contained in each of the numbered drawings.

The lettered figures are shown below:

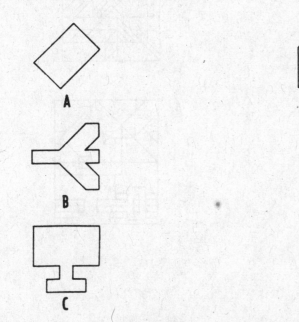

As an example, look at drawing X below:

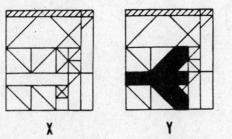

Which one of the five figures is contained in drawing X? Now look at drawing Y, which is exactly like drawing X except that the outline of figure B has been shaded to show where to look for it. Thus, B is the answer to sample item X.

Each numbered drawing contains only *one* of the lettered figures. The correct figure in each drawing will always be of the same size and in the same position as it appears at the top of the page. Therefore, do not rotate the page in order to find it. Look at each numbered drawing and decide which one of the five lettered figures is contained in it.

Directions: Decide which of the following lettered figures best matches each numbered drawing. Answers are on page 149.

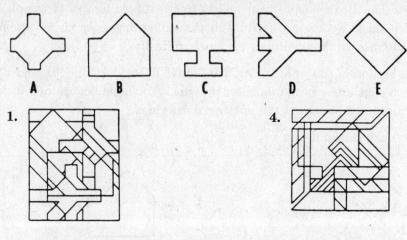

A   B   C   D   E

1.
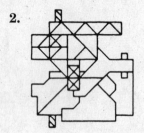

4.
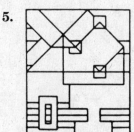

2.

5.

3.

COMPLEX MOVEMENTS

The Complex Movements subtest of the AFAST measures the test taker's ability to judge distance and visualize motion.

For these test items, the test taker must determine how to move a dot that is outside a circle into the center of the circle using a direction key and a distance key. First, the test taker must figure out the horizontal (right or left) direction, then the vertical direction (up or down), and finally the distance of movement, using the direction key and the distance key provided.

For example, let's look at the following situation:

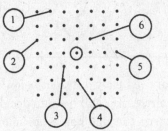

The dot to be moved may be in any of the 48 positions surrounding the circled dot. The dot must be moved first horizontally and then vertically a certain number of spaces to reach the center of the circle.

We will number several of the dots and see specifically how the dots are to be moved.

- Dot 1 should be moved 2 spaces to the right and 3 spaces down.
- Dot 2 should be moved 3 spaces to the right and 1 space down.
- Dot 3 should be moved 1 space to the right and 1 space up.
- Dot 4 is directly under the circled dot and need not be moved horizontally but should be moved up 2 spaces.
- Dot 5 should be moved to the left 3 spaces but need not be moved vertically, as it is in direct line with the circled dot.
- Dot 6 should be moved 1 space to the left and 1 space down.

Using the same practice grid, let's try with just one outside dot and the circled dot.

It should be moved 2 spaces to the right and 2 spaces down.

•

⊙

It should be moved 3 spaces to the left and 3 spaces down.

⊙ •

It should be moved 3 spaces to the left.

⊙

•

It should be moved 1 space to the right and 1 space up.

After this preliminary practice session, we are now ready for the "real" instructions using the "real" direction and distance keys. For each question, you must move the dot from outside the circle into the center of the circle. Five pairs of symbols are given representing direction and distance. You must choose the one pair that represents the amount and direction of movement to move the dot from outside the circle into the center of the circle.

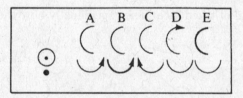

In the example above, look at the heavy dark dot below the circle. Your task is to move this dot to the center of the circle. You will have to decide which *direction* or *directions* (right or left and up or down) the dot has to be moved and the *distance* in each direction moved to reach the center of the circle.

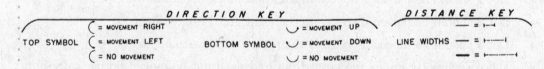

Look at the KEYS above. These show the meaning of the symbols in the test. There is a *Direction Key* that shows the meaning of the *top row of symbols* for movement *right* or *left* (horizontal movement) and the *bottom row of symbols* for movement *up* or *down* (vertical movement). Notice in each there is a symbol for no movement. The *Distance Key* shows the three line widths in which the arrows can be drawn. The thinnest line width represents movement of approximately $\frac{1}{8}$ inch. The medium width line represents approximately $\frac{2}{8}$ inch and the thickest line represents approximately $\frac{3}{8}$ inch.

Now decide which answer is correct by looking at the arrows in the top row and the arrows in the bottom row *and* the width of the line in which the arrows are drawn. Only one pair of symbols is correct.

The correct answer is (A). No horizontal movement is needed but it must be moved up one width.

Directions: Decide which one of the lettered answer choices is best. Answers are on page 149.

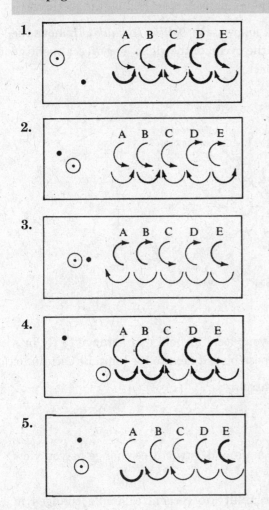

CYCLIC ORIENTATION

The Cyclic Orientation subtest of the AFAST is designed to measure your ability to recognize simple changes in helicopter position and to indicate the corresponding cyclic (stick) movement.

For each question in Cyclic Orientation, you are shown a series of three sequential pictures that represent the pilot's view of a helicopter windshield. The three pictures change from top to bottom showing the view from an aircraft in a climb, dive, bank to the left or right, or a combination of these maneuvers. You must determine which position the cyclic would be in to perform the maneuver indicated by the pictures.

For items in this test, the cyclic is moved as follows: For *banks*: To *bank left,* move the cyclic stick to the left; to *bank right,* move the cyclic to the right. For *dives*: push the cyclic forward. For *climbs*: pull the cyclic back.

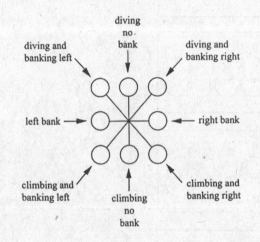

It is strongly recommended that you visit your local airfield and arrange to fly in a light, fixed-wing plane or in a helicopter. If possible, sit next to the pilot. Be certain to:

- Observe the instrument panels and controls
- Observe the pilot using the controls
- Study the terrain in front of you
- Notice how the natural landscape and man-made structures change as you view them from different heights and angles

Such flight orientation will sharpen your ability to recognize simple changes in aircraft position and the control movement required to achieve such changes.

Directions: For sample questions 1 and 2, assume that you are a pilot of a helicopter with a constant power setting going through a maneuver as shown in the pictures. The helicopter can be climbing, diving, banking (turning) to the right or left, or in a climbing and diving bank. Look at the pictures from top to bottom and determine which maneuver is being performed. Next, decide which position the cyclic (stick) would be in to perform the maneuver.

1.

As the aircraft is climbing but not banking, the correct answer is as follows:

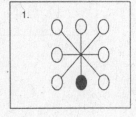

2.

As the aircraft is diving and banking to the right, the correct answer is as follows:

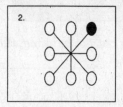

Directions: Decide in which position the cyclic would be to perform the maneuver indicated by the pictures. Answers are on page 150.

1.

2.

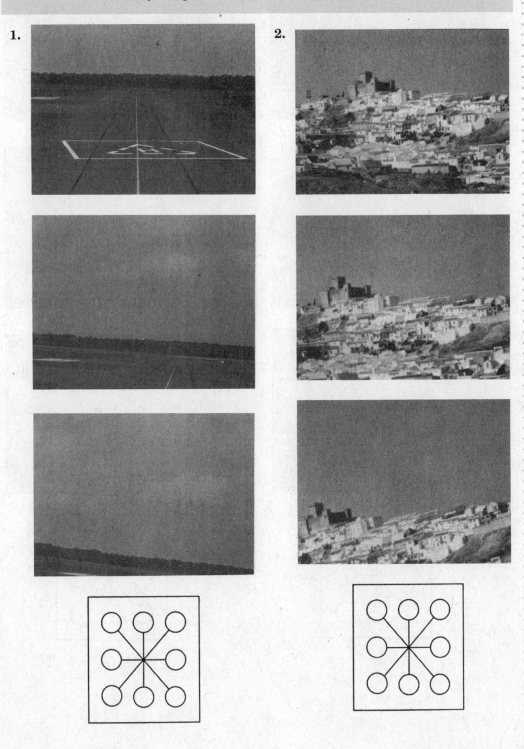

5.

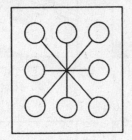

SPATIAL APPERCEPTION

Questions on spatial apperception appear in the Spatial Apperception Test of the Navy and Marine Corps Aviation Selection Test Battery. They are also used in constructing the Pilot Flight Aptitude Rating (PFAR) and the Flight Officer Flight Aptitude Rating (FOFAR).

These questions measure your ability to determine the position or attitude of an airplane in flight by viewing through the windshield of the cockpit the natural horizon and terrain. You must determine whether the airplane is flying straight and level, or climbing, diving, banking to the right or left, or any combination of these maneuvers. You must also determine the general direction of flight of the plane.

Sketches of the view of the horizon and terrain from an airplane in various attitudes are shown below.

View of Horizon and Terrain from Airplanes in Various Attitudes

Diving—Banking Left

Diving—No Bank

Diving—Banking Right

Level Flight—Banking Left

Straight and Level

Level Flight—Banking Right

Climbing—Banking Left

Climbing—No Bank

Climbing—Banking Right

Notice that the view is out to sea. The land is darkened, the coastline separates the land from the sea, and the horizon is shown where the sea meets the sky. The direction of flight can be determined by looking at the coastline. In all views shown, the planes are flying out to sea.

Note that when the airplane is flying straight and level, the horizon is horizontal and is in the middle of the pictured view. When in a level flight but banking to the left, the horizon appears tilted to the right, with the center point of the horizon still at the middle of the pictured view. When the plane is in level flight but banking to the right, the horizon appears tilted to the left, with the center point of the horizon still at the middle of the pictured view.

When the airplane is nose-down (diving) but not banking left or right, the horizon appears horizontal and in the upper half of the pictured view. When the plane is nose-down and banking to the left, the horizon appears tilted to the right, with the center point of the horizon in the upper half of the pictured view. When the plane is nose-down and banking to the right, the horizon appears tilted to the left, with the center point of the horizon in the upper half of the pictured view.

When the airplane is nose-up (climbing) but not banking left or right, the horizon is horizontal and is in the lower half of the pictured view. When the plane is nose-up and banking to the left, the horizon appears tilted to the right, with the center point of the horizon in the lower half of the pictured view. When the plane is nose-up and banking to the right, the horizon appears tilted to the left, with the center point of the horizon in the lower half of the pictured view. Note that when the horizon is tilted, the coastline also appears tilted.

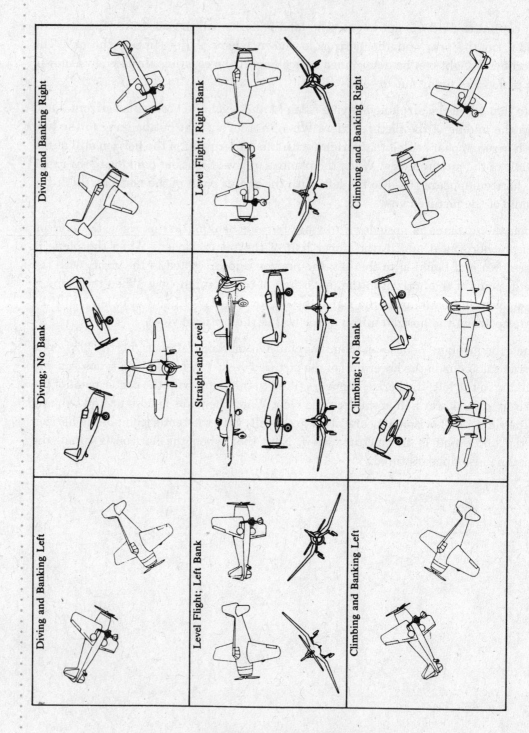

Airplanes in Various Attitudes

Sketches of airplanes in various attitudes are shown on page 128. Note that when the airplane is banked left or right, this means it is banked to the left or right of the pilot seated in the cockpit and looking directly forward, not as viewed from outside the airplane.

For each question, the picture at the upper left represents the view as the pilot looks straight ahead through the windshield. Below are five pictures, labeled (A), (B), (C), (D), or (E). Each picture shows a plane in a different position (or attitude) or in a different direction of flight. Determine from which plane the aerial view shown would have been seen.

1.

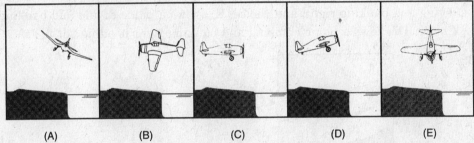

(A)   (B)   (C)   (D)   (E)

The correct answer is (C). Choice (A) shows a plane banking to the right; choice (B) shows one banking to the left; choice (D) shows a plane climbing; and choice (E) shows a plane diving. Choice (C) shows a plane in straight-and-level flight heading out to sea.

2.

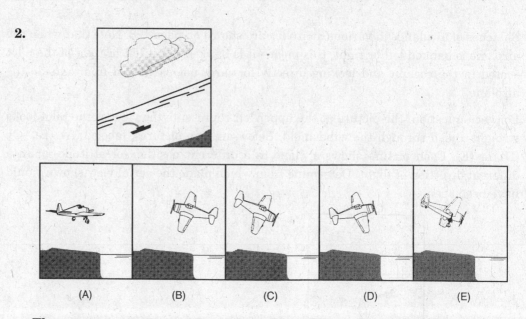

| (A) | (B) | (C) | (D) | (E) |

The correct answer is (D). Choice (A) shows a plane in straight-and-level flight; choice (B) shows one climbing and banking left; choice (C) shows a plane diving and banking right; and choice (E) shows a plane diving and banking left. Choice (D) shows a plane climbing and banking right heading out to sea.

3.

| (A) | (B) | (C) | (D) | (E) |

The correct answer is (A). Choice (B) shows a plane diving and banking to the left heading toward land; choice (C) shows one diving but not banking; choice (D) shows a plane diving and banking to the right; and choice (E) shows a plane banking to the right. Choice (A) shows a plane diving and banking to the left heading out to sea.

Note that in examples 1 and 2, the sea is to the right of the coastline. In example 3, the sea is to the left of the coastline. The sea may be above or below the coastline or be in any other position, depending on how the coastline is drawn.

Directions: In each of the following five questions, the view at the upper left represents what a pilot sees looking straight ahead through the windshield. Five sketches labeled (A), (B), (C), (D), and (E) are shown below. Each lettered sketch shows a plane in a different attitude and in a different direction of flight. From the aerial view shown, determine which of the sketches most nearly represents the attitude of the plane and the direction of flight from which the view would be seen by the pilot. Answers are on page 151.

1.

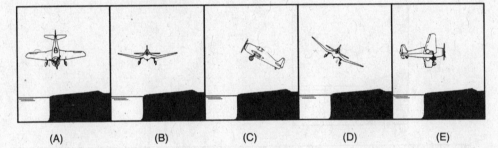

(A)   (B)   (C)   (D)   (E)

2.

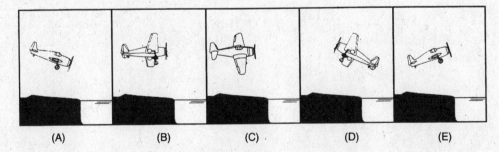

(A)   (B)   (C)   (D)   (E)

3.

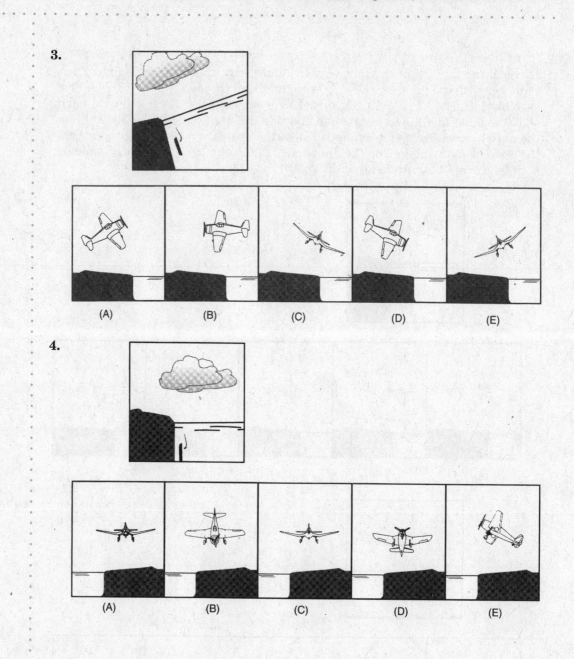

4.

5.

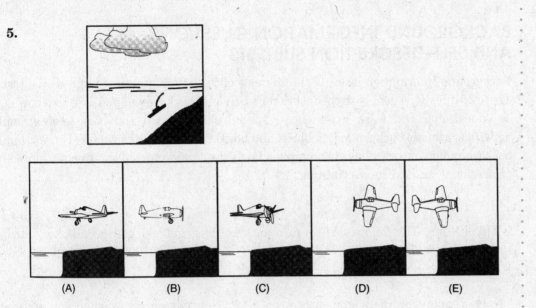

BACKGROUND INFORMATION QUESTIONS AND SELF-DESCRIPTION SUBTESTS

Background Information is one of the subtests of the AFAST, but it is not a scored test. These 25 questions deal with the test taker's personal background and cover such areas as educational and work experiences, special skills, social activities, recreational activities, athletic background, hobbies, and home conditions. Biographical or personal background inventories have been proven fairly good predictors of success in technical, professional, and executive training.

> **Directions:** The following two questions are biographical and pertain to your general background. Answer each question to the best of your ability and recollection.

1. How many brothers and sisters do you have in your family?

   (A) 0
   (B) 1
   (C) 2
   (D) 3
   (E) 4

2. How old were you when you entered college?

   (A) 16 years or younger
   (B) 17 years
   (C) 18 years
   (D) 19 years
   (E) 20 years or older

Self-Description Subtests

The AFAST and AFOQT include personality test subsections. Personality testing helps identify candidates who are truly motivated to become pilots and who have a good attitude about their work.

Because personality test questions have no right or wrong answers, it is difficult to prepare for taking such a test. Here are a few guidelines you can follow, however, that can improve your chances of doing well on a personality subtest. Keep the following three tips in mind when answering questions:

❶ **Always tell the truth.** Personality tests are designed in part to identify people who are not being candid. One of the main reasons some people do poorly on personality tests is because they answer questions in a way that they think makes them look perfect. This is a big mistake: No one is perfect.

❷ **Go with your first thought.** Because personality test questions have no right or wrong answers, it's easy to read too much into them. The questions are usually straightforward and should be answered as such. Don't try to second-guess the intent of the questions or look for hidden meanings; doing so will certainly lower your performance.

❸ **Don't be afraid to say how you feel.** The answers to many questions on personality tests are stated in terms of the extent to which you agree or disagree with a particular statement. For example, on the AFOQT Self-Description

Inventory, your answer choices are: (A) Strongly Disagree; (B) Moderately Disagree; (C) Neither Agree nor Disagree; (D) Moderately Agree; (E) Strongly Agree. If you feel strongly about a particular statement, don't be afraid to answer with an (A) or (E). It's usually not wise to respond with answer choice (C) too often, unless you're really not certain of how you feel.

AFAST Self-Description Form

The Self-Description subtest of the AFAST consists of 75 questions about the test taker's interests, likes, dislikes, opinions, and attitudes. Here are some examples of the types of questions you are likely to encounter in the five sections of this subtest.

Directions: Questions 1 and 2 each consist of a set of five descriptive words. Select the choice that MOST accurately describes you or the choice that LEAST describes you.

1. Which one of the following MOST accurately describes you?

   (A) Argumentative
   (B) Dependable
   (C) Impatient
   (D) Loyal
   (E) Stubborn

2. Which one of the following LEAST accurately describes you?

   (A) Argumentative
   (B) Dependable
   (C) Impatient
   (D) Loyal
   (E) Stubborn

Directions: Questions 3 and 4 should be answered either with "Yes" or "No."

3. Are you generally suspicious of most people you meet?

   (Y) Yes
   (N) No

4. Do you enjoy reading books?

   (Y) Yes
   (N) No

Directions: Questions 5 and 6 list occupations. Some may appeal to you; others may not. For each of the listed occupations you would like for a life career, answer by selecting "Like." For each of the listed occupations you would *not* like for a life career, answer by selecting "Dislike."

5. Singer

   (L) Like
   (D) Dislike

6. Writer

   (L) Like
   (D) Dislike

Directions: Questions 7 and 8 each consist of a pair of statements describing personal characteristics and preferences. For each question, select the statement that describes you best.

7. **(A)** I like keeping a set of office files in order.

   (B) I like keeping a piece of machinery in order.

8. **(A)** I often feel tense on the job.

   (B) I enjoy socializing on the job.

Directions: Questions 9 and 10 each consist of a statement that may be considered somewhat controversial. Select one of the answer choices that best describes the extent to which you agree or disagree with the statement in the question stem.

9. The United States should reduce its military involvement in Iraq.

   (A) Strongly agree
   (B) Tend to agree
   (C) Tend to disagree
   (D) Strongly disagree

10. Most people take life too seriously.

   (A) Strongly agree
   (B) Tend to agree
   (C) Tend to disagree
   (D) Strongly disagree

Remember that there are no right or wrong answers to these questions. Answer the self-description questions truthfully and to the best of your ability and recollection.

AFOQT Self-Description Inventory

On the AFOQT, the 220 questions of the Self-Description Inventory subtest measure personality traits and attitudes. Your responses to these questions are not used in calculating any of the composite scores on the AFOQT, and as with the AFAST, there are no right or wrong answers. You must read each statement carefully and decide how well each one describes you.

In the old version of the AFOQT (before August 2005), the Self-Description Inventory subtest measured five basic personality characteristics:

1 openness

2 conscientiousness

3 extroversion

4 agreeableness

5 neuroticism

The current version of the AFOQT Self-Description Inventory subtest measures two additional personality characteristics:

6 service orientation

7 team orientation

Service Orientation refers to an individual's organizational commitment. Team Orientation assesses one's preference for working as a member of a group or alone. These new factors (80 of the 220 statements) help measure the degree to which a candidate is likely to make a career commitment to the Armed Forces, and it also assesses one's ability to accept differing roles under changing conditions.

The acronym "OCEAN ST" is sometimes used to describe the AFOQT Self-Description Inventory. The official title is Self-Description Inventory Plus (SDI+).

Here's an example of the type of question you may encounter on the Self-Description subtest of the AFOQT or the SDI+:

Directions: Decide whether this statement is characteristic of you and indicate your agreement using the scale below.

1. I enjoy reading poetry.

A	B	C	D	E
Strongly Disagree	Moderately Disagree	Neither Agree nor Disagree	Moderately Agree	Strongly Agree

If you strongly agree that the statement describes you, select answer choice E. If you strongly disagree, select answer choice A on the scale. Choose B, C, or D to indicate another level of agreement.

On this type of subtest, work quickly but answer each test item—even if you do not feel entirely certain of your answer. Don't spend very much time considering what your answer should be; simply respond according to how well the statement describes you.

Don't be fooled by statements that seem to be negative or that appear to have a "correct" answer. Remember: There are no right or wrong answers in self-description inventory tests.

The ten sample test items below are representative of statements you will encounter on the AFOQT Self-Description Inventory subtest.

1. I always try to finish what I start.

2. I generally work well with others.

3. I get nervous if I have to speak in front of a large group of people.

4. I am always punctual and often show up early for events.

5. I generally wait for others to lead the way.

6. I tend to let my work goals take priority over my personal interests.

7. I am uncomfortable supervising others.

8. I am pleased when friends drop in to see me.

9. I prefer individual rather than group activities.

10. I have higher work standards than do most people.

ANSWER KEY AND EXPLANATIONS

Synonyms

1. C	3. A	5. B	7. C	9. E
2. A	4. E	6. B	8. C	10. D

For questions 1–10, refer to a good abridged dictionary for the meaning of those words that are giving you trouble.

Verbal Analogies

1. E	2. B	3. E	4. C	5. C

1. **The correct answer is (E).** *Botany* is the study of *plants*; *entomology* is the study of *insects*.

2. **The correct answer is (B).** *Epilogue* is a speech after the conclusion of a play; *prologue* is an introductory speech to a play. *Appendix* is material added after the end of the book; *preface* is an introductory part of a book.

3. **The correct answer is (E).** *Octagon* is an eight-sided figure; *square* is a four-sided figure (one-half of eight). *Hexagon* is a six-sided figure; *triangle* is a three-sided figure (one-half of six).

4. **The correct answer is (C).** *Glow* is to burn without any flame; *blaze* is to burn intensely. *Glance* is to look briefly; *stare* is to look intently.

5. **The correct answer is (C).** Absence of *water* results in *thirst*; absence of *food* results in *hunger*.

Reading/Paragraph Comprehension

1. C	5. C	9. B	13. C	17. A
2. D	6. D	10. D	14. D	18. D
3. C	7. A	11. B	15. C	19. A
4. A	8. A	12. A	16. A	20. A

1. **The correct answer is (C).** Safety education must be a continuous process because it is common for people to be careless.

2. **The correct answer is (D).** During times of stress, law enforcement becomes committed to reducing that stress between population groups.

3. **The correct answer is (C).** The uneven saturation of energy would result in unevenly cooked food.

4. **The correct answer is (A).** The watt is a measure of electrical energy. Electrical power in the home is measured in watts or kilowatts.

5. **The correct answer is (C).** The magnetron within the microwave oven generates the energy.

6. **The correct answer is (D).** The first three choices are not supported by the passage. The second sentence in the passage states that steel bars, deeply embedded in the concrete, are sinews to take the stresses.

7. **The correct answer is (A).** The third sentence in the passage states that when the heart contracts, the blood in the arteries is at its greatest pressure.

8. **The correct answer is (A).** The first sentence in the passage states that arsonists set fires deliberately or intentionally.

9. **The correct answer is (B).** The last sentence in the passage states that some arsonists just like the excitement of seeing the fire burn, and watching the firefighters at work, and even helping fight the fire.

10. **The correct answer is (D).** The first three choices are not supported by the passage. Different types of arsonists described in the passage lead to the conclusion that arsonists are not all alike.

11. **The correct answer is (B).** For the students to solve the problem with ease, the teacher's explanation must have been clearly expressed or explicit.

12. **The correct answer is (A).** To differentiate between fact and fiction requires that the listeners have keen discernment or be shrewd.

13. **The correct answer is (C).** If corn is native or indigenous to the region, it is readily available and is generally inexpensive as transportation costs are reduced or eliminated.

14. **The correct answer is (D).** It is difficult to change the mind of a stubborn or obdurate individual, even when he is in error.

15. **The correct answer is (C).** Of the choices given, the only one that gives the sentence meaning states that one who is immature can readily be deceived or deluded.

16. **The correct answer is (A).** Of the choices given, the only one that gives the sentence meaning states that compulsory education was established to prevent exploitation of young children and to give them a minimum of education.

17. **The correct answer is (A).** The only choice that provides a meaningful sentence states that a person in custody awaiting trial is considered innocent until found guilty.

18. **The correct answer is (D).** The word *large* appears to be inconsistent. Substituting *small* for *large* restores the intended meaning of the quotation.

19. **The correct answer is (A).** The word *legislators* appears to be inconsistent. Substituting *citizens* for *legislators* helps convey the meaning intended.

20. **The correct answer is (A).** The word *cannot* appears to be the cause for confusion. By substituting *eventually* for *cannot,* the intended meaning of the sentence is restored.

Arithmetic Reasoning

1. C   2. D   3. A   4. B   5. E

1. **The correct answer is (C).** Calculate in inches.

    $48 \times 24 \times 18 = 20{,}736 \text{ in}^3$
    (Vol. of bin)
    $8 \times 4 \times 2 = 64 \text{ in}^3$
    (Vol. of each brick)
    $20{,}736 \div 64 = 324 \text{ bricks}$

2. **The correct answer is (D).** Let $x =$ actual length of the room.

    $2 : 5 = 7 : x$
    $2x = 35$
    $x = 17\frac{1}{2} \text{ feet}$

3. **The correct answer is (A).** 4 hours at 6 mph = 24 miles

    2 hours at 10 mph = 20 miles
    4 hours at 5 mph = 20 miles
    Total = 10 hours for 64 miles =
    6.4 mph

4. **The correct answer is (B).** $240 − $192 = $48 discount

    $\dfrac{48}{240} = \dfrac{1}{5} = 20\%$

5. **The correct answer is (E).** 2.35 − .82 = 1.53, cost of weight above 5 ounces

    $\dfrac{1.53}{.09} = 20\%$

    5 ounces + 17 ounces =
    22 ounces = 1 pound, 6 ounces

Math Knowledge

1. C   2. E   3. A   4. B   5. C

1. **The correct answer is (C).** The 3s, 4s, 5s, 6s, and 7s cancel out leaving

    $\dfrac{2}{8} = \dfrac{1}{4}$

2. **The correct answer is (E).** All except choice (E) are equivalent.
    $115\% = 1.15$

3. **The correct answer is (A).** When logarithms with the same base are multiplied, the exponents are added.
    $10^4 \times 10^3 \times 10^2 = 10^{(4+3+2)} = 10^9$

4. **The correct answer is (B).** The Pythagorean theorem states that for any right triangle, the sum of the squares of the legs is equal to the square of the length of the hypotenuse.

    $3^2 + 4^2 = h^2$
    $9 + 16 = h^2$
    $h^2 = 25$
    $h = \sqrt{25}$

5. **The correct answer is (C).** $a = 4b$;

    $\dfrac{3}{4}a = \dfrac{3}{4}(4b) = \dfrac{12b}{4} = 3b$

Mechanical Comprehension

1. B	3. C	5. B	7. B	9. A
2. D	4. C	6. A	8. B	10. A

1. **The correct answer is (B).** Wood is an insulator. Silver is a better conductor than steel.

2. **The correct answer is (D).** Choice (A) does not permit airflow through G and S; choice (B) does not permit airflow through S; choice (C) does not permit airflow through G; choice (D) is correct; choice (E) does not permit airflow through G and S.

3. **The correct answer is (C).** The total weight of 32 pounds is balanced equally between the two scales. Each records one half of the total weight or 16 pounds.

4. **The correct answer is (C).** If the block is moved toward the brick, the moment for a given force exerted will increase (being farther from the force) making it easier to lift; the height will be made smaller, hardly raising the brick when moved to the limit (directly underneath it).

5. **The correct answer is (B).** Each time the rotating arm makes a complete revolution, it moves the slotted disc $\frac{1}{4}$ of a turn.

6. **The correct answer is (A).** The film of water inside the loop would form a lens that would enlarge the printing on the page. If you looked through a water-filled globe, objects will also appear larger.

7. **The correct answer is (B).** The metal key has the highest conductivity. Metals are the best conductors of heat. The other choices can be used as insulators.

8. **The correct answer is (B).** This is a mechanical or solderless connector. It does away with the need to solder wires and is found in house wiring.

9. **The correct answer is (A).** An inclined plane is a sloping, triangular shape, used here as a wedge to force open an axe-cut made in the wood.

10. **The correct answer is (A).** The weight is not centered but is closer to choice (A). The distance from the center of the load to choice (A) is less than the distance from the center of the load to choice (B). Therefore, choice (A) would support the greater part of the load.

Instrument Comprehension

1. B	3. D	5. C	7. C	9. B
2. A	4. B	6. B	8. D	10. A

1. **The correct answer is (B).** Climbing; 15° right; heading 60°.

2. **The correct answer is (A).** Neither climbing nor diving; 30° right bank; heading 360° (north).

3. **The correct answer is (D).** Neither climbing nor diving; 90° right bank; heading 360° (west).

4. **The correct answer is (B).** Climbing; 15° left bank; heading 300°.

5. **The correct answer is (C).** Climbing; 30° left bank; heading 60°.

6. **The correct answer is (B).** Diving; no bank; heading $22\frac{1}{2}°$ (north-northeast).

7. **The correct answer is (C).** Neither climbing nor diving; no bank; heading 240°.

8. **The correct answer is (D).** Diving; 30° right bank; heading 315° (north-west).

9. **The correct answer is (B).** Neither climbing nor diving; 30° left bank; heading 300°.

10. **The correct answer is (A).** Diving; no bank; heading 150°.

Block Counting

1. E	3. E	5. E	7. A	9. E
2. B	4. B	6. D	8. B	10. A

1. **The correct answer is (E).** There are 9 blocks on the bottom tier, 5 on the middle tier, and 1 on the top tier. 9 + 5 + 1 = 15

2. **The correct answer is (B).** There are 14 blocks on the lower tier and 10 blocks on the upper tier. 14 + 10 = 24

3. **The correct answer is (E).** There are 16 blocks on the bottom tier, 16 on the middle tier, and 12 on the top tier. 16 + 16 + 12 = 44

4. **The correct answer is (B).** There are 24 blocks from top to bottom on the left column, 24 blocks from top to bottom on the right column, and 8 blocks in the center. 24 + 24 + 8 = 56

5. **The correct answer is (E).** There are 15 blocks on the bottom tier, 14 on the middle tier, and 9 on the top tier. 15 + 14 + 9 = 38

6. **The correct answer is (D).** There are 4 alongside and 2 below. 4 + 2 = 6

7. The correct answer is (A). There are 3 alongside and 1 below.
$3 + 1 = 4$

8. The correct answer is (B). There is 1 alongside and 1 below.
$1 + 1 = 2$

9. The correct answer is (E). There are 2 above, 3 alongside, and 3 below.
$2 + 3 + 3 = 8$

10. The correct answer is (A). There are 3 above and 1 alongside.
$3 + 1 = 4$

Table Reading

1. A	2. E	3. C	4. D	5. D

1. The correct answer is (A). The entry that occurs at the intersection of an X-value of -1 and a Y-value of 0 is 29.

2. The correct answer is (E). The entry that occurs at the intersection of an X-value of -2 and a Y-value of -2 is 30.

3. The correct answer is (C). The entry that occurs at the intersection of an X-value of $+2$ and a Y-value of -1 is 35.

4. The correct answer is (D). The entry that occurs at the intersection of an X-value of 0 and a Y-value of $+3$ is 27.

5. The correct answer is (D). The entry that occurs at the intersection of an X-value of $+1$ and a Y-value of -2 is 35.

Aviation Information

1. B	6. B	11. D	16. C	21. D
2. A	7. A	12. A	17. D	22. D
3. C	8. A	13. A	18. A	23. B
4. D	9. D	14. C	19. D	24. B
5. A	10. E	15. D	20. D	25. A

1. The correct answer is (B). The upward angle formed by the wings, called *dihedral,* counteracts any balance upset caused by a gust of wind and returns the airplane to a wing-level attitude.

2. The correct answer is (A). The flight path and relative wind are parallel but travel in opposite directions. If an airfoil moves forward and upward, the relative wind moves backward and downward.

3. The correct answer is (C). The lift and drag acting on a wing are proportional to the wing area. If the wing area is doubled and the other variables remain the same, the lift and drag created by the wing will be doubled.

4. The correct answer is (D). Tetraethyl lead is the best available knock inhibitor. It is added to improve the antiknock quality of a fuel.

5. **The correct answer is (A).** The standard weight for gasoline is 6 lbs./U.S. gal., that for oil is 7.5 lbs./U.S. gal., and that for water is 8.35 lbs./U.S. gal.

6. **The correct answer is (B).** Bernocilli's principle and Newton's third law of motion are the basis for explaining how an airplane wing produces lift.

7. **The correct answer is (A).** The rearward or retarding force acting on an airplane during flight is called drag.

8. **The correct answer is (A).** The angle of attack is the angle between the chord line of the airfoil and the direction of the relative wind.

9. **The correct answer is (D).** Lift varies directly with the density of air. As the density of air increases, lift and drag increase.

10. **The correct answer is (E).** The trailing edge of the airfoil or wing is the aft end of the airfoil, where the airflow over the upper surface meets the airflow from the lower surface.

11. **The correct answer is (D).** The empennage is the tail section and generally consists of a vertical stabilizer, a horizontal stabilizer, a movable rudder, and a movable elevator.

12. **The correct answer is (A).** The ailerons, located on the rear edge of the wings near the outer tips, are used to bank or roll the airplane around its longitudinal axis.

13. **The correct answer is (A).** The pitot is used to ascertain the impact pressure of the air as the airplane moves forward.

14. **The correct answer is (C).** Applying forward pressure on the control causes the elevator surfaces to move downward. The flow of air striking the deflected surfaces exerts an upward force, pushing the airplane's tail upward and the nose downward.

15. **The correct answer is (D).** Runway numbers are different at each end of the runway strip because the magnetic directions are 180 degrees apart. The approximate magnetic direction for runway numbered 3 is 30 degrees. The other end would be numbered 21 as it has a magnetic direction of 210 degrees.

16. **The correct answer is (C).** The tower operator uses a flashing red signal to instruct pilots not to land because the airport is unsafe.

17. **The correct answer is (D).** White lights are used to illuminate airport runways.

18. **The correct answer is (A).** The arrow of the weathervane points into the wind midway between north and east, or northeast.

19. **The correct answer is (D).** The 24-hour system consists of a four-digit number with 0000 as midnight to 2400 the following midnight. The time 2:00 p.m. would be expressed as 1400 hours in the 24-hour system.

20. **The correct answer is (D).** Note the tail assembly on the airplane. The pilot has banked the airplane 45 degrees to the left.

21. **The correct answer is (D).** Foot pedals in the cockpit permit the helicopter to increase or decrease tail-rotor thrust, as needed, to neutralize torque effect.

22. The correct answer is (D). A red radial line is placed on the airspeed indicator to show the airspeed limit beyond that operation is dangerous.

23. The correct answer is (B). In the event of engine failure while hovering or on takeoff below 10 feet, apply collective pitch as necessary to cushion the landing.

24. The correct answer is (B). The useful load (payload) is the weight of the pilot, passengers, baggage, removable ballast, and usable fuel. Oil is considered to be part of the empty weight.

25. The correct answer is (A). For any given gross weight, the higher the density altitude, the less the rate of climb for any helicopter.

Nautical Information

1. C	7. B	13. B	19. D	25. C
2. E	8. B	14. E	20. C	26. A
3. C	9. B	15. B	21. C	27. A
4. D	10. A	16. C	22. E	28. A
5. A	11. A	17. E	23. E	29. B
6. C	12. B	18. B	24. C	30. A

1. The correct answer is (C). "Zulu time" or Greenwich mean time is used in communications between ships in different time zones.

2. The correct answer is (E). The foghorn is a type of *sound* communication; facsimile, radiotelegraph, and satellite are types of *electronic* communication; and semiphore is a type of *visual* communication using hand flags.

3. The correct answer is (C). The plane intersects the earth's surface at the equator and divides the earth into the northern and southern hemispheres.

4. The correct answer is (D). Nylon is a synthetic fiber of great strength and is much stronger than manila rope.

5. The correct answer is (A). Amsterdam with coordinates of 52°22′N and 4°53′E is closest to Greenwich.

6. The correct answer is (C). Hawaii is located at a latitude of 21°N and longitude of 159°W.

7. The correct answer is (B). If unlighted, a green channel marker is can-shaped.

8. The correct answer is (B). It would be 1400 − 3, or 1100 Greenwich mean time.

9. The correct answer is (B). *Red* is for port; *green* is starboard. *White* navigation lights inform an observer in which direction a vessel is going. *Yellow* is for special circumstances.

10. The correct answer is (A). The stern is the after part of the ship. To go in that direction is to go *aft*.

11. **The correct answer is (A).** *Draft* is the vertical distance from the waterline to the lowest part of the ship's bottom. *Freeboard* is the vertical distance from the waterline to the edge of the lowest outside deck.

12. **The correct answer is (B).** The forward part of the main deck is generally the *forecastle*. The after part is the *fantail*.

13. **The correct answer is (B).** The 180th meridian is also known as the International Date Line. Greenwich, England, is located at 0 meridian, or prime meridian.

14. **The correct answer is (E).** The magnetic north pole and true north are not at the same location. The magnetic compass does not usually point directly north in most places. This compass error is termed *variation*.

15. **The correct answer is (B).** The lubber's line indicates the fore-and-aft line of the ship.

16. **The correct answer is (C).** When the tide is falling after high tide, it is called ebb tide.

17. **The correct answer is (E).** Stratus clouds are gray clouds found at low altitude and consist of a uniform layer of water droplets.

18. **The correct answer is (B).** The Beaufort scale of wind force is useful in estimating wind speed.

19. **The correct answer is (D).** The sextant is a precision instrument used in celestial navigation to measure angles.

20. **The correct answer is (C).** Life buoys should be thrown over immediately.

21. **The correct answer is (C).** A fathometer is an electronic device used in making deep-sea soundings.

22. **The correct answer is (E).** 12:00 noon would be written as 1200; 6:00 p.m. would be written as 1800.

23. **The correct answer is (E).** In marine navigation, the four methods of determining position are piloting, dead reckoning, celestial navigation, and electronic navigation.

24. **The correct answer is (C).** The gunwale is the deck edge, the intersection of the main deck with the shell or side plating.

25. **The correct answer is (C).** A *pier* is built at right angle to the shore; a *wharf* is parallel. The space between adjacent piers is called a *slip*.

26. **The correct answer is (A).** A balanced rudder with part of the area of the blade surface projected ahead of the rudder stock has a great effect in reducing the strain on the steering gear and in making steering easier.

27. **The correct answer is (A).** With left rudder (to port), water flowing past the hull hits the rudder at the port side forcing the stern to starboard, and the boat's bow swings to port.

28. **The correct answer is (A).** With left rudder (to port) and going astern, the stern swings to port.

29. **The correct answer is (B).** With right rudder (to starboard), water

flowing past the hull hits the rudder at the starboard side forcing the stern to port, and the boat's bow swings to starboard.

30. The correct answer is (A). With left rudder (to port) and going astern, the stem swings to port.

Rotated Blocks

1. C   2. E   3. B   4. D   5. A

If you examine each set of blocks carefully, you will find that only one of the five choices is just like the pictured block at the left, although turned in a different position. You may have to mentally turn blocks over, turn them around, or turn them both over and around.

General Science

1. C   2. C   3. B   4. D   5. E

1. **The correct answer is (C).** Meteors, or "shooting stars," come into the earth's atmosphere from outer space with high velocity. The resistance offered by the earth's atmosphere makes these meteors incandescent in flight.

2. **The correct answer is (C).** Organisms that live on or in the body of other living organisms from which food is obtained are called parasites.

3. **The correct answer is (B).** Substances are classified as elements or compounds. A compound is a substance composed of the atoms of two or more different elements.

4. **The correct answer is (D).** The greater the number of vibrations per second produced by the sounding object, the higher will be the pitch produced. Playing a $33\frac{1}{3}$ rpm phonograph record at a faster speed (45 rpm) will produce a higher-pitched sound.

5. **The correct answer is (E).** Combustion cannot occur in the absence of oxygen.

Hidden Figures

| 1. A | 2. E | 3. E | 4. C | 5. B |

1. The correct answer is (A).

2. The correct answer is (E).

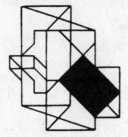

3. The correct answer is (E).

4. The correct answer is (C).

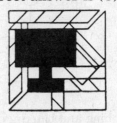

5. The correct answer is (B).

Complex Movements

| 1. B | 2. D | 3. C | 4. D | 5. B |

1. The correct answer is (B). (2 left and 2 up).

2. The correct answer is (D). (1 right and 1 down).

3. The correct answer is (C). (1 left, no vertical movement).

4. The correct answer is (D). (3 right and 3 down).

5. The correct answer is (B). (no horizontal movement, 2 down).

Cyclic Orientation

1. Climbing and banking left

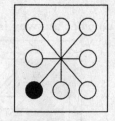

4. Climbing and banking right

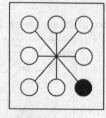

2. Climbing and banking right

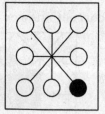

5. Climbing and banking left

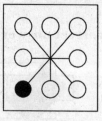

3. Diving; no bank

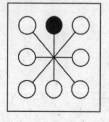

Spatial Apperception

| 1. B | 2. E | 3. C | 4. D | 5. A |

1. **The correct answer is (B).** Straight-and-level flight along the coastline.

2. **The correct answer is (E).** Climbing; no bank; flying out to sea.

3. **The correct answer is (C).** Level flight; right bank; flying up the coastline.

4. **The correct answer is (D).** Climbing, no bank; flying down the coastline. (Note that the sea is left of the coastline in the lettered choices but right of the coastline in the aerial view.)

5. **The correct answer is (A).** Straight-and-level flight heading 45 degrees left of coastline.

SUMMING IT UP

- Synonym questions appear in the Word Knowledge subtest of the AFOQT.

- Verbal analogy questions appear in the Verbal Analogies subtest of the AFOQT; they test your knowledge of word meanings, your vocabulary level, and your ability to reason.

- The Reading Comprehension subtest is no longer a part of the AFOQT, but this type of question appears in the Paragraph Comprehension subtest of the ASVAB. Sentence comprehension questions also appear in the Reading Skills Test of the ASTB.

- Arithmetic reasoning questions appear in the Arithmetic Reasoning subtest of the AFOQT and are used to construct the Pilot, Navigator-Technical, Academic Aptitude, and Quantitative composite scores. This type of test item also appears in the Math Skills Test of the ASTB, and it is a subtest of the ASVAB.

- The Math Knowledge subtest of the AFOQT is used in calculating the Pilot, Navigator-Technical, Academic Aptitude, and Quantitative composite scores. These questions also appear in the Math Skills Test of the ASTB.

- Questions on mechanical comprehension are part of the Mechanical Functions subtest of the AFAST and in the Mechanical Comprehension Test of the ASTB. They are used to calculate the Pilot Flight Aptitude Rating (PFAR) and the Flight Officer Flight Aptitude Rating (FOFAR).

- Instrument Comprehension subtests of the AFOQT and the AFAST measure one's ability to determine the position of an airplane in flight.

- The Block Counting subtest of the AFOQT is used in calculating the Navigator-Technical composite score. These test items are designed to assess your ability to "see into" a three-dimensional group of blocks.

- The Table Reading subtest of the AFOQT is used to calculate the Pilot and Navigator-Technical composite scores. These test items measure your ability to read tabular material quickly and accurately.

- The Rotated Blocks subtest of the AFOQT is designed to test your ability to visualize and manipulate objects in three-dimensional space.

- The Aviation Information subtest of the AFOQT is used to calculate the Pilot composite score. It also appears on the ASTB's Aviation and Nautical Information Test and is used to calculate the PFAR and the FOFAR.

- Nautical information questions appear in the ASTB's Aviation and Nautical Information Test. The score is used to calculate the PFAR and the FOFAR.

- The General Science subtest of the AFOQT is used to calculate the Navigator-Technical composite score. The questions assess one's knowledge of life science, physical science, and earth science.

- The Hidden Figures subtest of the AFOQT measures one's ability to see simple figures in complex drawings.

- The Background Information and Self-Description subtests on the AFAST and the Self-Description Inventory subtest of the AFOQT contain questions about one's background, interests, likes and dislikes, personality traits, opinions, and attitudes. There are no correct answers for these.

PART IV
THREE PRACTICE TESTS

ANSWER SHEET

Part 1: Verbal Analogies

1. Ⓐ Ⓑ Ⓒ Ⓓ Ⓔ   10. Ⓐ Ⓑ Ⓒ Ⓓ Ⓔ   18. Ⓐ Ⓑ Ⓒ Ⓓ Ⓔ
2. Ⓐ Ⓑ Ⓒ Ⓓ Ⓔ   11. Ⓐ Ⓑ Ⓒ Ⓓ Ⓔ   19. Ⓐ Ⓑ Ⓒ Ⓓ Ⓔ
3. Ⓐ Ⓑ Ⓒ Ⓓ Ⓔ   12. Ⓐ Ⓑ Ⓒ Ⓓ Ⓔ   20. Ⓐ Ⓑ Ⓒ Ⓓ Ⓔ
4. Ⓐ Ⓑ Ⓒ Ⓓ Ⓔ   13. Ⓐ Ⓑ Ⓒ Ⓓ Ⓔ   21. Ⓐ Ⓑ Ⓒ Ⓓ Ⓔ
5. Ⓐ Ⓑ Ⓒ Ⓓ Ⓔ   14. Ⓐ Ⓑ Ⓒ Ⓓ Ⓔ   22. Ⓐ Ⓑ Ⓒ Ⓓ Ⓔ
6. Ⓐ Ⓑ Ⓒ Ⓓ Ⓔ   15. Ⓐ Ⓑ Ⓒ Ⓓ Ⓔ   23. Ⓐ Ⓑ Ⓒ Ⓓ Ⓔ
7. Ⓐ Ⓑ Ⓒ Ⓓ Ⓔ   16. Ⓐ Ⓑ Ⓒ Ⓓ Ⓔ   24. Ⓐ Ⓑ Ⓒ Ⓓ Ⓔ
8. Ⓐ Ⓑ Ⓒ Ⓓ Ⓔ   17. Ⓐ Ⓑ Ⓒ Ⓓ Ⓔ   25. Ⓐ Ⓑ Ⓒ Ⓓ Ⓔ
9. Ⓐ Ⓑ Ⓒ Ⓓ Ⓔ

Part 2: Arithmetic Reasoning

1. Ⓐ Ⓑ Ⓒ Ⓓ Ⓔ   10. Ⓐ Ⓑ Ⓒ Ⓓ Ⓔ   18. Ⓐ Ⓑ Ⓒ Ⓓ Ⓔ
2. Ⓐ Ⓑ Ⓒ Ⓓ Ⓔ   11. Ⓐ Ⓑ Ⓒ Ⓓ Ⓔ   19. Ⓐ Ⓑ Ⓒ Ⓓ Ⓔ
3. Ⓐ Ⓑ Ⓒ Ⓓ Ⓔ   12. Ⓐ Ⓑ Ⓒ Ⓓ Ⓔ   20. Ⓐ Ⓑ Ⓒ Ⓓ Ⓔ
4. Ⓐ Ⓑ Ⓒ Ⓓ Ⓔ   13. Ⓐ Ⓑ Ⓒ Ⓓ Ⓔ   21. Ⓐ Ⓑ Ⓒ Ⓓ Ⓔ
5. Ⓐ Ⓑ Ⓒ Ⓓ Ⓔ   14. Ⓐ Ⓑ Ⓒ Ⓓ Ⓔ   22. Ⓐ Ⓑ Ⓒ Ⓓ Ⓔ
6. Ⓐ Ⓑ Ⓒ Ⓓ Ⓔ   15. Ⓐ Ⓑ Ⓒ Ⓓ Ⓔ   23. Ⓐ Ⓑ Ⓒ Ⓓ Ⓔ
7. Ⓐ Ⓑ Ⓒ Ⓓ Ⓔ   16. Ⓐ Ⓑ Ⓒ Ⓓ Ⓔ   24. Ⓐ Ⓑ Ⓒ Ⓓ Ⓔ
8. Ⓐ Ⓑ Ⓒ Ⓓ Ⓔ   17. Ⓐ Ⓑ Ⓒ Ⓓ Ⓔ   25. Ⓐ Ⓑ Ⓒ Ⓓ Ⓔ
9. Ⓐ Ⓑ Ⓒ Ⓓ Ⓔ

Part 3: Word Knowledge

1. Ⓐ Ⓑ Ⓒ Ⓓ Ⓔ   10. Ⓐ Ⓑ Ⓒ Ⓓ Ⓔ   18. Ⓐ Ⓑ Ⓒ Ⓓ Ⓔ
2. Ⓐ Ⓑ Ⓒ Ⓓ Ⓔ   11. Ⓐ Ⓑ Ⓒ Ⓓ Ⓔ   19. Ⓐ Ⓑ Ⓒ Ⓓ Ⓔ
3. Ⓐ Ⓑ Ⓒ Ⓓ Ⓔ   12. Ⓐ Ⓑ Ⓒ Ⓓ Ⓔ   20. Ⓐ Ⓑ Ⓒ Ⓓ Ⓔ
4. Ⓐ Ⓑ Ⓒ Ⓓ Ⓔ   13. Ⓐ Ⓑ Ⓒ Ⓓ Ⓔ   21. Ⓐ Ⓑ Ⓒ Ⓓ Ⓔ
5. Ⓐ Ⓑ Ⓒ Ⓓ Ⓔ   14. Ⓐ Ⓑ Ⓒ Ⓓ Ⓔ   22. Ⓐ Ⓑ Ⓒ Ⓓ Ⓔ
6. Ⓐ Ⓑ Ⓒ Ⓓ Ⓔ   15. Ⓐ Ⓑ Ⓒ Ⓓ Ⓔ   23. Ⓐ Ⓑ Ⓒ Ⓓ Ⓔ
7. Ⓐ Ⓑ Ⓒ Ⓓ Ⓔ   16. Ⓐ Ⓑ Ⓒ Ⓓ Ⓔ   24. Ⓐ Ⓑ Ⓒ Ⓓ Ⓔ
8. Ⓐ Ⓑ Ⓒ Ⓓ Ⓔ   17. Ⓐ Ⓑ Ⓒ Ⓓ Ⓔ   25. Ⓐ Ⓑ Ⓒ Ⓓ Ⓔ
9. Ⓐ Ⓑ Ⓒ Ⓓ Ⓔ

answer sheet

Part 4: Math Knowledge

1. Ⓐ Ⓑ Ⓒ Ⓓ Ⓔ
2. Ⓐ Ⓑ Ⓒ Ⓓ Ⓔ
3. Ⓐ Ⓑ Ⓒ Ⓓ Ⓔ
4. Ⓐ Ⓑ Ⓒ Ⓓ Ⓔ
5. Ⓐ Ⓑ Ⓒ Ⓓ Ⓔ
6. Ⓐ Ⓑ Ⓒ Ⓓ Ⓔ
7. Ⓐ Ⓑ Ⓒ Ⓓ Ⓔ
8. Ⓐ Ⓑ Ⓒ Ⓓ Ⓔ
9. Ⓐ Ⓑ Ⓒ Ⓓ Ⓔ

10. Ⓐ Ⓑ Ⓒ Ⓓ Ⓔ
11. Ⓐ Ⓑ Ⓒ Ⓓ Ⓔ
12. Ⓐ Ⓑ Ⓒ Ⓓ Ⓔ
13. Ⓐ Ⓑ Ⓒ Ⓓ Ⓔ
14. Ⓐ Ⓑ Ⓒ Ⓓ Ⓔ
15. Ⓐ Ⓑ Ⓒ Ⓓ Ⓔ
16. Ⓐ Ⓑ Ⓒ Ⓓ Ⓔ
17. Ⓐ Ⓑ Ⓒ Ⓓ Ⓔ

18. Ⓐ Ⓑ Ⓒ Ⓓ Ⓔ
19. Ⓐ Ⓑ Ⓒ Ⓓ Ⓔ
20. Ⓐ Ⓑ Ⓒ Ⓓ Ⓔ
21. Ⓐ Ⓑ Ⓒ Ⓓ Ⓔ
22. Ⓐ Ⓑ Ⓒ Ⓓ Ⓔ
23. Ⓐ Ⓑ Ⓒ Ⓓ Ⓔ
24. Ⓐ Ⓑ Ⓒ Ⓓ Ⓔ
25. Ⓐ Ⓑ Ⓒ Ⓓ Ⓔ

Part 5: Instrument Comprehension

1. Ⓐ Ⓑ Ⓒ Ⓓ
2. Ⓐ Ⓑ Ⓒ Ⓓ
3. Ⓐ Ⓑ Ⓒ Ⓓ
4. Ⓐ Ⓑ Ⓒ Ⓓ
5. Ⓐ Ⓑ Ⓒ Ⓓ
6. Ⓐ Ⓑ Ⓒ Ⓓ
7. Ⓐ Ⓑ Ⓒ Ⓓ

8. Ⓐ Ⓑ Ⓒ Ⓓ
9. Ⓐ Ⓑ Ⓒ Ⓓ
10. Ⓐ Ⓑ Ⓒ Ⓓ
11. Ⓐ Ⓑ Ⓒ Ⓓ
12. Ⓐ Ⓑ Ⓒ Ⓓ
13. Ⓐ Ⓑ Ⓒ Ⓓ
14. Ⓐ Ⓑ Ⓒ Ⓓ

15. Ⓐ Ⓑ Ⓒ Ⓓ
16. Ⓐ Ⓑ Ⓒ Ⓓ
17. Ⓐ Ⓑ Ⓒ Ⓓ
18. Ⓐ Ⓑ Ⓒ Ⓓ
19. Ⓐ Ⓑ Ⓒ Ⓓ
20. Ⓐ Ⓑ Ⓒ Ⓓ

Part 6: Block Counting

1. Ⓐ Ⓑ Ⓒ Ⓓ Ⓔ
2. Ⓐ Ⓑ Ⓒ Ⓓ Ⓔ
3. Ⓐ Ⓑ Ⓒ Ⓓ Ⓔ
4. Ⓐ Ⓑ Ⓒ Ⓓ Ⓔ
5. Ⓐ Ⓑ Ⓒ Ⓓ Ⓔ
6. Ⓐ Ⓑ Ⓒ Ⓓ Ⓔ
7. Ⓐ Ⓑ Ⓒ Ⓓ Ⓔ

8. Ⓐ Ⓑ Ⓒ Ⓓ Ⓔ
9. Ⓐ Ⓑ Ⓒ Ⓓ Ⓔ
10. Ⓐ Ⓑ Ⓒ Ⓓ Ⓔ
11. Ⓐ Ⓑ Ⓒ Ⓓ Ⓔ
12. Ⓐ Ⓑ Ⓒ Ⓓ Ⓔ
13. Ⓐ Ⓑ Ⓒ Ⓓ Ⓔ
14. Ⓐ Ⓑ Ⓒ Ⓓ Ⓔ

15. Ⓐ Ⓑ Ⓒ Ⓓ Ⓔ
16. Ⓐ Ⓑ Ⓒ Ⓓ Ⓔ
17. Ⓐ Ⓑ Ⓒ Ⓓ Ⓔ
18. Ⓐ Ⓑ Ⓒ Ⓓ Ⓔ
19. Ⓐ Ⓑ Ⓒ Ⓓ Ⓔ
20. Ⓐ Ⓑ Ⓒ Ⓓ Ⓔ

Part 7: Table Reading

1. Ⓐ Ⓑ Ⓒ Ⓓ Ⓔ
2. Ⓐ Ⓑ Ⓒ Ⓓ Ⓔ
3. Ⓐ Ⓑ Ⓒ Ⓓ Ⓔ
4. Ⓐ Ⓑ Ⓒ Ⓓ Ⓔ
5. Ⓐ Ⓑ Ⓒ Ⓓ Ⓔ
6. Ⓐ Ⓑ Ⓒ Ⓓ Ⓔ
7. Ⓐ Ⓑ Ⓒ Ⓓ Ⓔ
8. Ⓐ Ⓑ Ⓒ Ⓓ Ⓔ
9. Ⓐ Ⓑ Ⓒ Ⓓ Ⓔ
10. Ⓐ Ⓑ Ⓒ Ⓓ Ⓔ
11. Ⓐ Ⓑ Ⓒ Ⓓ Ⓔ
12. Ⓐ Ⓑ Ⓒ Ⓓ Ⓔ
13. Ⓐ Ⓑ Ⓒ Ⓓ Ⓔ
14. Ⓐ Ⓑ Ⓒ Ⓓ Ⓔ

15. Ⓐ Ⓑ Ⓒ Ⓓ Ⓔ
16. Ⓐ Ⓑ Ⓒ Ⓓ Ⓔ
17. Ⓐ Ⓑ Ⓒ Ⓓ Ⓔ
18. Ⓐ Ⓑ Ⓒ Ⓓ Ⓔ
19. Ⓐ Ⓑ Ⓒ Ⓓ Ⓔ
20. Ⓐ Ⓑ Ⓒ Ⓓ Ⓔ
21. Ⓐ Ⓑ Ⓒ Ⓓ Ⓔ
22. Ⓐ Ⓑ Ⓒ Ⓓ Ⓔ
23. Ⓐ Ⓑ Ⓒ Ⓓ Ⓔ
24. Ⓐ Ⓑ Ⓒ Ⓓ Ⓔ
25. Ⓐ Ⓑ Ⓒ Ⓓ Ⓔ
26. Ⓐ Ⓑ Ⓒ Ⓓ Ⓔ
27. Ⓐ Ⓑ Ⓒ Ⓓ Ⓔ
28. Ⓐ Ⓑ Ⓒ Ⓓ Ⓔ

29. Ⓐ Ⓑ Ⓒ Ⓓ Ⓔ
30. Ⓐ Ⓑ Ⓒ Ⓓ Ⓔ
31. Ⓐ Ⓑ Ⓒ Ⓓ Ⓔ
32. Ⓐ Ⓑ Ⓒ Ⓓ Ⓔ
33. Ⓐ Ⓑ Ⓒ Ⓓ Ⓔ
34. Ⓐ Ⓑ Ⓒ Ⓓ Ⓔ
35. Ⓐ Ⓑ Ⓒ Ⓓ Ⓔ
36. Ⓐ Ⓑ Ⓒ Ⓓ Ⓔ
37. Ⓐ Ⓑ Ⓒ Ⓓ Ⓔ
38. Ⓐ Ⓑ Ⓒ Ⓓ Ⓔ
39. Ⓐ Ⓑ Ⓒ Ⓓ Ⓔ
40. Ⓐ Ⓑ Ⓒ Ⓓ Ⓔ

Part 8: Aviation Information

1. Ⓐ Ⓑ Ⓒ Ⓓ Ⓔ
2. Ⓐ Ⓑ Ⓒ Ⓓ Ⓔ
3. Ⓐ Ⓑ Ⓒ Ⓓ Ⓔ
4. Ⓐ Ⓑ Ⓒ Ⓓ Ⓔ
5. Ⓐ Ⓑ Ⓒ Ⓓ Ⓔ
6. Ⓐ Ⓑ Ⓒ Ⓓ Ⓔ
7. Ⓐ Ⓑ Ⓒ Ⓓ Ⓔ

8. Ⓐ Ⓑ Ⓒ Ⓓ Ⓔ
9. Ⓐ Ⓑ Ⓒ Ⓓ Ⓔ
10. Ⓐ Ⓑ Ⓒ Ⓓ Ⓔ
11. Ⓐ Ⓑ Ⓒ Ⓓ Ⓔ
12. Ⓐ Ⓑ Ⓒ Ⓓ Ⓔ
13. Ⓐ Ⓑ Ⓒ Ⓓ Ⓔ
14. Ⓐ Ⓑ Ⓒ Ⓓ Ⓔ

15. Ⓐ Ⓑ Ⓒ Ⓓ Ⓔ
16. Ⓐ Ⓑ Ⓒ Ⓓ Ⓔ
17. Ⓐ Ⓑ Ⓒ Ⓓ Ⓔ
18. Ⓐ Ⓑ Ⓒ Ⓓ Ⓔ
19. Ⓐ Ⓑ Ⓒ Ⓓ Ⓔ
20. Ⓐ Ⓑ Ⓒ Ⓓ Ⓔ

Part 9: Rotated Blocks

1. Ⓐ Ⓑ Ⓒ Ⓓ Ⓔ
2. Ⓐ Ⓑ Ⓒ Ⓓ Ⓔ
3. Ⓐ Ⓑ Ⓒ Ⓓ Ⓔ
4. Ⓐ Ⓑ Ⓒ Ⓓ Ⓔ
5. Ⓐ Ⓑ Ⓒ Ⓓ Ⓔ

6. Ⓐ Ⓑ Ⓒ Ⓓ Ⓔ
7. Ⓐ Ⓑ Ⓒ Ⓓ Ⓔ
8. Ⓐ Ⓑ Ⓒ Ⓓ Ⓔ
9. Ⓐ Ⓑ Ⓒ Ⓓ Ⓔ
10. Ⓐ Ⓑ Ⓒ Ⓓ Ⓔ

11. Ⓐ Ⓑ Ⓒ Ⓓ Ⓔ
12. Ⓐ Ⓑ Ⓒ Ⓓ Ⓔ
13. Ⓐ Ⓑ Ⓒ Ⓓ Ⓔ
14. Ⓐ Ⓑ Ⓒ Ⓓ Ⓔ
15. Ⓐ Ⓑ Ⓒ Ⓓ Ⓔ

answer sheet

Part 10: General Science

1. Ⓐ Ⓑ Ⓒ Ⓓ Ⓔ
2. Ⓐ Ⓑ Ⓒ Ⓓ Ⓔ
3. Ⓐ Ⓑ Ⓒ Ⓓ Ⓔ
4. Ⓐ Ⓑ Ⓒ Ⓓ Ⓔ
5. Ⓐ Ⓑ Ⓒ Ⓓ Ⓔ
6. Ⓐ Ⓑ Ⓒ Ⓓ Ⓔ
7. Ⓐ Ⓑ Ⓒ Ⓓ Ⓔ

8. Ⓐ Ⓑ Ⓒ Ⓓ Ⓔ
9. Ⓐ Ⓑ Ⓒ Ⓓ Ⓔ
10. Ⓐ Ⓑ Ⓒ Ⓓ Ⓔ
11. Ⓐ Ⓑ Ⓒ Ⓓ Ⓔ
12. Ⓐ Ⓑ Ⓒ Ⓓ Ⓔ
13. Ⓐ Ⓑ Ⓒ Ⓓ Ⓔ
14. Ⓐ Ⓑ Ⓒ Ⓓ Ⓔ

15. Ⓐ Ⓑ Ⓒ Ⓓ Ⓔ
16. Ⓐ Ⓑ Ⓒ Ⓓ Ⓔ
17. Ⓐ Ⓑ Ⓒ Ⓓ Ⓔ
18. Ⓐ Ⓑ Ⓒ Ⓓ Ⓔ
19. Ⓐ Ⓑ Ⓒ Ⓓ Ⓔ
20. Ⓐ Ⓑ Ⓒ Ⓓ Ⓔ

Part 11: Hidden Figures

1. Ⓐ Ⓑ Ⓒ Ⓓ Ⓔ
2. Ⓐ Ⓑ Ⓒ Ⓓ Ⓔ
3. Ⓐ Ⓑ Ⓒ Ⓓ Ⓔ
4. Ⓐ Ⓑ Ⓒ Ⓓ Ⓔ
5. Ⓐ Ⓑ Ⓒ Ⓓ Ⓔ

6. Ⓐ Ⓑ Ⓒ Ⓓ Ⓔ
7. Ⓐ Ⓑ Ⓒ Ⓓ Ⓔ
8. Ⓐ Ⓑ Ⓒ Ⓓ Ⓔ
9. Ⓐ Ⓑ Ⓒ Ⓓ Ⓔ
10. Ⓐ Ⓑ Ⓒ Ⓓ Ⓔ

11. Ⓐ Ⓑ Ⓒ Ⓓ Ⓔ
12. Ⓐ Ⓑ Ⓒ Ⓓ Ⓔ
13. Ⓐ Ⓑ Ⓒ Ⓓ Ⓔ
14. Ⓐ Ⓑ Ⓒ Ⓓ Ⓔ
15. Ⓐ Ⓑ Ⓒ Ⓓ Ⓔ

Part 12: Self-Description Inventory

1. Ⓐ Ⓑ Ⓒ Ⓓ Ⓔ	29. Ⓐ Ⓑ Ⓒ Ⓓ Ⓔ	57. Ⓐ Ⓑ Ⓒ Ⓓ Ⓔ	85. Ⓐ Ⓑ Ⓒ Ⓓ Ⓔ
2. Ⓐ Ⓑ Ⓒ Ⓓ Ⓔ	30. Ⓐ Ⓑ Ⓒ Ⓓ Ⓔ	58. Ⓐ Ⓑ Ⓒ Ⓓ Ⓔ	86. Ⓐ Ⓑ Ⓒ Ⓓ Ⓔ
3. Ⓐ Ⓑ Ⓒ Ⓓ Ⓔ	31. Ⓐ Ⓑ Ⓒ Ⓓ Ⓔ	59. Ⓐ Ⓑ Ⓒ Ⓓ Ⓔ	87. Ⓐ Ⓑ Ⓒ Ⓓ Ⓔ
4. Ⓐ Ⓑ Ⓒ Ⓓ Ⓔ	32. Ⓐ Ⓑ Ⓒ Ⓓ Ⓔ	60. Ⓐ Ⓑ Ⓒ Ⓓ Ⓔ	88. Ⓐ Ⓑ Ⓒ Ⓓ Ⓔ
5. Ⓐ Ⓑ Ⓒ Ⓓ Ⓔ	33. Ⓐ Ⓑ Ⓒ Ⓓ Ⓔ	61. Ⓐ Ⓑ Ⓒ Ⓓ Ⓔ	89. Ⓐ Ⓑ Ⓒ Ⓓ Ⓔ
6. Ⓐ Ⓑ Ⓒ Ⓓ Ⓔ	34. Ⓐ Ⓑ Ⓒ Ⓓ Ⓔ	62. Ⓐ Ⓑ Ⓒ Ⓓ Ⓔ	90. Ⓐ Ⓑ Ⓒ Ⓓ Ⓔ
7. Ⓐ Ⓑ Ⓒ Ⓓ Ⓔ	35. Ⓐ Ⓑ Ⓒ Ⓓ Ⓔ	63. Ⓐ Ⓑ Ⓒ Ⓓ Ⓔ	91. Ⓐ Ⓑ Ⓒ Ⓓ Ⓔ
8. Ⓐ Ⓑ Ⓒ Ⓓ Ⓔ	36. Ⓐ Ⓑ Ⓒ Ⓓ Ⓔ	64. Ⓐ Ⓑ Ⓒ Ⓓ Ⓔ	92. Ⓐ Ⓑ Ⓒ Ⓓ Ⓔ
9. Ⓐ Ⓑ Ⓒ Ⓓ Ⓔ	37. Ⓐ Ⓑ Ⓒ Ⓓ Ⓔ	65. Ⓐ Ⓑ Ⓒ Ⓓ Ⓔ	93. Ⓐ Ⓑ Ⓒ Ⓓ Ⓔ
10. Ⓐ Ⓑ Ⓒ Ⓓ Ⓔ	38. Ⓐ Ⓑ Ⓒ Ⓓ Ⓔ	66. Ⓐ Ⓑ Ⓒ Ⓓ Ⓔ	94. Ⓐ Ⓑ Ⓒ Ⓓ Ⓔ
11. Ⓐ Ⓑ Ⓒ Ⓓ Ⓔ	39. Ⓐ Ⓑ Ⓒ Ⓓ Ⓔ	67. Ⓐ Ⓑ Ⓒ Ⓓ Ⓔ	95. Ⓐ Ⓑ Ⓒ Ⓓ Ⓔ
12. Ⓐ Ⓑ Ⓒ Ⓓ Ⓔ	40. Ⓐ Ⓑ Ⓒ Ⓓ Ⓔ	68. Ⓐ Ⓑ Ⓒ Ⓓ Ⓔ	96. Ⓐ Ⓑ Ⓒ Ⓓ Ⓔ
13. Ⓐ Ⓑ Ⓒ Ⓓ Ⓔ	41. Ⓐ Ⓑ Ⓒ Ⓓ Ⓔ	69. Ⓐ Ⓑ Ⓒ Ⓓ Ⓔ	97. Ⓐ Ⓑ Ⓒ Ⓓ Ⓔ
14. Ⓐ Ⓑ Ⓒ Ⓓ Ⓔ	42. Ⓐ Ⓑ Ⓒ Ⓓ Ⓔ	70. Ⓐ Ⓑ Ⓒ Ⓓ Ⓔ	98. Ⓐ Ⓑ Ⓒ Ⓓ Ⓔ
15. Ⓐ Ⓑ Ⓒ Ⓓ Ⓔ	43. Ⓐ Ⓑ Ⓒ Ⓓ Ⓔ	71. Ⓐ Ⓑ Ⓒ Ⓓ Ⓔ	99. Ⓐ Ⓑ Ⓒ Ⓓ Ⓔ
16. Ⓐ Ⓑ Ⓒ Ⓓ Ⓔ	44. Ⓐ Ⓑ Ⓒ Ⓓ Ⓔ	72. Ⓐ Ⓑ Ⓒ Ⓓ Ⓔ	100. Ⓐ Ⓑ Ⓒ Ⓓ Ⓔ
17. Ⓐ Ⓑ Ⓒ Ⓓ Ⓔ	45. Ⓐ Ⓑ Ⓒ Ⓓ Ⓔ	73. Ⓐ Ⓑ Ⓒ Ⓓ Ⓔ	101. Ⓐ Ⓑ Ⓒ Ⓓ Ⓔ
18. Ⓐ Ⓑ Ⓒ Ⓓ Ⓔ	46. Ⓐ Ⓑ Ⓒ Ⓓ Ⓔ	74. Ⓐ Ⓑ Ⓒ Ⓓ Ⓔ	102. Ⓐ Ⓑ Ⓒ Ⓓ Ⓔ
19. Ⓐ Ⓑ Ⓒ Ⓓ Ⓔ	47. Ⓐ Ⓑ Ⓒ Ⓓ Ⓔ	75. Ⓐ Ⓑ Ⓒ Ⓓ Ⓔ	103. Ⓐ Ⓑ Ⓒ Ⓓ Ⓔ
20. Ⓐ Ⓑ Ⓒ Ⓓ Ⓔ	48. Ⓐ Ⓑ Ⓒ Ⓓ Ⓔ	76. Ⓐ Ⓑ Ⓒ Ⓓ Ⓔ	104. Ⓐ Ⓑ Ⓒ Ⓓ Ⓔ
21. Ⓐ Ⓑ Ⓒ Ⓓ Ⓔ	49. Ⓐ Ⓑ Ⓒ Ⓓ Ⓔ	77. Ⓐ Ⓑ Ⓒ Ⓓ Ⓔ	105. Ⓐ Ⓑ Ⓒ Ⓓ Ⓔ
22. Ⓐ Ⓑ Ⓒ Ⓓ Ⓔ	50. Ⓐ Ⓑ Ⓒ Ⓓ Ⓔ	78. Ⓐ Ⓑ Ⓒ Ⓓ Ⓔ	106. Ⓐ Ⓑ Ⓒ Ⓓ Ⓔ
23. Ⓐ Ⓑ Ⓒ Ⓓ Ⓔ	51. Ⓐ Ⓑ Ⓒ Ⓓ Ⓔ	79. Ⓐ Ⓑ Ⓒ Ⓓ Ⓔ	107. Ⓐ Ⓑ Ⓒ Ⓓ Ⓔ
24. Ⓐ Ⓑ Ⓒ Ⓓ Ⓔ	52. Ⓐ Ⓑ Ⓒ Ⓓ Ⓔ	80. Ⓐ Ⓑ Ⓒ Ⓓ Ⓔ	108. Ⓐ Ⓑ Ⓒ Ⓓ Ⓔ
25. Ⓐ Ⓑ Ⓒ Ⓓ Ⓔ	53. Ⓐ Ⓑ Ⓒ Ⓓ Ⓔ	81. Ⓐ Ⓑ Ⓒ Ⓓ Ⓔ	109. Ⓐ Ⓑ Ⓒ Ⓓ Ⓔ
26. Ⓐ Ⓑ Ⓒ Ⓓ Ⓔ	54. Ⓐ Ⓑ Ⓒ Ⓓ Ⓔ	82. Ⓐ Ⓑ Ⓒ Ⓓ Ⓔ	110. Ⓐ Ⓑ Ⓒ Ⓓ Ⓔ
27. Ⓐ Ⓑ Ⓒ Ⓓ Ⓔ	55. Ⓐ Ⓑ Ⓒ Ⓓ Ⓔ	83. Ⓐ Ⓑ Ⓒ Ⓓ Ⓔ	
28. Ⓐ Ⓑ Ⓒ Ⓓ Ⓔ	56. Ⓐ Ⓑ Ⓒ Ⓓ Ⓔ	84. Ⓐ Ⓑ Ⓒ Ⓓ Ⓔ	

answer sheet

PART 1: VERBAL ANALOGIES

Directions: This part of the test has 25 questions designed to measure your ability to reason and see relationships between words. Each question begins with a pair of capitalized words. You are to choose the choice that best completes the analogy developed at the beginning of each question. That is, select the choice that shows a relationship similar to the one shown by the original pair of capitalized words. Then, mark the space on your answer form that has the same number and letter as your choice.

Now look at the two sample questions below:

1. FINGER is to HAND as TOOTH is to

   (A) TONGUE
   (B) LIPS
   (C) NOSE
   (D) MOUTH
   (E) MOLAR

   The correct answer is (D). A *finger* is part of the *hand*; a *tooth* is part of the *mouth*.

2. RACQUET is to COURT as

   (A) TRACTOR is to FIELD
   (B) BLOSSOM is to BLOOM
   (C) STALK is to PREY
   (D) PLAN is to STRATEGY
   (E) MOON is to PLANET

   The correct answer is (A). A *racquet* is used (by a tennis player) on the *court*; a *tractor* is used (by a farmer) on the *field*.

Your score on this test will be based on the number of questions you answer correctly. You should try to answer every question. You will not lose points or be penalized for guessing. Do not spend too much time on any one question.

When you begin, be sure to start with question number 1 of Part 1 of your test booklet and number 1 of Part 1 on your answer sheet.

STOP! DO NOT TURN THIS PAGE UNTIL TOLD TO DO SO.

25 Questions • 8 Minutes

1. BOOK is to CHAPTER as BUILDING is to
   - (A) ELEVATOR
   - (B) LOBBY
   - (C) ROOF
   - (D) STORY
   - (E) WING

2. ALPHA is to OMEGA as
   - (A) APPENDIX is to PREFACE
   - (B) BEGINNING is to END
   - (C) HEAD is to BODY
   - (D) INTERMISSION is to FINALE
   - (E) PRELUDE is to INTER-MISSION

3. CARROT is to VEGETABLE as
   - (A) DOGWOOD is to OAK
   - (B) FOOT is to PAW
   - (C) PEPPER is to SPICE
   - (D) SHEEP is to LAMB
   - (E) VEAL is to BEEF

4. MICROMETER is to MACHINIST as TROWEL is to
   - (A) BLACKSMITH
   - (B) ELECTRICIAN
   - (C) MASON
   - (D) PRESSMAN
   - (E) WELDER

5. CONCAVE is to CONVEX as
   - (A) CAVITY is to MOUND
   - (B) HILL is to HOLE
   - (C) OVAL is to OBLONG
   - (D) ROUND is to POINTED
   - (E) SQUARE is to ROUND

6. DOZEN is to SCORE as
   - (A) VII is to XII
   - (B) IIX is to XX
   - (C) IIX is to XL
   - (D) XII is to XX
   - (E) XII is to XL

7. GOWN is to GARMENT as GASOLINE is to
   - (A) COOLANT
   - (B) FUEL
   - (C) GREASE
   - (D) LUBRICANT
   - (E) OIL

8. EMERALD is to GREEN as
   - (A) CANARY is to YELLOW
   - (B) COCOA is to BROWN
   - (C) NAVY is to BLUE
   - (D) ROYAL is to PURPLE
   - (E) RUBY is to RED

9. HYPER- is to HYPO- as
   - (A) ACTUAL is to THEORETICAL
   - (B) DIASTOLIC is to SYSTOLIC
   - (C) OVER is to UNDER
   - (D) SMALL is to LARGE
   - (E) STALE is to FRESH

10. HORIZONTAL is to VERTICAL as WARP is to
    - (A) COUNT
    - (B) PILE
    - (C) SELVAGE
    - (D) WEAVE
    - (E) WOOF

GO ON TO THE NEXT PAGE.

11. IMMIGRATION is to EMIGRATION as

   (A) ARRIVAL is to DEPARTURE
   (B) FLIGHT is to VOYAGE
   (C) LEGAL is to ILLEGAL
   (D) MIGRATION is to TRAVEL
   (E) PASSPORT is to VISA

12. KILOMETER is to METER as

   (A) CENTURY is to DECADE
   (B) CENTURY is to YEAR
   (C) DECADE is to MONTH
   (D) MILLENNIUM is to CENTURY
   (E) MILLENNIUM is to YEAR

13. OCTAGON is to SQUARE as HEXAGON is to

   (A) CUBE
   (B) POLYGON
   (C) PYRAMID
   (D) RECTANGLE
   (E) TRIANGLE

14. ORDINATION is to PRIEST as

   (A) ELECTION is to OFFICIAL
   (B) INAUGURATION is to PRESIDENT
   (C) MATRICULATION is to STUDENT
   (D) NOMINATION is to OFFICER
   (E) RETIREMENT is to MINISTER

15. PERJURE is to STATE as

   (A) ABANDON is to DESERT
   (B) CONCENTRATE is to FOCUS
   (C) MARVEL is to WONDER
   (D) ROB is to STEAL
   (E) TRESPASS is to ENTER

16. ORDINANCE is to REGULATION as ORDNANCE is to

   (A) LAW
   (B) MILITARY
   (C) MUNITION
   (D) NUMERICAL
   (E) STATUTE

17. TELL is to TOLD as

   (A) RIDE is to RODE
   (B) SLAY is to SLEW
   (C) SINK is to SANK
   (D) WEAVE is to WOVE
   (E) WEEP is to WEPT

18. UNIT is to DOZEN as

   (A) DAY is to WEEK
   (B) HOUR is to DAY
   (C) MINUTE is to HOUR
   (D) MONTH is to YEAR
   (E) WEEK is to MONTH

19. SHEEP is to LAMB as HORSE is to

   (A) COLT
   (B) DOE
   (C) FAWN
   (D) MARE
   (E) RAM

20. ZENITH is to NADIR as

   (A) BEST is to WORST
   (B) HEAVIEST is to LIGHTEST
   (C) HIGHEST is to LOWEST
   (D) MOST is to LEAST
   (E) WIDEST is to NARROWEST

21. IGNORE is to OVERLOOK as

   (A) AGREE is to CONSENT
   (B) ATTACH is to SEPARATE
   (C) CLIMB is to WALK
   (D) DULL is to SHARPEN
   (E) LEARN is to REMEMBER

GO ON TO THE NEXT PAGE.

22. SQUARE is to CIRCLE as PERIMETER is to

(A) ARC
(B) CIRCUMFERENCE
(C) DIAMETER
(D) RADIUS
(E) SECTOR

23. FREQUENTLY is to SELDOM as

(A) ALWAYS is to NEVER
(B) EVERYBODY is to EVERYONE
(C) GENERALLY is to USUALLY
(D) OCCASIONALLY is to CONSTANTLY
(E) SORROW is to SYMPATHY

24. VEHICLE is to BUS as

(A) FOOTBALL is to HANDBALL
(B) GAME is to BASEBALL
(C) HUNTING is to FISHING
(D) PLAY is to SPORT
(E) SPORT is to RECREATION

25. TRICKLE is to GUSH as TEPID is to

(A) COLD
(B) COOL
(C) FROZEN
(D) HOT
(E) WARM

STOP! DO NOT GO ON UNTIL TIME IS UP.

practice test

PART 2: ARITHMETIC REASONING

Directons: This part of the test has 25 questions that measure mathematical reasoning or your ability to arrive at solutions to problems. Each problem is followed by five possible answers. Decide which one of the five choices is most nearly correct. Then, mark the space on your answer form that has the same number and letter as your choice. Use the scratch paper that has been given to you to do any figuring.

Now look at the two sample problems below.

1. A field with an area of 420 square yards is twice as large in area as a second field. If the second field is 15 yards long, how wide is it?

   (A) 7 yards
   (B) 14 yards
   (C) 28 yards
   (D) 56 yards
   (E) 90 yards

   The correct answer is (B). The second field has an area of 210 square yards. If one side is 15 yards, the other side must be 14 yards ($15 \times 14 = 210$).

2. An applicant took three typing tests. The average typing speed on these three tests was 48 words per minute. If the applicant's speed on two of these tests was 52 words per minute, what was the applicant's speed on the third test?

   (A) 46 words per minute
   (B) 44 words per minute
   (C) 42 words per minute
   (D) 40 words per minute
   (E) 38 words per minute

   The correct answer is (D). The formula for finding an average is as follows:

   $$\text{average} = \frac{\text{sum of terms}}{\text{number of terms}}$$

   In this case the problem provides the average (48), two of the terms (52 + 52), and the number of terms (3). Substitute this information into the formula for average and then solve for x (the missing term).

   $$48 = \frac{52 + 52 + x}{3}$$
   $$48 \times 3 = 104 + x$$
   $$144 = 104 + x$$
   $$40 = x$$

Your score on this test will be based on the number of questions you answer correctly. You should try to answer every question. You will not lose points or be penalized for guessing. Do not spend too much time on any one question.

When you begin, be sure to start with question number 1 of Part 2 of your test booklet and number 1 of Part 2 on your answer sheet.

STOP! DO NOT TURN THIS PAGE UNTIL TOLD TO DO SO.

25 Questions • 29 Minutes

1. An athlete jogs 15 laps around a circular track. If the total distance jogged is 3 kilometers, what is the distance around the track?

   (A) 0.2 meters
   (B) 2 meters
   (C) 20 meters
   (D) 200 meters
   (E) 2,000 meters

2. The floor area in an Air Force warehouse measures 200 feet by 200 feet. What is the maximum safe floor load if the maximum weight the floor area can hold is 4,000 tons?

   (A) 100 pounds per square foot
   (B) 120 pounds per square foot
   (C) 140 pounds per square foot
   (D) 160 pounds per square foot
   (E) 200 pounds per square foot

3. A crate containing a tool weighs 12 pounds. If the tool weighs 9 pounds, 9 ounces, how much does the crate weigh?

   (A) 2 pounds, 7 ounces
   (B) 2 pounds, 9 ounces
   (C) 3 pounds, 3 ounces
   (D) 3 pounds, 7 ounces
   (E) 3 pounds, 9 ounces

4. Assume that the U.S. Mint produces one million nickels a month. The total value of the nickels produced during a year is

   (A) $50,000
   (B) $60,000
   (C) $250,000
   (D) $500,000
   (E) $600,000

5. In order to check on a shipment of 500 articles, a sampling of 50 articles was carefully inspected. Of the sample, 4 articles were found to be defective. On this basis, what is the probable percentage of defective articles in the original shipment?

   (A) 8 percent
   (B) 4 percent
   (C) 0.8 percent
   (D) 0.4 percent
   (E) 0.04 percent

6. There are 20 cigarettes in one pack and 10 packs of cigarettes in a carton. A certain brand of cigarette contains 12 mg of tar per cigarette. How many grams of tar are contained in one carton of these cigarettes? (1 gram = 1,000 milligrams)

   (A) 0.024 grams
   (B) 0.24 grams
   (C) 2.4 grams
   (D) 24 grams
   (E) 240 grams

7. Assume that it takes an average of 3 man-hours to stack 1 ton of a particular item. In order to stack 36 tons in 6 hours, the number of people required is

   (A) 9
   (B) 12
   (C) 15
   (D) 18
   (E) 21

GO ON TO THE NEXT PAGE.

8. Two office workers have been assigned to address 750 envelopes. One addresses twice as many envelopes per hour as the other. If it takes 5 hours for them to complete the job, what was the rate of the slower worker?

   (A) 50 envelopes per hour
   (B) 75 envelopes per hour
   (C) 100 envelopes per hour
   (D) 125 envelopes per hour
   (E) 150 envelopes per hour

9. A room measuring 15 feet wide, 25 feet long, and 12 feet high is scheduled to be painted shortly. If there are two windows in the room, each 7 feet by 5 feet, and a glass door, 6 feet by 4 feet, then the area of wall space to be painted measures

   (A) 842 square feet.
   (B) 866 square feet.
   (C) 901 square feet.
   (D) 925 square feet.
   (E) 4,406 square feet.

10. A pound of margarine contains four equal sticks of margarine. The wrapper of each stick has markings that indicate how to divide the stick into eight sections, each section measuring one tablespoon. If a recipe calls for four tablespoons of margarine, the amount to use is

    (A) $\frac{1}{16}$ lb.

    (B) $\frac{1}{8}$ lb.

    (C) $\frac{1}{4}$ lb.

    (D) $\frac{1}{2}$ lb.

    (E) $\frac{3}{4}$ lb.

11. The price of a one-hundred-dollar item after successive discounts of 10 percent and 15 percent is

    (A) $75.00
    (B) $75.50
    (C) $76.00
    (D) $76.50
    (E) $77.00

12. A certain governmental agency had a budget last year of $1,100,500. Its budget this year was 7 percent higher than that of last year. The budget for next year is 8 percent higher than this year's budget. Which one of the following is the agency's budget for next year?

    (A) $1,117,600
    (B) $1,161,600
    (C) $1,261,700
    (D) $1,265,600
    (E) $1,271,700

13. The length of a rectangle is 4 times the width. If the area of the rectangle is 324 square feet, the dimensions of the rectangle are

    (A) 8' × 32'
    (B) 8' × 42'
    (C) 9' × 36'
    (D) 9' × 40'
    (E) 9' × 46'

GO ON TO THE NEXT PAGE.

14. On a scaled drawing of an office building floor, $\frac{1}{2}$ inch represents 3 feet of actual floor dimension. A floor that is actually 75 feet wide and 132 feet long would have which of the following dimensions on the scaled drawing?

    (A) 12.5 inches wide and 22 inches long
    (B) 17 inches wide and 32 inches long
    (C) 25 inches wide and 44 inches long
    (D) 29.5 inches wide and 52 inches long
    (E) None of the above

15. If the weight of water is 62.4 pounds per cubic foot, the weight of the water that fills a rectangular container 6 inches by 6 inches by 1 foot is

    (A) 3.9 pounds.
    (B) 7.8 pounds.
    (C) 15.6 pounds.
    (D) 31.2 pounds.
    (E) 62.4 pounds.

16. If there are red, green, and yellow marbles in a jar, and 20 percent of these marbles are either red or green, what are the chances of blindly picking a yellow marble out of the jar?

    (A) 1 out of 3
    (B) 1 out of 5
    (C) 2 out of 3
    (D) 2 out of 5
    (E) 4 out of 5

17. An Air Force recruiting station enlisted 560 people. Of these, 25 percent were under 20 years old and 35 percent were 20–22 years old. How many of the recruits were over 22 years old?

    (A) 196
    (B) 224
    (C) 244
    (D) 280
    (E) 336

18. A passenger plane can carry 2 tons of cargo. A freight plane can carry 6 tons of cargo. If an equal number of both kinds of planes are used to ship 160 tons of cargo and each plane carries its maximum cargo load, how many tons of cargo are shipped on the passenger planes?

    (A) 40 tons
    (B) 60 tons
    (C) 80 tons
    (D) 100 tons
    (E) 120 tons

19. The area of a square is 36 square inches. If the side of this square is doubled, the area of the new square will be

    (A) 72 square inches.
    (B) 108 square inches.
    (C) 216 square inches.
    (D) 244 square inches.
    (E) None of the above

20. When 550 gallons of oil are added to an oil tank that is $\frac{1}{8}$ full, the tank becomes $\frac{1}{2}$ full. The capacity of the oil tank is most nearly

    (A) 1,350 gals.
    (B) 1,390 gals.
    (C) 1,430 gals.
    (D) 1,470 gals.
    (E) 1,510 gals.

21. If an aircraft is traveling at 630 miles per hour, how many miles does it cover in 1,200 seconds?

    (A) 180 miles
    (B) 210 miles
    (C) 240 miles
    (D) 280 miles
    (E) 310 miles

GO ON TO THE NEXT PAGE.

22. If your watch gains 20 minutes per day and you set it to the correct time at 7:00 a.m., the correct time when the watch indicates 1:00 p.m. is

(A) 12:45 p.m.

(B) 12:50 p.m.

(C) 12:55 p.m.

(D) 1:05 p.m.

(E) 1:10 p.m.

23. It takes a runner 9 seconds to run a distance of 132 feet. What is the runner's speed in miles per hour? (5,280 ft = 1 mile)

(A) 5

(B) 10

(C) 12

(D) 15

(E) 16

24. The arithmetic mean of the salaries paid to 5 employees earning $18,400, $19,300, $18,450, $18,550, and $17,600, respectively, is

(A) $18,450

(B) $18,460

(C) $18,470

(D) $18,475

(E) $18,500

25. How many meters will a point on the rim of a wheel travel if the wheel makes 35 rotations and its radius is one meter?

(A) 110

(B) 120

(C) 210

(D) 220

(E) 240

practice test

STOP! DO NOT GO ON UNTIL TIME IS UP.

PART 3: WORD KNOWLEDGE

Directions: This part of the test has 25 questions designed to measure verbal comprehension involving your ability to understand written language. For each question, you are to select the option that means the same or most nearly the same as the capitalized word. Then mark the space on your answer form that has the same number and letter as your choice.

Here are two sample questions:

1. CRIMSON:
   - **(A)** bluish
   - **(B)** colorful
   - **(C)** crisp
   - **(D)** lively
   - **(E)** reddish

   The correct answer is (E). *Crimson* means "a deep purple red." Choice (E) has almost the same meaning. None of the other options has the same or a similar meaning.

2. CEASE:
   - **(A)** continue
   - **(B)** fold
   - **(C)** start
   - **(D)** stop
   - **(E)** transform

The correct answer is (D). *Cease* means "to stop." Choice (D) is the only option with the same meaning.

Your score on this test will be based on the number of questions you answer correctly. You should try to answer every question. You will not lose points or be penalized for guessing. Do not spend too much time on any one question.

When you begin, be sure to start with question number 1 of Part 3 of your test booklet and number 1 of Part 3 on your answer sheet.

STOP! DO NOT TURN THIS PAGE UNTIL TOLD TO DO SO.

practice test

25 Questions • 5 Minutes

1. ADAMANT:
   (A) belligerent
   (B) cowardly
   (C) inflexible
   (D) justified
   (E) petty

2. ALTERCATION:
   (A) controversy
   (B) defeat
   (C) irritation
   (D) substitution
   (E) vexation

3. ASSENT:
   (A) acquire
   (B) climb
   (C) consent
   (D) emphasize
   (E) participate

4. ATTRITION:
   (A) act of expanding
   (B) act of giving up
   (C) act of purifying
   (D) act of solving
   (E) act of wearing down

5. AUTHENTIC:
   (A) detailed
   (B) genuine
   (C) literary
   (D) practical
   (E) precious

6. CONDUCIVE:
   (A) confusing
   (B) cooperative
   (C) energetic
   (D) helpful
   (E) respectful

7. COUNTERACT:
   (A) criticize
   (B) conserve
   (C) erode
   (D) neutralize
   (E) retreat

8. DELETERIOUS:
   (A) delightful
   (B) frail
   (C) harmful
   (D) late
   (E) tasteful

9. DILATED:
   (A) cleared
   (B) clouded
   (C) decreased
   (D) enlarged
   (E) tightened

10. FLEXIBLE:
    (A) flammable
    (B) fragile
    (C) pliable
    (D) rigid
    (E) separable

11. FORTNIGHT:
    (A) two days
    (B) one week
    (C) two weeks
    (D) one month
    (E) two months

12. IMPARTIAL:
    (A) complete
    (B) fair
    (C) incomplete
    (D) sincere
    (E) watchful

GO ON TO THE NEXT PAGE.

13. INCIDENTAL:

   (A) minor
   (B) eventful
   (C) infrequent
   (D) unexpected
   (E) unnecessary

14. INDOLENT:

   (A) hopeless
   (B) lazy
   (C) lenient
   (D) rude
   (E) selfish

15. NOTORIOUS:

   (A) annoying
   (B) condemned
   (C) ill-mannered
   (D) official
   (E) well known

16. REBUFF:

   (A) forget
   (B) ignore
   (C) recover
   (D) polish
   (E) snub

17. SPURIOUS:

   (A) false
   (B) maddening
   (C) obvious
   (D) odd
   (E) stimulating

18. SUCCINCT:

   (A) concise
   (B) helpful
   (C) important
   (D) misleading
   (E) sweet

19. SULLEN:

   (A) angrily silent
   (B) grayish yellow
   (C) mildly nauseated
   (D) soaking wet
   (E) very dirty

20. SYMPTOM:

   (A) cure
   (B) disease
   (C) mistake
   (D) sign
   (E) test

21. TEDIOUS:

   (A) demanding
   (B) dull
   (C) hard
   (D) simple
   (E) surprising

22. TERSE:

   (A) faulty
   (B) lengthy
   (C) oral
   (D) pointed
   (E) written

23. TRIVIAL:

   (A) distressing
   (B) enjoyable
   (C) exciting
   (D) important
   (E) petty

24. VERIFY:

   (A) alarm
   (B) confirm
   (C) explain
   (D) guarantee
   (E) question

GO ON TO THE NEXT PAGE.

25. VIGILANT:
    (A) cross
    (B) patient
    (C) suspicious
    (D) understanding
    (E) watchful

STOP! DO NOT GO ON UNTIL TIME IS UP.

PART 4: MATH KNOWLEDGE

Directions: This part of the test has 25 questions designed to measure your ability to use learned mathematical relationships. Each problem is followed by five possible answers. Decide which one of the five choices is most nearly correct. Then, mark the space on your answer form that has the same number and letter as your choice. Use scratch paper to do any figuring.

Here are three sample questions:

1. The reciprocal of 5 is
   - **(A)** 0.1
   - **(B)** 0.2
   - **(C)** 0.5
   - **(D)** 1.0
   - **(E)** 2.0

   The correct answer is (B). The reciprocal of 5 is $\frac{1}{5}$ or 0.2.

2. The expression "3 factorial" equals
   - **(A)** $\frac{1}{9}$
   - **(B)** $\frac{1}{6}$
   - **(C)** 6
   - **(D)** 9
   - **(E)** 27

   The correct answer is (C). "3 factorial" or 3! equals $3 \times 2 \times 1 = 6$.

3. The logarithm to the base 10 of 1000 is
   - **(A)** 1
   - **(B)** 1.6
   - **(C)** 2
   - **(D)** 2.7
   - **(E)** 3

   The correct answer is (E). $10 \times 10 \times 10 = 1000$. The logarithm of 1000 is the exponent 3 to which the base 10 must be raised.

Your score on this test will be based on the number of questions you answer correctly. You should try to answer every question. You will not lose points or be penalized for guessing. Do not spend too much time on any one question.

When you begin, be sure to start with question number 1 of Part 4 of your test booklet and number 1 of Part 4 on your answer sheet.

STOP! DO NOT TURN THIS PAGE UNTIL TOLD TO DO SO.

25 Questions • 22 Minutes

1. Which of the following integers is NOT a prime number?

   (A) 3
   (B) 5
   (C) 7
   (D) 9
   (E) 11

2. The distance in miles around a circular course with a radius of 35 miles is (use pi $= \frac{22}{7}$)

   (A) 110 miles.
   (B) 156 miles.
   (C) 220 miles.
   (D) 440 miles.
   (E) 880 miles.

3. If $5x + 3y = 29$ and $x - y = 1$, then $x =$

   (A) 1
   (B) 2
   (C) 3
   (D) 4
   (E) 5

4. Solve for x: $\frac{2x}{7} = 2x^2$

   (A) $\frac{1}{7}$

   (B) $\frac{2}{7}$

   (C) 2
   (D) 7
   (E) 14

5. If x is an odd integer, which one of the following is an even integer?

   (A) $2x + 1$
   (B) $2x - 1$
   (C) $x^2 - x$
   (D) $x^2 + x - 1$
   (E) None of the above

6. $\frac{x - 2}{x^2 - 6x + 8}$ can be reduced to

   (A) $\frac{1}{x - 4}$

   (B) $\frac{1}{x - 2}$

   (C) $\frac{x - 2}{x + 2}$

   (D) $\frac{1}{x + 2}$

   (E) $\frac{1}{x + 4}$

7. 10^x divided by 10^y equals

   (A) $10^{x/y}$
   (B) 10^{xy}
   (C) $10^{x + y}$
   (D) $10^{x - y}$
   (E) None of the above

8. $(-3)^3 =$

   (A) 9
   (B) -9
   (C) 27
   (D) -27
   (E) None of the above

9. One million may be represented as

   (A) 10^4
   (B) 10^5
   (C) 10^6
   (D) 10^7
   (E) 10^8

GO ON TO THE NEXT PAGE.

10. $\left(\dfrac{2}{5}\right)^2$ equals

(A) $\dfrac{4}{5}$

(B) $\dfrac{2}{10}$

(C) $\dfrac{4}{10}$

(D) $\dfrac{2}{25}$

(E) $\dfrac{4}{25}$

11. If $3^n = 9$, what is the value of 4^{n+1}?

(A) 24
(B) 48
(C) 64
(D) 108
(E) None of the above

12. 10^{-2} is equal to

(A) 0.001
(B) 0.01
(C) 0.1
(D) 1.0
(E) 100.0

13. The expression $\sqrt{28} - \sqrt{7}$ reduces to

(A) $\sqrt{4}$

(B) $\sqrt{7}$

(C) $3\sqrt{7}$

(D) $\sqrt{21}$

(E) $-\sqrt{35}$

14. The hypotenuse of a right triangle whose legs are 5″ and 12″ is

(A) 7″
(B) 13″
(C) 14″
(D) 17″
(E) None of the above

15. The sum of the angle measures of a pentagon is

(A) 360 degrees.
(B) 540 degrees.
(C) 720 degrees.
(D) 900 degrees.
(E) 1,180 degrees.

16. If the ratio of $3x$ to $5y$ is 1:2, what is the ratio of x to y?

(A) 1:2
(B) 2:3
(C) 3:4
(D) 4:5
(E) 5:6

17. A scale of $\dfrac{1}{24,000}$ is the same as a scale of

(A) $\dfrac{1}{32}$ inch $\cong$ 1 yard

(B) 1 inch $\cong$ 2,000 feet

(C) 1 foot $\cong \dfrac{1}{2}$ mile

(D) 1 yard $\cong$ 2 miles

(E) None of the above

18. The distance between two points on a graph whose rectangular coordinates are (2,4) and (5,8) is most nearly

(A) 4.7
(B) 4.8
(C) 4.9
(D) 5.0
(E) 5.1

19. The volume of a cylinder with a radius of r and a height of h is

(A) $\pi r h$
(B) $2\pi r h$
(C) $2\pi r^2 h$
(D) $4\pi r^2 h$
(E) None of the above

GO ON TO THE NEXT PAGE.

20. Which of the following lengths of a side of an equilateral triangle has a perimeter divisible by both 3 and 5?

    (A) 3
    (B) 4
    (C) 5
    (D) 6
    (E) 7

21. The numerical value of $\frac{4!}{3!}$ is

    (A) .75
    (B) 1
    (C) 1.25
    (D) 1.33
    (E) 4

22. The cube root of 729 is equal to the square of

    (A) 11
    (B) 9
    (C) 7
    (D) 5
    (E) 3

23. If one angle of a triangle measures 115°, then the sum of the other two angles is

    (A) 245°
    (B) 75°
    (C) 195°
    (D) 65°
    (E) None of the above

24. What is the appropriate number that would follow the last number in the following series of numbers arranged in a logical order?

    2   4   12   48   __

    (A) 96
    (B) 144
    (C) 192
    (D) 204
    (E) 240

25. What is the appropriate choice for the next two letters in the following series of letters that follow some definite pattern?

    A R C S E T G __ __

    (A) UH
    (B) HI
    (C) UI
    (D) IU
    (E) IH

STOP! DO NOT GO ON UNTIL TIME IS UP.

PART 5: INSTRUMENT COMPREHENSION

Directions: This part of the test has 20 questions designed to measure your ability to determine the position of an airplane in flight from reading instruments showing its compass heading, its amount of climb or dive, and its degree of bank to right or left. In each item, the left-hand dial is labeled ARTIFICIAL HORIZON. On the face of this dial the small aircraft silhouette remains stationary, while the positions of the heavy black line and the black pointer vary with changes in the position of the airplane in which the instrument is located.

HOW TO READ THE ARTIFICIAL HORIZON DIAL

The heavy black line represents the HORIZON LINE. The black pointer shows the degree of BANK to the right or left. The HORIZON LINE tilts as the aircraft is banked and is always at a right angle to the pointer.

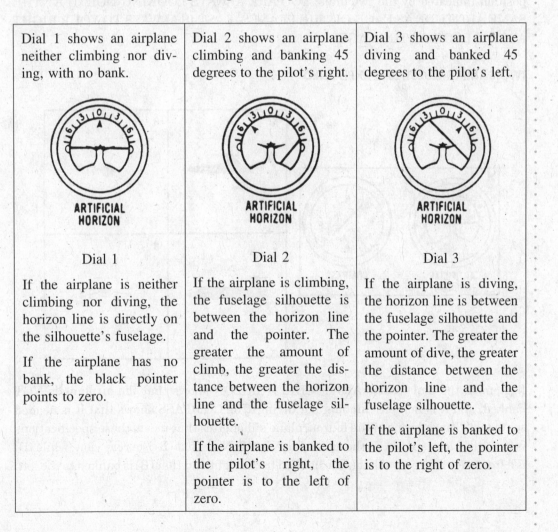

Dial 1 shows an airplane neither climbing nor diving, with no bank.	Dial 2 shows an airplane climbing and banking 45 degrees to the pilot's right.	Dial 3 shows an airplane diving and banked 45 degrees to the pilot's left.
Dial 1	Dial 2	Dial 3
If the airplane is neither climbing nor diving, the horizon line is directly on the silhouette's fuselage. If the airplane has no bank, the black pointer points to zero.	If the airplane is climbing, the fuselage silhouette is between the horizon line and the pointer. The greater the amount of climb, the greater the distance between the horizon line and the fuselage silhouette. If the airplane is banked to the pilot's right, the pointer is to the left of zero.	If the airplane is diving, the horizon line is between the fuselage silhouette and the pointer. The greater the amount of dive, the greater the distance between the horizon line and the fuselage silhouette. If the airplane is banked to the pilot's left, the pointer is to the right of zero.

GO ON TO THE NEXT PAGE.

On each item, the right dial is labeled COMPASS. On this dial, the arrow shows the compass direction in which the airplane is headed at the moment. Dial 4 shows it headed north; dial 5 shows it headed west; and dial 6 shows it headed northwest.

Each item in this test consists of two dials and four silhouettes of airplanes in flight. Your task is to determine which one of the four airplanes is MOST NEARLY in the position indicated by the two dials. YOU ARE ALWAYS LOOKING NORTH AT THE SAME ALTITUDE AS EACH OF THE PLANES. EAST IS ALWAYS TO YOUR RIGHT AS YOU LOOK AT THE PAGE.

TWO SAMPLE QUESTIONS EXPLAINED

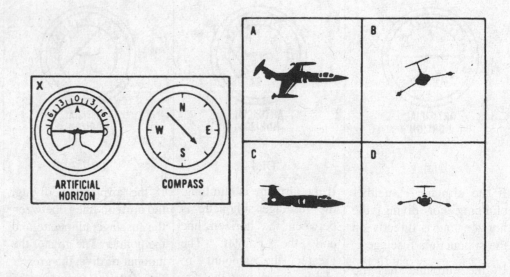

In item X, the dial labeled ARTIFICIAL HORIZON shows that the airplane is NOT banked, and it is neither climbing nor diving. The COMPASS shows that it is headed southeast. The only one of the four airplane silhouettes that meets these specifications is in the box lettered (C), so the answer to X is (C). Note that (B) is a rear view, while (D) is a front view. Note also that (A) is banked to the right and that (B) is banked to the left.

GO ON TO THE NEXT PAGE.

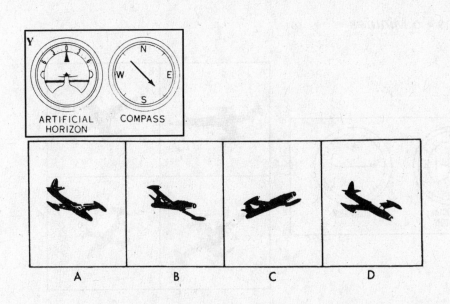

In item Y, the dial labeled ARTIFICIAL HORIZON shows that the airplane is NOT banked, and it is climbing to a slight extent. The COMPASS shows that it is headed southeast. The only one of the four airplane silhouettes that meets these specifications is choice (C), so the answer to Y is (C). Note that (A) is diving and is headed southeast; (B) is neither diving nor climbing and is banking to the pilot's right; (D) is in a slight dive, headed southeast.

STOP! DO NOT TURN THIS PAGE UNTIL TOLD TO DO SO.

20 Questions • 6 Minutes

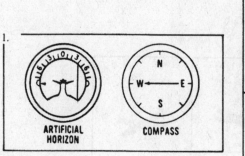 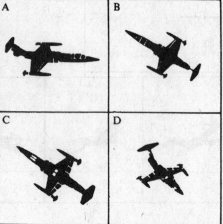

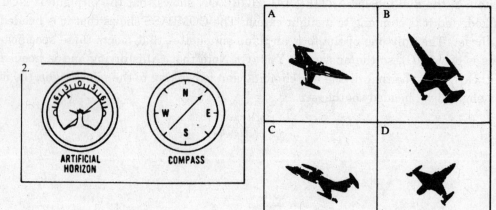

GO ON TO THE NEXT PAGE.

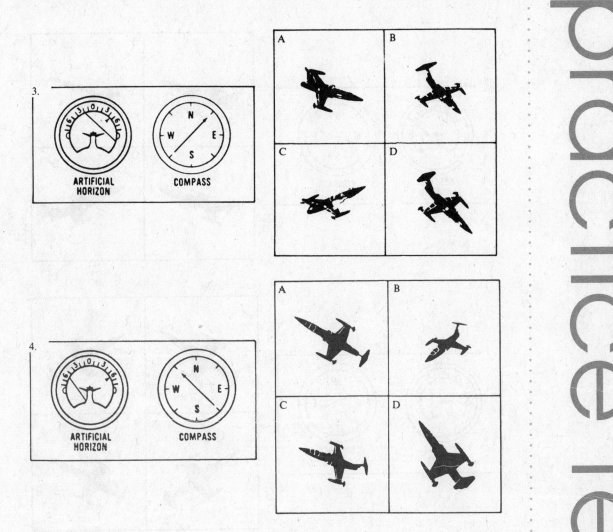

practice test

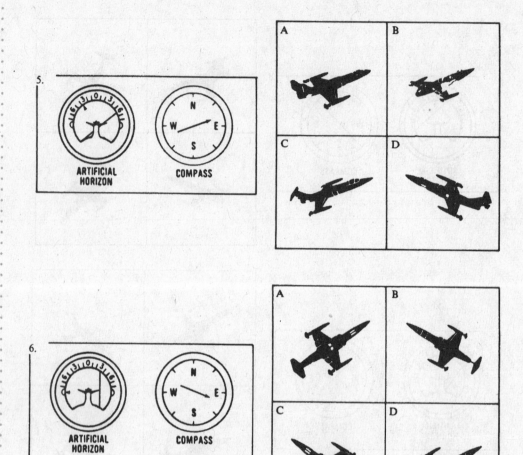

GO ON TO THE NEXT PAGE.

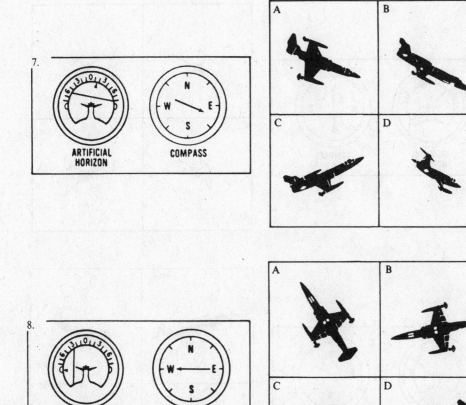

9.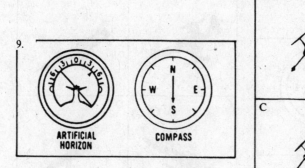

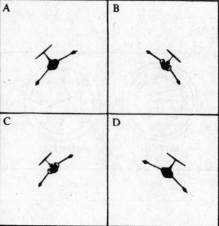

10.

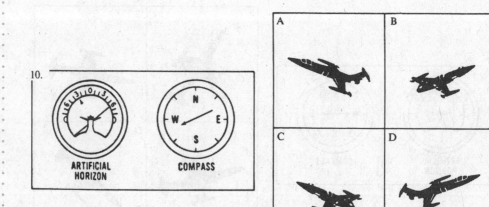

GO ON TO THE NEXT PAGE.

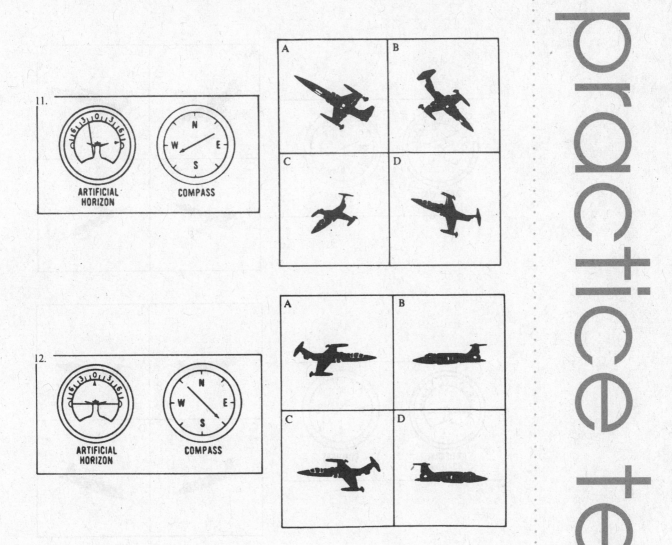

13.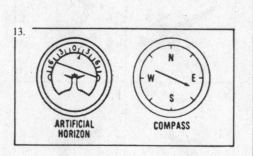

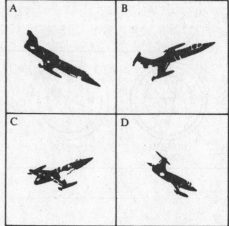

14.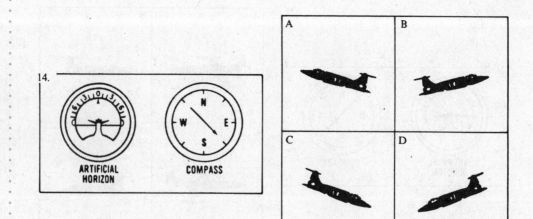

GO ON TO THE NEXT PAGE.

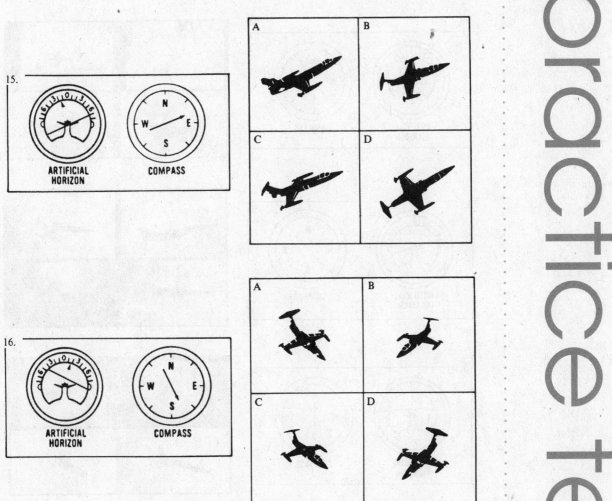

practice test

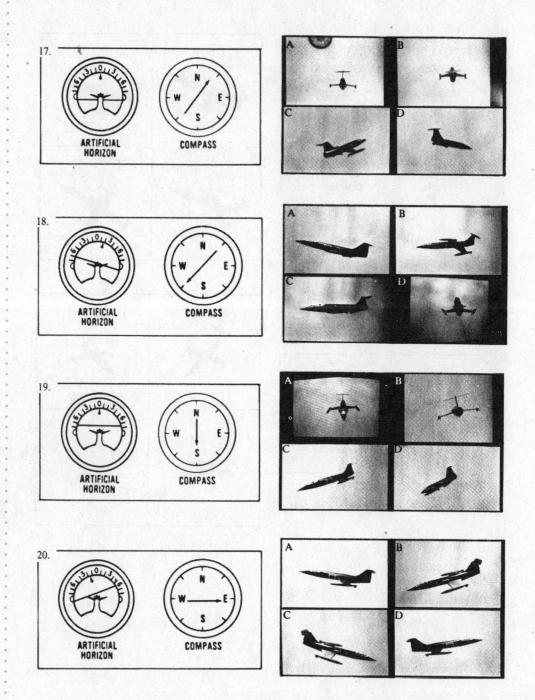

STOP! DO NOT GO ON UNTIL TIME IS UP.

PART 6: BLOCK COUNTING

Directions: This part of the test has 20 questions designed to measure your ability to "see into" a three-dimensional pile of blocks and determine how many pieces are touched by certain numbered blocks. *All of the blocks in each pile are the same size and shape.* A block is considered to touch the numbered block if any part, even a corner or an edge, touches. Look at the sample below:

	KEY				
Block	**A**	**B**	**C**	**D**	**E**
1	1	2	3	4	5
2	3	4	5	6	7
3	5	6	7	8	9
4	2	3	4	5	6
5	2	3	4	5	6

1. **The correct answer is (D).** Block 1 touches the other 2 top blocks and the 2 blocks directly below it. The total number of blocks touched by 1 is, therefore, 4.

2. **The correct answer is (A).** Block 2 touches blocks 1 and 3, and the unnumbered block to the right of block 3. Since block 2 touches 3 other blocks, the answer is 3.

3. **The correct answer is (C).** Now look at sample problem 3. It touches 3 blocks above, 3 blocks below, and one block on the right. Therefore, the correct answer is 7.

4. **The correct answer is (D).** The total number of blocks touched by block 4 is 5.

5. **The correct answer is (C).** Block 5 touches 4 other blocks.

Your score on this test is based on the number of questions you answer correctly. You should try to answer every question. You will not lose points or be penalized for guessing. Do not spend too much time on any one question.

When you begin, be sure to start with question number 1 of Part 6 of your test booklet and number 1 of Part 6 on your answer sheet.

STOP! DO NOT TURN THIS PAGE UNTIL TOLD TO DO SO.

20 Questions • 3 Minutes

Block	KEY				
	A	B	C	D	E
1	3	4	5	6	7
2	5	6	7	8	9
3	5	6	7	8	9
4	4	5	6	7	8
5	4	5	6	7	8

Block	KEY				
	A	B	C	D	E
6	1	2	3	4	5
7	2	3	4	5	6
8	5	6	7	8	9
9	4	5	6	7	8
10	2	3	4	5	6

GO ON TO THE NEXT PAGE.

Block	KEY				
	A	B	C	D	E
11	3	4	5	6	7
12	4	5	6	7	8
13	5	6	7	8	9
14	4	5	6	7	8
15	2	3	4	5	6

Block	KEY				
	A	B	C	D	E
16	3	4	5	6	7
17	5	6	7	8	9
18	3	4	5	6	7
19	2	3	4	5	6
20	1	2	3	4	5

PART 7: TABLE READING

Directions: This part of the test has 40 questions designed to test your ability to read tables quickly and accurately.

Now, look at the following sample items based on the tabulation of turnstile readings shown below:

TABULATION OF TURNSTILE READINGS

Turnstile Number	Turnstile Readings At					
	5:30 a.m.	6:00 a.m.	7:00 a.m.	8:00 a.m.	9:00 a.m.	9:30 a.m.
1	79078	79090	79225	79590	79860	79914
2	24915	24930	25010	25441	25996	26055
3	39509	39530	39736	40533	41448	41515
4	58270	58291	58396	58958	59729	59807
5	43371	43378	43516	43888	44151	44217

For each question, determine the turnstile reading for the turnstile number and time given. Choose as your answer the letter of the column in which the correct reading is found.

	Turnstile Number	Time	A	B	C	D	E
1.	1	8:00 a.m.	25441	25996	79225	79590	79860
2.	2	6:00 a.m.	24915	24930	25010	39530	79090
3.	4	9:30 a.m.	41515	44217	44151	59729	59807
4.	5	7:00 a.m.	39530	39736	43516	58291	58396
5.	3	5:30 a.m.	39509	39530	39736	58270	58291

1. **The correct answer is (D).** The reading for Turnstile 1 at 8:00 a.m. is 79590.

2. **The correct answer is (B).** At 6:00 a.m., the reading for Turnstile 2 is 24930.

3. **The correct answer is (E).** The 9:30 a.m. reading for Turnstile 4 is 59807.

4. **The correct answer is (C).** At 7:00 a.m., Turnstile 5's reading is 43516.

5. **The correct answer is (A).** Turnstile 3's reading at 5:30 a.m. is 39509.

Your score on this test is based on the number of questions you answer correctly. You should try to answer every question. You will not lose points or be penalized for guessing. Do not spend too much time on any one question.

When you begin, be sure to start with question number 1 of Part 7 of your test booklet and number 1 of Part 7 on your answer sheet.

STOP! DO NOT TURN THIS PAGE UNTIL TOLD TO DO SO.

40 Questions • 7 Minutes

Questions 1–5 are based on the table below. Note that the X-values are shown at the top of the table and the Y-values are shown on the left of the table. Find the entry that occurs at the intersection of the row and the column corresponding to the values given.

X-VALUE

Y-VALUE		−3	−2	−1	0	+1	+2	+3
	+3	22	23	25	27	28	29	30
	+2	23	25	27	29	30	31	32
	+1	24	26	28	30	32	33	34
	0	**26**	**27**	**29**	**31**	**33**	**34**	**35**
	−1	27	29	30	32	34	35	37
	−2	28	30	31	33	35	36	38
	−3	29	31	32	34	36	37	39

	X	Y	A	B	C	D	E
1.	0	−1	29	33	32	35	34
2.	−3	−3	22	29	23	31	28
3.	−1	+2	25	31	29	30	27
4.	+3	0	30	34	35	37	39
5.	−2	+1	26	23	29	25	22

GO ON TO THE NEXT PAGE.

Questions 6–10 are based on the following table showing height–weight standards used by the Air Force in its commissioning program.

COMMISSION HEIGHT–WEIGHT STANDARDS

Men Height Inches	Weight Min.	Weight Max.	Women Height Inches	Weight Min.	Weight Max.
60	100	153	60	92	130
61	102	155	61	95	132
62	103	158	62	97	134
63	105	164	63	100	136
64	105	169	64	103	139
65	106	169	65	106	144
66	107	174	66	108	148
67	111	179	67	111	152
68	115	184	68	114	156
69	119	189	69	117	161
70	123	194	70	119	165
71	127	199	71	122	169
72	131	205	72	125	174
73	135	211	73	128	179
74	139	218	74	130	185
75	143	224	75	133	190
76	147	230	76	136	196
77	151	236	77	139	201
78	153	242	78	141	206
79	157	248	79	144	211
80	161	254	80	147	216

		A	B	C	D	E
6.	The maximum weight for 66″ women is	152	148	169	144	174
7.	The minimum weight for 72″ men is	128	125	127	231	131
8.	The maximum weight for 68″ men is	189	156	179	184	161
9.	The minimum weight for 62″ women is	100	97	95	92	103
10.	The maximum weight for 75″ men is	224	190	236	196	230

Questions 11–15 are based on the table below showing the blood alcohol content in relation to body weight and the number of drinks consumed during a 2-hour period. For each question, ascertain the blood alcohol content-percent.

BLOOD ALCOHOL CONTENT (BAC)—PERCENT

No. of Drinks* (2-hour period)	Body Weight (in pounds)							
	100	120	140	160	180	200	220	240
12	.33	.25	.21	.19	.17	.16	.15	.14
11	.29	.23	.19	.18	.16	.15	.14	.14
10	.26	.21	.18	.17	.15	.14	.13	.13
9	.23	.19	.16	.15	.14	.13	.12	.12
8	.20	.17	.15	.14	.13	.12	.11	.11
7	.17	.15	.14	.13	.12	.11	.10	.10
6	.15	.13	.12	.11	.11	.10	.09	.08
5	.13	.11	.10	.10	.09	.08	.08	.07
4	.10	.09	.08	.08	.07	.06	.06	.06
3	.08	.07	.06	.05	.05	.04	.04	.04
2	.05	.04	.04	.03	.03	.03	.02	.02
1	.03	.02	.02	.02	.01	.01	.01	.01

* One drink is equivalent to $1\frac{1}{2}$ oz. 85-proof liquor, 6 oz. wine, or 12 oz. beer.

		A	B	C	D	E
11.	A 160-pound person—2 drinks	.01	.02	.03	.04	.05
12.	A 200-pound person—3 drinks	.01	.02	.03	.04	.05
13.	A 180-pound person—4 drinks	.06	.07	.08	.09	.10
14.	A 100-pound person—2 drinks	.01	.02	.03	.04	.05
15.	A 240-pound person—3 drinks	.04	.05	.06	.07	.08

GO ON TO THE NEXT PAGE.

Questions 16–20 are based on the weekly train schedule given below for the Dumont Line:

WEEKDAY TRAIN LINE SCHEDULE—DUMONT LINE

Train #	Eastbound			Magic Mall		Westbound		
	Harvard Square Leave	Pleasure Plaza Leave	Harding Street Leave	Arrive	Leave	Harding Street Leave	Pleasure Plaza Leave	Harvard Square Leave
69	7:48	7:51	7:56	8:00	8:06	8:10	8:15	8:18
70	7:54	7:57	8:02	8:06	8:12	8:16	8:21	8:24
71	8:00	8:03	8:08	8:12	8:18	8:22	8:27	8:30
72	8:04	8:07	8:13	8:17	8:22	8:26	8:31	8:34
73	8:08	8:11	8:17	8:21	8:26	8:30	8:35	8:38
74	8:12	8:15	8:20	8:24	8:30	8:34	8:39	8:42
75	8:16	8:19	8:24	8:28	8:34	8:38	8:43	8:46
69	8:20	8:23	8:28	8:32	8:38	8:42	8:47	8:50
70	8:26	8:29	8:34	8:38	8:44	8:48	8:53	8:56

16. Train 73 is scheduled to arrive at Magic Mall at

(A) 8:26
(B) 8:21
(C) 8:22
(D) 8:17
(E) 8:24

17. Train 75 is scheduled to leave Harvard Square at

(A) 8:20
(B) 8:12
(C) 8:15
(D) 8:19
(E) 8:16

18. Train 70 is scheduled to leave Pleasure Plaza on its second westbound trip to Harvard Square at

(A) 8:48
(B) 8:21
(C) 8:53
(D) 8:24
(E) 8:56

19. Going toward Harvard Square, what time is Train 71 scheduled to leave Pleasure Plaza?

(A) 8:27
(B) 8:03
(C) 8:22
(D) 8:08
(E) 8:18

20. Passengers boarding at Harding Street and wishing to get to Harvard Square by 8:42 would have to board a train that is scheduled to leave Magic Mall no later than

(A) 8:34
(B) 8:24
(C) 8:39
(D) 8:30
(E) 8:28

GO ON TO THE NEXT PAGE.

Questions 21–30 are based on the mileage between the two cities:

Albuquerque	Atlanta	Boston	Chicago	Cleveland	Dallas	Denver	Detroit	Los Angeles	Miami	Minneapolis	New Orleans	New York City	St. Louis	Salt Lake City	San Francisco	Seattle	Washington, D.C.
1,420																	
2,255	1,070																
1,350	730	1,000															
1,620	740	640	350														
660	800	1,800	930	1,200													
445	1,470	2,010	1,040	1,355	805												
1,605	755	825	295	170	1,190	1,300											
845	2,270	3,080	2,200	2,440	1,500	1,160	2,450										
2,000	665	1,545	1,400	1,350	1,330	2,140	1,420	2,840									
1,260	1,190	1,410	410	760	1,020	945	710	2060	1,860								
1,170	485	1,580	955	1,060	500	1,300	1,070	2,010	880	1,260							
2,040	860	210	840	505	1,600	1,850	660	2,890	1,360	1,220	1,380						
1,050	620	1,210	300	560	635	885	550	1,900	1,290	570	705	990					
620	2,050	2,440	1,460	1,775	1,280	560	1,750	715	2,610	1,370	1,790	2,270	1,450				
1,140	2,550	3,200	2,210	2,530	1,790	1,320	2,500	410	3,120	2,120	2,300	3,030	2,200	755			
1,450	2,850	3,110	2,100	2,430	2,110	1,370	2,420	1,160	3,440	1,700	2,620	2,920	2,550	830	840		
1,920	645	435	705	370	1,360	1,730	525	2,720	1,120	1,080	1,130	225	940	2,080	2,835	2,810	

		A	**B**	**C**	**D**	**E**
21.	Chicago to Dallas	1,040	930	1,200	1,355	825
22.	New Orleans to Miami	1,360	1,260	570	880	715
23.	Albuquerque to Denver	660	845	825	755	445
24.	Washington, D.C. to Seattle	2,835	2,080	2,200	2,810	2,250
25.	Atlanta to Salt Lake City	2,050	2,850	1,920	2,440	2,210
26.	San Francisco to Boston	3,200	3,110	2,850	2,440	2,530
27.	Cleveland to Minneapolis	410	1,060	1,020	760	1,350
28.	St. Louis to Detroit	660	550	560	885	715
29.	Los Angeles to Detroit	2,010	2,060	2,840	2,140	2,450
30.	New York City to Dallas	1,300	1,850	1,600	1,060	1,280

GO ON TO THE NEXT PAGE.

Questions 31–40 are based on the table below. Note that the *X*-values are shown at the top of the table and the *Y*-values are shown on the left of the table. Find the entry that occurs at the intersection of the row and the column corresponding to the values given.

X-VALUE

Y-VALUE	−5	−4	−3	−2	−1	0	+1	+2	+3	+4	+5
+5	32	30	29	28	27	25	23	22	21	19	17
+4	34	32	31	30	29	27	25	23	22	20	18
+3	36	34	33	32	30	28	26	24	23	21	19
+2	37	35	34	33	31	29	27	26	25	23	21
+1	39	37	35	34	32	30	29	27	26	24	22
0	40	38	36	35	33	31	30	28	27	25	23
−1	41	39	37	36	34	32	31	29	28	26	25
−2	43	41	39	38	36	34	33	31	30	28	26
−3	44	42	40	39	37	36	34	33	32	30	28
−4	46	44	42	41	39	38	36	35	33	31	30
−5	48	46	44	43	41	40	38	37	35	33	31

	X	Y	A	B	C	D	E
31.	0	−3	34	38	37	35	36
32.	−4	+2	36	35	33	37	34
33.	+2	−2	31	36	33	38	30
34.	−5	−5	46	19	17	44	48
35.	+1	−3	27	33	36	34	26
36.	−3	+4	28	32	29	31	30
37.	+4	+1	26	39	24	36	25
38.	−1	−5	41	43	37	40	39
39.	+3	+1	27	24	28	25	26
40.	+5	0	4	23	6	25	22

STOP! DO NOT GO ON UNTIL TIME IS UP.

PART 8: AVIATION INFORMATION

Directions: This part of the test has 20 questions designed to measure your knowledge of aviation. Each of the questions or incomplete statements is followed by five choices. Decide which one of the choices best answers the question or completes the statement.

Now look at the two sample questions below:

1. The force necessary to overcome gravitational force to keep the airplane flying is termed

   (A) power.
   (B) drag.
   (C) lift.
   (D) thrust.
   (E) weight.

   The correct answer is (C). To keep the airplane flying, *lift* must overcome gravitational force.

2. The ailerons are used primarily to

   (A) bank the airplane.
   (B) control the direction of yaw.
   (C) permit a slower landing speed.
   (D) permit a steep angle of descent.
   (E) control the pitch attitude.

   The correct answer is (A). The ailerons, located on the trailing edge of each wing near the outer tip, are used primarily to bank (roll) the airplane around its longitudinal axis. The banking of the wing results in the airplane turning in the direction of the bank.

Your score on this test will be based on the number of questions you answer correctly. You should try to answer every question. You will not lose points or be penalized for guessing. Do not spend too much time on any one question.

When you begin, be sure to start with question number 1 of Part 8 of your test booklet and number 1 of Part 8 on your answer sheet.

STOP! DO NOT TURN THIS PAGE UNTIL TOLD TO DO SO.

20 Questions • 8 Minutes

1. The four aerodynamic forces acting on an airplane are

   (A) drag, gravity, power, and velocity.

   (B) drag, friction, power, and velocity.

   (C) drag, lift, thrust, and weight.

   (D) friction, power, velocity, and weight.

   (E) gravity, lift, thrust, and weight.

2. An airplane wing is designed to produce lift resulting from relatively

   (A) positive air pressure below and above the wing's surface.

   (B) negative air pressure below the wing's surface and positive air pressure above the wing's surface.

   (C) positive air pressure below the wing's surface and negative air pressure above the wing's surface.

   (D) negative air pressure below and above the wing's surface.

   (E) neutral air pressure below and above the wing's surface.

3. Operation of modern airplanes is dependent upon the use of instruments. These instrument dials, displayed in the airplane's cockpit, are referred to as "flight instruments" or "engine instruments." Which one of the following is NOT a "flight instrument"?

   (A) Airspeed indicator

   (B) Altimeter

   (C) Attitude indicator

   (D) Tachometer

   (E) Vertical velocity indicator

4. Which statement is true regarding the forces acting on an aircraft in a steady flight condition (no change in speed or flightpath)?

   (A) Lift equals weight and thrust equals drag.

   (B) Lift equals thrust and weight equals drag.

   (C) Lift equals drag and thrust equals weight.

   (D) Lift is greater than weight and thrust is less than drag.

   (E) Lift is less than weight and thrust is greater than drag.

5. A flashing green air traffic control signal directed to an aircraft on the surface is a signal that the pilot

   (A) is cleared to taxi.

   (B) is cleared for takeoff.

   (C) should exercise extreme caution.

   (D) should taxi clear of the runway in use.

   (E) should stop taxiing.

GO ON TO THE NEXT PAGE.

6. What is the difference between a steady red and a flashing red light signal from the tower to an aircraft approaching to land?

   (A) Both light signals mean the same except the flashing red light requires a more urgent reaction.

   (B) Both light signals mean the same except the steady red light requires a more urgent reaction.

   (C) A steady red light signals to continue circling and a flashing red light signals that the airport is unsafe for landing.

   (D) A steady red light signals to continue circling and a flashing red light signals to continue, but exercise extreme caution.

   (E) A steady red light signals that the airport is unsafe and a flashing red light signals to use a different runway.

7. The propeller blades are curved on one side and flat on the other side to

   (A) increase its strength.
   (B) produce thrust.
   (C) provide proper balance.
   (D) reduce air friction.
   (E) reduce drag.

8. When in the down (extended) position, wingflaps provide

   (A) decreased wing camber (curvature).
   (B) less lift and less drag.
   (C) less lift but more drag.
   (D) greater lift but less drag.
   (E) greater lift and more drag.

9. What makes an airplane turn?

   (A) Centrifugal force
   (B) Horizontal component of lift
   (C) Rudder and aileron
   (D) Rudder, aileron, and elevator
   (E) Vertical component of lift

10. What is one advantage of an airplane said to be inherently stable?

   (A) The airplane will not spin.
   (B) The airplane will be difficult to stall.
   (C) The airplane will require less fuel.
   (D) The airplane will require less effort to control.
   (E) The airplane will not overbank during steep turns.

11. If the elevator trim tabs on a plane are lowered, the plane will tend to

   (A) nose up.
   (B) nose down.
   (C) pitch fore and aft.
   (D) go into a slow roll.
   (E) wing over.

12. The pilot always advances the throttle during a

   (A) nose dive.
   (B) landing.
   (C) turn.
   (D) spin.
   (E) climb.

GO ON TO THE NEXT PAGE.

13. The pilot of an airplane can best detect the approach of a stall by the

(A) increase in speed of the engine.
(B) increase in pitch and intensity of the sound of the air moving past the plane.
(C) increase in effectiveness of the rudder.
(D) ineffectiveness of the ailerons and elevator.
(E) decrease in pitch and intensity of the sound of the air moving past the plane.

14. It is ordinarily desirable to provide an unusually long flight strip at municipal airports for the take-off of

(A) military planes in echelon.
(B) heavily loaded ships in still air.
(C) small airplanes in rainy weather.
(D) any airplane across the wind.
(E) airplanes that have high climbing speeds.

Questions 15–17 are based on the airport diagram shown below:

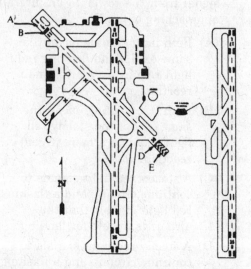

15. According to the above diagram, which of the following is correct?

(A) Takeoffs and landings are permissible at position C.
(B) The takeoff and landing portion of Runway 12 begins at position B.
(C) Runway 30 is equipped at position E with emergency arresting gear to provide a means of stopping military aircraft.
(D) Takeoffs may be started at position A on Runway 12, and the landing portion of this runway begins at position B.
(E) Light airplanes only may land in position A on Runway 12.

GO ON TO THE NEXT PAGE.

16. What is the difference between Area A and Area E, as shown in the diagram?

    (A) A may be used only for takeoff; E may be used for all operations.

    (B) A may be used only for taxi and takeoff; E may be used for all operations except landing.

    (C) A may be used only for taxi and takeoff; E may be used only for landing.

    (D) A may be used for all operations except heavy aircraft landing; E may be used only as an overrun.

    (E) A may be used for taxi and takeoff; E may be used only as an overrun.

17. Area C on the airport depicted in the diagram is classified as a(n)

    (A) STOL runway.

    (B) parking ramp.

    (C) closed runway.

    (D) multiple heliport.

    (E) active runway.

Questions 18–20 are based on the figure shown below:

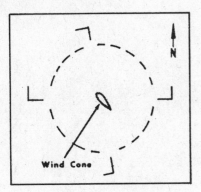

Wind Cone

18. The segmented circle shown indicates that the airport traffic is

    (A) left for Runway 17 and right for Runway 35.

    (B) right for Runway 9 and left for Runway 27.

    (C) right for Runway 35 and right for Runway 9.

    (D) left for Runway 17 and right for Runway 9.

    (E) left for Runway 35 and right for Runway 17.

19. The segmented circle indicates that a landing on Runway 27 will be with a

    (A) right-quartering headwind.

    (B) left-quartering headwind.

    (C) right-quartering tailwind.

    (D) left-quartering tailwind.

    (E) 90-degree crosswind.

20. Which runways and traffic pattern should be used as indicated by the wind cone in the segmented circle?

    (A) Right traffic on Runway 35 or left traffic on Runway 27

    (B) Left traffic on Runway 35 or right traffic on Runway 27

    (C) Right traffic on Runway 17 or left traffic on Runway 9

    (D) Left traffic on Runway 17 or right traffic on Runway 9

    (E) Left traffic on Runways 9 or 27

STOP! DO NOT GO ON UNTIL TIME IS UP.

PART 9: ROTATED BLOCKS

> **Directions:** This part of the test has 15 questions designed to measure your ability to visualize and manipulate objects in space. In each item, you are shown a picture of a block. You must find a second block that is just like the first.

Look at the two blocks below. Although viewed from different points, the blocks are the same shape.

Look at the two blocks below. They are not alike. They can never be turned so that they will be alike.

Now look at the sample item below. Which of the five choices is just like the first block?

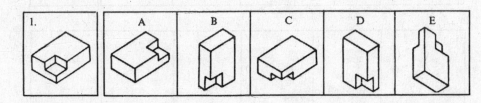

For sample problem 1, the correct answer is (D). It is the same block as seen from a different side.

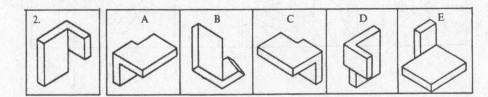

For sample problem 2, the correct answer is (C).

Your score on this test will be based on the number of questions you answer correctly. You should try to answer every question.

When you begin, be sure to start with question number 1 of Part 9 of your test booklet and number 1 on Part 9 of your answer sheet.

STOP! DO NOT TURN THIS PAGE UNTIL TOLD TO DO SO.

15 Questions • 13 Minutes

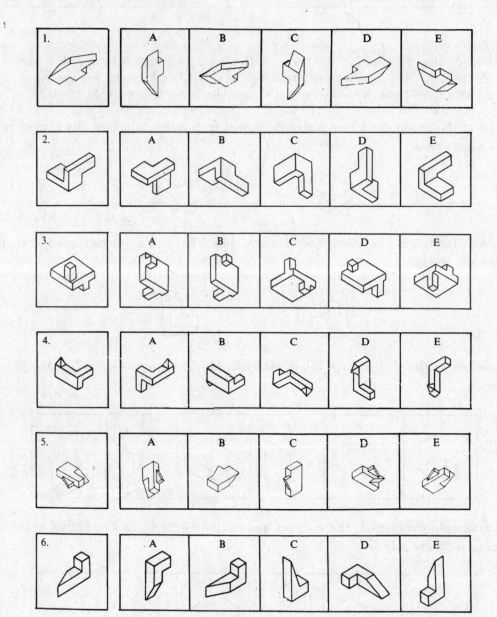

GO ON TO THE NEXT PAGE.

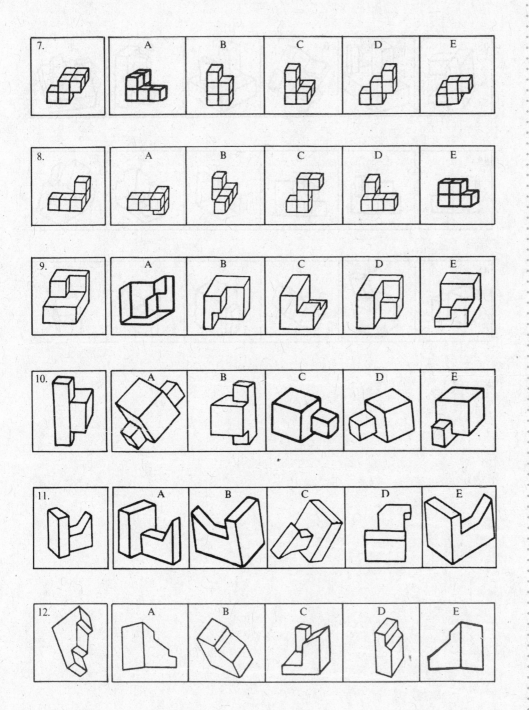

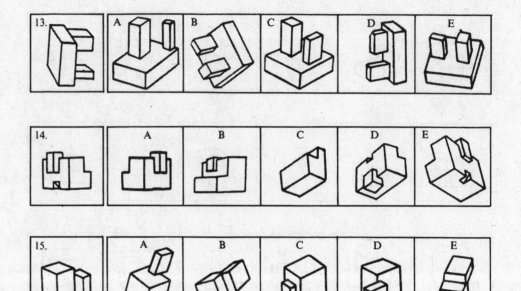

PART 10: GENERAL SCIENCE

Directions: This part of the test has 20 questions designed to measure your scientific knowledge. Each of the questions or incomplete statements is followed by five choices. Decide which one of the choices best answers the question or completes the statement.

Now look at the three sample questions below:

1. An eclipse of the sun throws the shadow of the

   (A) moon on the sun.
   (B) earth on the sun.
   (C) sun on the earth.
   (D) earth on the moon.
   (E) moon on the earth.

   The correct answer is (E).

2. Substances that hasten a chemical reaction without themselves undergoing change are called

   (A) buffers.
   (B) catalysts.
   (C) colloids.
   (D) reducers.
   (E) polymers.

   The correct answer is (B).

3. Lack of iodine is often related to which of the following diseases?

   (A) Beriberi
   (B) Scurvy
   (C) Rickets
   (D) Goiter
   (E) Asthma

   The correct answer is (D).

Your score on this test will be based on the number of questions you answer correctly. You should try to answer every question. You will not lose points or be penalized for guessing. Do not spend too much time on any one question.

When you begin, be sure to start with question number 1 of Part 10 of your test booklet and number 1 of Part 10 on your answer sheet.

STOP! DO NOT TURN THIS PAGE UNTIL TOLD TO DO SO.

20 Questions • 10 Minutes

1. Under natural conditions, large quantities of organic matter decay after each year's plant growth has been completed. As a result of such conditions,

   (A) many animals are deprived of adequate food supplies.
   (B) soil erosion is accelerated.
   (C) soil maintains its fertility.
   (D) earthworms are added to the soil.
   (E) pollution increases.

2. The thin, clear layer that forms the front part of the eyeball is called the

   (A) pupil.
   (B) iris.
   (C) lens.
   (D) retina.
   (E) cornea.

3. The most likely reason why dinosaurs became extinct was that they

   (A) were killed by erupting volcanoes.
   (B) were eaten as adults by the advancing mammalian groups.
   (C) failed to adapt to a changing environment.
   (D) killed each other in combat.
   (E) were destroyed by meteorites.

4. Which of the following is a chemical change?

   (A) Magnetizing a rod of iron
   (B) Burning one pound of coal
   (C) Mixing flake graphite with oil
   (D) Vaporizing one gram of mercury in a vacuum
   (E) Melting ice

5. A person with high blood pressure should

   (A) take frequent naps.
   (B) avoid salt.
   (C) eat only iodized salt.
   (D) exercise vigorously.
   (E) avoid proteins.

6. The chief nutrient in lean meat is

   (A) starch.
   (B) protein.
   (C) fat.
   (D) carbohydrates.
   (E) Vitamin B.

7. Spiders can be distinguished from insects by the fact that spiders have

   (A) hard outer coverings.
   (B) large abdomens.
   (C) four pairs of legs.
   (D) biting mouth parts.
   (E) jointed appendages.

8. An important ore of uranium is called

   (A) hematite.
   (B) chalcopyrite.
   (C) bauxite.
   (D) pitchblende.
   (E) feldspar.

9. Of the following, the lightest element known on Earth is

   (A) hydrogen.
   (B) oxygen.
   (C) helium.
   (D) air.
   (E) nitrogen.

GO ON TO THE NEXT PAGE.

10. Of the following gases in the air, the most plentiful is

    (A) argon.
    (B) oxygen.
    (C) nitrogen.
    (D) carbon dioxide.
    (E) hydrogen.

11. The time it takes for light from the sun to reach the earth is approximately

    (A) four years.
    (B) eight minutes.
    (C) four months.
    (D) eight years.
    (E) one week.

12. Of the following types of clouds, the ones that occur at the greatest height are called

    (A) cirrus.
    (B) nimbus.
    (C) cumulus.
    (D) stratus.
    (E) altostratus.

13. A new drug for treatment of tuberculosis was being tested in a hospital. Patients in Group A actually received doses of the new drug; those patients in Group B were given only sugar pills. Group B represents a(n)

    (A) scientific experiment.
    (B) scientific method.
    (C) experimental error.
    (D) experimental control.
    (E) hypothesis.

14. After adding salt to water, the freezing point of the water is

    (A) variable.
    (B) inverted.
    (C) the same.
    (D) raised.
    (E) lowered.

15. Radium is stored in lead containers because

    (A) the lead absorbs the harmful radiation.
    (B) radium is a heavy substance.
    (C) lead prevents the disintegration of the radium.
    (D) lead is cheap.
    (E) lead is brittle.

16. The type of joint that attaches the arm to the shoulder blade is known as a(n)

    (A) hinge.
    (B) pivot.
    (C) immovable.
    (D) gliding.
    (E) ball and socket.

17. Limes were eaten by British sailors in order to prevent

    (A) anemia.
    (B) beriberi.
    (C) night blindness.
    (D) rickets.
    (E) scurvy.

18. The time that it takes for the earth to rotate 45 degrees is

    (A) 2 hours.
    (B) 4 hours.
    (C) 1 hour.
    (D) 3 hours.
    (E) 5 hours.

19. Of the following planets, the one that has the shortest revolutionary period around the sun is

    (A) Mercury.
    (B) Jupiter.
    (C) Earth.
    (D) Venus.
    (E) Mars.

GO ON TO THE NEXT PAGE.

20. What is the name of the negative particle that circles the nucleus of the atom?

(A) Neutron

(B) Meson

(C) Proton

(D) Electron

(E) Isotope

STOP! DO NOT GO ON UNTIL TIME IS UP.

PART 11: HIDDEN FIGURES

Directions: This part of the test has 15 questions designed to measure your ability to see a simple figure in a complex drawing. At the top of each page are five figures, lettered A, B, C, D, and E. Below these on each page are several numbered drawings. You are to determine which lettered figure is contained in each of the numbered drawings.

The lettered figures are:

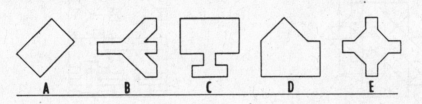

As an example, look at drawing X below. Which one of the five figures is contained in drawing X?

Now look at drawing Y, which is exactly like drawing X except that figure B has been blackened to show where to look for it. Thus, the correct answer is (B).

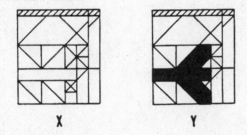

Each numbered drawing contains only *one* of the lettered figures. The correct figure in each drawing will always be of the same size and in the same position as it appears at the top of the page. Therefore, do not rotate the page in order to find it. Look at each numbered drawing and decide which one of the five lettered figures is contained in it.

Your score on this test is based on the number of questions you answer correctly. You should try to answer every question. You will not lose points or be penalized for guessing. Do not spend too much time on any one question.

When you begin, be sure to start with question number 1 of Part 11 of your test booklet and number 1 of Part 11 of your answer sheet.

STOP! DO NOT TURN THIS PAGE UNTIL TOLD TO DO SO.

15 Questions • 8 Minutes

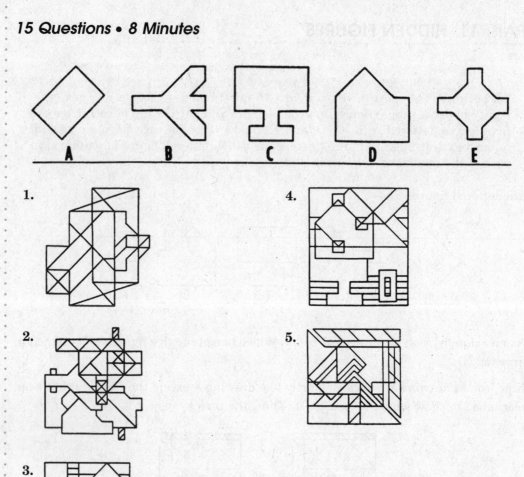

A   B   C   D   E

1.

2.

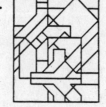

3.

4.

5.

GO ON TO THE NEXT PAGE.

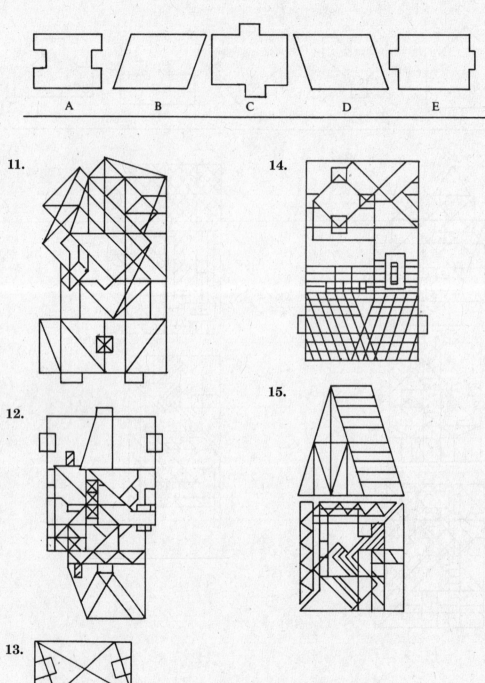

11.

14.

12.

15.

13.

STOP! DO NOT GO ON UNTIL TIME IS UP.

PART 12: SELF-DESCRIPTION INVENTORY

110 Questions • 20 Minutes

The Self-Description Inventory subtest measures personal traits and attitudes. On this section of the AFOQT, you are presented with 220 statements (test items). This practice test, which consists of 110 statements, will give you a good idea of what the Self-Description Inventory subtest is all about.

Directions: This inventory measures personal traits and attitudes. The inventory consists of a list of statements. The task is to read each statement carefully and decide how well each one describes you.

Look at the sample statement below:

1. I enjoy reading poetry.

   Decide whether statement 1 is characteristic of you and indicate your agreement using the scale below.

A	B	C	D	E
Strongly Disagree	Moderately Disagree	Neither Agree nor Disagree	Moderately Agree	Strongly Agree

If you <u>strongly agree</u> that the statement describes you, select (E) on your answer sheet next to the statement number. If you <u>strongly disagree</u>, select (A) on the answer sheet. You would mark (B), (C), or (D) to indicate other levels of agreement.

You should work quickly but reply to all statements. Give your first impression about how well each statement describes you by comparing yourself to people in your same sex and age group. Don't spend a long time deciding what your answer should be. There is no right or wrong answer to each statement. Answer all statements, even if you're not sure of your answer.

When you begin, be sure to start with question 1 of Part 12 of your test booklet and number 1 of Part 12 on your answer sheet. If you complete all of the statements before the allotted time has elapsed, you may return to this section to review.

STOP! DO NOT TURN THIS PAGE UNTIL TOLD TO DO SO.

110 Questions • 20 Minutes

(Note: On the AFOQT, you will have 40 minutes to answer 220 Questions)

A	B	C	D	E
Strongly Disagree	Moderately Disagree	Neither Agree nor Disagree	Moderately Agree	Strongly Agree

1. I try to find a balance between my work and personal interests.
2. I am very comfortable supervising others.
3. I get annoyed when friends drop by unexpectedly.
4. I like being involved in group activities.
5. I always set high work standards for myself.
6. I am quiet and reserved.
7. I enjoy being the center of attention.
8. I like to have a daily routine.
9. I always think hard before making decisions.
10. I am easily hurt.
11. I am quite talkative.
12. I worry more about pleasing others than myself.
13. I do things at my own pace.
14. I am more stressed than relaxed.
15. I am extremely organized.
16. I keep my emotions under control.
17. I dislike large parties.
18. I worry about things.
19. I make friends easily.
20. I have a vivid imagination.
21. I trust others.
22. I complete tasks successfully.
23. I get angry easily.
24. I believe in the importance of art.
25. I use others for my own ends.
26. I like to tidy up.
27. I often feel blue.
28. I tend to take charge.
29. I experience my emotions intensely.
30. I love helping others.
31. I keep my promises.
32. I find it difficult to approach others.
33. I'm always busy.
34. I prefer variety to routine.
35. I love a good fight.
36. I work hard.
37. I occasionally go on binges.
38. I love excitement.
39. I love reading challenging material.
40. I believe that I am better than others.
41. I'm always prepared.
42. I panic easily.
43. I radiate joy.
44. I tend to vote for liberal political candidates.
45. I sympathize with the homeless.
46. I tend to jump into things without thinking.
47. I often fear for the worst.
48. I put little time and effort into my work.
49. I enjoy wild flights of fantasy.
50. I generally believe that others have good intentions.
51. I excel in what I do.
52. I am easily irritated.
53. I talk to a lot of different people when I'm at a party.
54. I like to see beauty in things that others might not notice.
55. I would cheat to get ahead.

GO ON TO THE NEXT PAGE.

56. I often forget to put things back in their proper place.

57. I tend to waste my time.

58. I try to lead others.

59. I feel others' emotions.

60. I generally tell the truth.

61. I am concerned about others.

62. I'm afraid to draw attention to myself.

63. I'm always on the go.

64. I prefer to stick with what I know.

65. I tend to yell at people.

66. I often do more than what's expected of me.

67. I rarely overindulge.

68. I seek adventure.

69. I avoid philosophical discussions.

70. I think highly of myself.

71. I carry out my plans.

72. I sometimes become overwhelmed by events.

73. I like to have a lot of fun.

74. I believe that there is no absolute right or wrong.

75. I sympathize with those who are worse off than me.

76. I tend to make rash decisions.

77. I'm afraid of many things.

78. I avoid contacts with others.

79. I love to daydream.

80. I trust what people say.

81. I usually handle tasks smoothly.

82. I tend to lose my temper.

83. I prefer to be alone.

84. I do not like poetry.

85. I take advantage of others.

86. I leave a mess in my room.

87. I'm often down in the dumps.

88. I take control of things.

89. I rarely notice my emotional reactions.

90. I'm indifferent to the feelings of others.

91. I break rules.

92. I only feel comfortable with friends.

93. I do a lot in my spare time.

94. I dislike changes.

95. I insult people.

96. I do just enough work to get by.

97. I can easily resist temptations.

98. I enjoy being reckless.

99. I have trouble understanding abstract ideas.

100. I love life.

101. I'm able to control my cravings.

102. I act wild and crazy.

103. I'm not interested in theoretical discussions.

104. I boast about my virtues.

105. I have difficulty starting tasks.

106. I remain calm under pressure.

107. I look at the bright side of life.

108. I believe that we should be tough on crime.

109. I try not to think about the needy.

110. I act without thinking.

STOP! END OF TEST.

ANSWER KEY AND EXPLANATIONS

Use this answer key to determine the number of questions you answered correctly on each subtest and to note questions you answered incorrectly or of which you were unsure.

Be certain to review carefully and understand the rationale for arriving at the correct answer for all items you answered incorrectly or correctly but were unsure of. This is essential to helping you obtain the maximum scores possible on the subtests of the real AFOQT.

Part 1: Verbal Analogies

1. D	6. D	11. A	16. C	21. A
2. B	7. B	12. E	17. E	22. B
3. C	8. E	13. E	18. D	23. A
4. C	9. C	14. B	19. A	24. B
5. A	10. E	15. E	20. C	25. D

1. **The correct answer is (D).** A *chapter* is a numbered division of a *book*; a *story* is a numbered floor of a *building*.

2. **The correct answer is (B).** *Alpha* is the first letter, or the *beginning*, of the Greek alphabet; *omega* is the last letter, or *end*, of the Greek alphabet.

3. **The correct answer is (C).** *Carrot* is a type of *vegetable*; *pepper* is a type of *spice*.

4. **The correct answer is (C).** A *micrometer* is a tool used by a *machinist*. A *trowel* is a tool used by a *mason*.

5. **The correct answer is (A).** *Concave* is hollow and curved like a *cavity*; *convex* is bulging and curved like a *mound*.

6. **The correct answer is (D).** *Dozen*, or 12, is represented by Roman numeral *XII*. *Score*, or 20, is represented by Roman numeral *XX*.

7. **The correct answer is (B).** *Gown* is a type of *garment*; *gasoline* is a type of *fuel*.

8. **The correct answer is (E).** An *emerald* is a *green* gem; a *ruby* is a *red* gem.

9. **The correct answer is (C).** *Hyper-* is a prefix meaning *over*; *hypo-* is a prefix meaning *under*.

10. **The correct answer is (E).** *Horizontal* is at right angle to the *vertical*. In yarns, *warp* is at right angle to the *woof*.

11. **The correct answer is (A).** *Immigration* is the act of *arriving* in a new country. *Emigration* is the act of leaving or *departing* one country to settle in another.

12. **The correct answer is (E).** A *kilometer* is equal to 1,000 *meters*. A *millennium* is equal to a period of 1,000 *years*.

13. **The correct answer is (E).** An *octagon* is an eight-sided polygon; a *square* is a four-sided one. A *hexagon* is a six-sided polygon; a *triangle* is a three-sided one.

14. **The correct answer is (B).** A *priest* is inducted into office by a formal ceremony termed *ordination*. A *president* is inducted into office by a formal ceremony termed *inauguration*.

15. **The correct answer is (E).** *Perjure* is to willfully make a false *statement* under oath; *trespass* is to wrongfully *enter* the property of another. Both are illegal actions.

16. **The correct answer is (C).** An *ordinance* is a rule or *regulation*; *ordnance* is *munition* (weapons and ammunition).

17. **The correct answer is (E).** *Told* is the past and past participle of *tell*; *wept* is the past and past participle of *weep*.

18. **The correct answer is (D).** A *dozen* contains 12 *units*; a *year* consists of 12 *months*.

19. **The correct answer is (A).** A *lamb* is a young *sheep*; a *colt* is a young *horse*.

20. **The correct answer is (C).** *Zenith* is the *highest* point; *nadir* is the *lowest* point.

21. **The correct answer is (A).** *Ignore* and *overlook* have the same or a similar meaning; *agree* and *consent* are synonyms.

22. **The correct answer is (B).** The outer boundary of a *square* is its *perimeter*. The outer boundary of a *circle* is its *circumference*.

23. **The correct answer is (A).** *Frequently* and *seldom* have opposite meanings; *always* and *never* are antonyms.

24. **The correct answer is (B).** A *bus* is a type of *vehicle*; *baseball* is a type of *game*.

25. **The correct answer is (D).** *Trickle* means to flow or fall gently; *gush* means to flow plentifully and is much more forceful than a trickle. *Tepid* means moderately warm; *hot* is a much higher temperature than moderately warm.

answers practice test 1

Part 2: Arithmetic Reasoning

1. D	6. C	11. D	16. E	21. B
2. E	7. D	12. E	17. B	22. C
3. A	8. A	13. C	18. A	23. B
4. E	9. B	14. A	19. E	24. B
5. A	10. B	15. C	20. D	25. D

1. **The correct answer is (D).** 3 kilometers = 3,000 meters; $\frac{3,000}{15} = 200$ meters.

2. **The correct answer is (E).** 200 feet × 200 feet = 40,000 square feet of floor area; 4,000 tons × 2,000 = 8,000,000 pounds; $\frac{8,000,000}{40,000} = 200$ pounds.

3. **The correct answer is (A).** 12 pounds = 11 pounds, 16 ounces; weight of tool = 9 pounds, 9 ounces. 11 pounds, 16 ounces minus 9 pounds, 9 ounces = 2 pounds, 7 ounces.

4. **The correct answer is (E).** One million × 12 = 12 million = 12,000,000 (nickels per year); 12,000,000 × .05 = $600,000

5. **The correct answer is (A).** Sample size is 50. Number of defects found in sample = 4. $\frac{4}{50} = 8\%$. If 8% defects were found in the sample, it is probable that the percentage of defective articles in the original shipment is also 8%.

6. **The correct answer is (C).** There are 200 cigarettes in a carton (20 × 10 = 200). 12 mg × 200 = 2,400 mg of tar in 200 cigarettes. 2,400 mg = 2.4 grams.

7. **The correct answer is (D).** 36 tons × 3 man-hours = 108 man-hours to stack 36 tons. $\frac{108}{6} = 18$ people needed to complete stacking in 6 hours.

8. **The correct answer is (A).** Let x = number of envelopes addressed in 1 hour by slower worker. $2x$ = number of envelopes addressed in 1 hour by faster worker. $3x \times 5 = 750$; $15x = 750$; $x = 50$ envelopes per hour for slower worker.

9. **The correct answer is (B).** 25 × 12 = 300 sq. ft. = area of long wall; (300 × 2 = 600 sq. ft.) 15 × 12 = 180 sq. ft. = area of short wall; (180 × 2 = 360 sq. ft.) 600 + 360 = 960 sq. ft. = total wall area. 7 × 5 = 35 sq. ft. = area of window; 35 × 2 = 70 sq. ft. = area of windows. 6 × 4 = 24 sq. ft. = area of glass door; 70 + 24 = 94 sq. ft. = total glass area. 960 − 94 = 866 sq. ft. of wall space to be painted.

10. **The correct answer is (B).** Each stick of margarine = $\frac{1}{4}$ lb. Each stick consists of eight sections or tablespoons. Four sections or tablespoons = $\frac{1}{2}$ of $\frac{1}{4}$ lb. = $\frac{1}{8}$ lb.

11. **The correct answer is (D).** $100 × .10 = $10; $100 − $10 = $90. $90 × .15 = $13.50; $90 − 13.50 = $76.50.

12. **The correct answer is (E).** $1,100,500 \times .07 = $77,035$; $1,100,500 + $77,035 = $1,177,535$ = this year's budget. $1,177,535 \times .08 = $94,203$; $1,177,535 + $94,203 = $1,271,738$, which is closest to choice (E).

13. **The correct answer is (C).** Let $x =$ width of rectangle; $4x =$ length of rectangle, $x \times 4x = 324$; $4x^2 = 324$; $x^2 = \dfrac{324}{4} = 81$; $x = 9$ feet; $4x = 36$ feet.

14. **The correct answer is (A).** $\dfrac{1}{2}$ inch on scaled drawing = 3 feet of actual floor dimension. $\dfrac{75}{3} = 25\dfrac{1}{2}$ inches = 12.5 inches; $\dfrac{132}{3} = 44\dfrac{1}{2}$ inches = 22 inches.

15. **The correct answer is (C).** $\dfrac{1}{2} \times \dfrac{1}{2} \times 1 = \dfrac{1}{4}$ cu. ft.; $\dfrac{1}{4}$ of 62.4 = 15.6 pounds.

16. **The correct answer is (E).** If 20% are either red or green, 80% are yellow. The chance of blindly picking a yellow marble is 4 out of 5 (80%).

17. **The correct answer is (B).** 25% + 35% = 60%. 60% were 22 years old or under 22 years of age. 40% were over 22 years old. $560 \times .40 = 224$.

18. **The correct answer is (A).** 2 tons + 6 tons = 8 tons carried by 1 passenger and 1 freight plane. $\dfrac{160 \text{ tons}}{8}$ = 20 pairs of passenger and freight planes needed. 20 passenger planes carrying 2 tons each = 40 tons of cargo.

19. **The correct answer is (E).** The square root of 36 = 6. Each side of the square = 6″. 6″ × 2 = 12″. 12″ × 12″ = 144 square inches.

20. **The correct answer is (D).** Let $x =$ the capacity of the tank.

$\dfrac{1}{8}$ of x + 550 = $\dfrac{1}{2}$ of x.

$550 = \dfrac{x}{2} - \dfrac{x}{8} = \dfrac{3x}{8}$

$x = \dfrac{8}{3} \times 550 = 1,467$ gallons

21. **The correct answer is (B).** 1,200 seconds = 20 minutes $\left(\dfrac{1,200}{60} = 20 \right)$. 20 minutes = $\dfrac{1}{3}$ hour. $\dfrac{1}{3}$ of 630 = 210.

22. **The correct answer is (C).** Interval between 7:00 a.m. and 1:00 p.m is 6 hours or $\dfrac{1}{4}$ of a day. $\dfrac{1}{4}$ of 20 minutes = 5 minutes. Subtracting 5 minutes from watch reading of 1:00 p.m. = 12:55 p.m.

23. **The correct answer is (B).** 132 feet $= \dfrac{132}{5,280} = \dfrac{1}{40}$ mile

9 seconds $= \dfrac{9}{3,600} = \dfrac{1}{400}$ hour

$\dfrac{1}{40}$ mile in $\dfrac{1}{400}$ hour =

1 mile in $\dfrac{1}{10}$ hour =

10 miles in 1 hour = 10 mph

24. **The correct answer is (B).**

$18,400$
$19,300$
$18,450$
$18,550$
$17,600$
$92,300$

$\dfrac{92,300}{5} = 18,460$, or $18,460$

25. The correct answer is (D). If the radius of the wheel is 1 meter, its diameter is 2 meters. The circumference is $\pi \times$ diameter $= 2 \times \dfrac{22}{7}$.

The distance traveled is $35 \times 2 \times \dfrac{22}{7}$ $= 70 \times \dfrac{22}{7} = 220$.

Part 3: Word Knowledge

1. C	6. D	11. C	16. E	21. B
2. A	7. D	12. B	17. A	22. D
3. C	8. C	13. A	18. A	23. E
4. E	9. D	14. B	19. A	24. B
5. B	10. C	15. E	20. D	25. E

Review questions you did not answer correctly and those you did answer correctly but are unsure of. Refer to any good dictionary for the meaning of words that are giving you trouble.

Developing your own list of troublesome words and their meanings will enable you to review these words periodically. Practice helps you increase your vocabulary and raise your exam scores on word knowledge.

Add to your vocabulary list whenever you come across a word whose meaning is unclear to you.

Part 4: Math Knowledge

1. D	6. A	11. C	16. E	21. E
2. C	7. D	12. B	17. B	22. E
3. D	8. D	13. B	18. D	23. D
4. A	9. C	14. B	19. E	24. E
5. C	10. E	15. B	20. C	25. C

1. **The correct answer is (D).** A natural number that has no other factors except 1 and itself is a prime number. 9 is divisible by 1, 3, and 9.

2. **The correct answer is (C).** Circumference $= \pi \times$ diameter; circumference $= \dfrac{22}{7} \times 70 = 220$ miles.

3. **The correct answer is (D).**
$$5x + 3(x - 1) = 29$$
$$5x + 3x - 3 = 29$$
$$8x = 32$$
$$x = 4$$

4. **The correct answer is (A).**
$\dfrac{2x}{7} = 2x^2; \dfrac{2x}{14} = x^2; \dfrac{2}{14} = \dfrac{x^2}{x}; x = \dfrac{1}{7}$.

5. **The correct answer is (C).** Squaring an odd integer results in an odd integer. Adding an odd integer to it results in an even integer. Choices (A), (B), and (D) remain odd.

6. **The correct answer is (A).**
$\dfrac{x-2}{x^2-6x+8} = \dfrac{x-2}{(x-2)(x-4)} = \dfrac{1}{x-4}$

7. **The correct answer is (D).** To divide powers of the same base, subtract the exponent of the denominator from the exponent of the numerator. 10^x divided by 10^y equals 10^{x-y}.

8. **The correct answer is (D).** The odd integer power of a negative number is negative; the even integer power of a negative number is positive.

9. **The correct answer is (C).** $1{,}000{,}000 = 10^6$.

10. **The correct answer is (E).** $\left(\dfrac{2}{5}\right)^2 = \dfrac{2}{5} \times \dfrac{2}{5} = \dfrac{4}{25}$

11. **The correct answer is (C).** $3^n = 9$; $n = 2$; $4^{n+1} = 4^3 = 64$.

12. **The correct answer is (B).** $10^{-2} = \dfrac{1}{10^2} = \dfrac{1}{100} = 0.01$.

13. **The correct answer is (B).** $\sqrt{28} - \sqrt{7} = \sqrt{7 \times 4} - \sqrt{7} = 2\sqrt{7} - \sqrt{7} = \sqrt{7}$.

14. **The correct answer is (B).** $h^2 = 5^2 + 12^2$; $h^2 = 25 + 144$; $h^2 = 169$; $\sqrt{169}$; $h = 13''$.

15. **The correct answer is (B).** A pentagon has 5 sides. (Number of sides − 2) × 180 degrees = sum of angles. 3 × 180 degrees = 540°.

16. **The correct answer is (E).** $\dfrac{3x}{5y} = \dfrac{1}{2}$; $6x = 5y$; $\dfrac{6x}{y} = 5$; $\dfrac{x}{y} = \dfrac{5}{6}$

17. **The correct answer is (B).** 1 inch $\cong$ 2,000 feet; 1 inch $\cong$ 2,000 × 12 inches $\cong$ 24,000 inches. No other choice, converted into common terms, shows a scale of $\dfrac{1}{24{,}000}$.

18. **The correct answer is (D).**

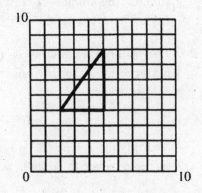

The coordinates form a right triangle with a horizontal leg of 3 and a vertical leg of 4.

The distance between the two points is the hypotenuse of the right triangle.

$\text{Hypotenuse}^2 = 3^2 + 4^2 = 25$; $\text{Hypotenuse} = \sqrt{25} = 5$.

19. **The correct answer is (E).** The base of the cylinder, πr^2, times the height, h, = volume of the cylinder. $\pi r^2 h$ is not one of the answers listed.

20. **The correct answer is (C).** $5 \times 3 = 15$, which is divisible by both 3 and 5; 9, 12, 18, and 21 are not divisible by 5.

21. **The correct answer is (E).** $\dfrac{4!}{3!} = \dfrac{4 \times 3 \times 2 \times 1}{3 \times 2 \times 1} = 4$.

22. **The correct answer is (E).** The cube root of 729 is 9 ($9 \times 9 \times 9$). 9 is the square of 3 (3×3).

23. The correct answer is (D). The sum of the angles of a triangle is 180°. Therefore 180° − 115° = 65°.

24. The correct answer is (E). The pattern for the arrangement is shown below:

$$2 \quad 4 \quad 12 \quad 48 \quad \underline{\hspace{1cm}}$$
$$\times 2 \times 3 \times 4 \times 5$$

Multiplying 48 by 5, we find the correct answer to be 240.

25. The correct answer is (C). The first and each subsequent odd letter in the series are in regular alphabetical order skipping one letter each time: A C E G . . . The second and each subsequent even letter in the series are in straight alphabetical order: R S T . . . Accordingly, the next two letters in the series are U I.

Part 5: Instrument Comprehension

1. C	5. A	9. B	13. A	17. C
2. D	6. D	10. C	14. B	18. B
3. B	7. B	11. D	15. A	19. A
4. D	8. D	12. D	16. C	20. C

1. The correct answer is (C). Nose up 40°; 90° right bank; heading 270° (west).

2. The correct answer is (D). Nose up 45°; 40° right bank; heading 45° (northeast).

3. The correct answer is (B). Nose down 45°; 45° left bank; heading 45° (northeast).

4. The correct answer is (D). Nose up 45°; 60° left bank; heading 315° (northwest).

5. The correct answer is (A). Nose up 25°; 35° right bank; heading 80°.

6. The correct answer is (D). Nose up 30°; 90° right bank; heading 100°.

7. The correct answer is (B). Nose down 40°; 15° left bank; heading 110°.

8. The correct answer is (D). Nose down 45°; 90° right bank; heading 270° (west).

9. The correct answer is (B). No climb, no dive; 45° left bank; heading 180° (south).

10. The correct answer is (C). Nose up slightly; 30° right bank; heading 250°.

11. The correct answer is (D). Nose up slightly; 80° left bank; heading 250°.

12. The correct answer is (D). Straight and level; heading 135° (southeast).

13. The correct answer is (A). Nose down 30°; 15° left bank; heading 115°.

14. The correct answer is (B). Nose up 20°; heading 135° (southeast).

15. **The correct answer is (A).** Nose up slightly; 15° right bank; heading 70°.

16. **The correct answer is (C).** Nose down 30°; 20° left bank; heading 150°.

17. **The correct answer is (C).** Nose up slightly; heading 45° (northeast).

18. **The correct answer is (B).** No climb, no dive; 15° left bank; heading 225° (southwest).

19. **The correct answer is (A).** Nose down slightly; heading 180° (south).

20. **The correct answer is (C).** Nose down slightly; 15° right bank; heading 90° (east).

Part 6: Block Counting

1. E	5. D	9. E	13. A	17. E
2. C	6. C	10. A	14. B	18. C
3. A	7. D	11. B	15. E	19. C
4. E	8. A	12. C	16. D	20. B

1. **The correct answer is (E).** 4 on the side + 3 on and along the bottom = 7.

2. **The correct answer is (C).** 5 on the side + 2 on and along the bottom = 7.

3. **The correct answer is (A).** 4 on the side + 1 on the bottom = 5.

4. **The correct answer is (E).** 2 on the top + 3 on the side + 3 on the bottom = 8.

5. **The correct answer is (D).** 4 on and along the top + 3 on the side = 7.

6. **The correct answer is (C).** 3 on the bottom = 3.

7. **The correct answer is (D).** 1 on the top + 1 on the side + 3 on the bottom = 5.

8. **The correct answer is (A).** 3 on the top + 1 on the side + 1 on the bottom = 5.

9. **The correct answer is (E).** 3 on the top + 3 on the side + 2 on and along the bottom = 8.

10. **The correct answer is (A).** 1 on the top + 1 on the side = 2.

11. **The correct answer is (B).** 3 on the side + 1 on the bottom = 4.

12. **The correct answer is (C).** 5 on the side + 1 on the bottom = 6.

13. **The correct answer is (A).** 1 on the top + 1 on the side + 3 on the bottom = 5.

14. **The correct answer is (B).** 3 on the top + 1 on the side + 1 on the bottom = 5.

15. **The correct answer is (E).** 3 on the top + 3 on the side = 6.

16. **The correct answer is (D).** 3 on the side + 3 on the bottom = 6.

answers practice test 1

17. The correct answer is (E). 3 on the top + 3 on the side + 3 on the bottom = 9.

18. The correct answer is (C). 3 on the top + 1 on the side + 1 on the bottom = 5.

19. The correct answer is (C). 3 on the top + 1 on the side = 4.

20. The correct answer is (B). 1 on the top + 1 on the side = 2.

Part 7: Table Reading

1. C	9. B	17. E	25. A	33. A
2. B	10. A	18. C	26. A	34. E
3. E	11. C	19. A	27. D	35. D
4. C	12. D	20. D	28. B	36. D
5. A	13. B	21. B	29. E	37. C
6. B	14. E	22. D	30. C	38. A
7. E	15. A	23. E	31. E	39. E
8. D	16. B	24. D	32. B	40. B

1. The correct answer is (C). 32

2. The correct answer is (B). 29

3. The correct answer is (E). 27

4. The correct answer is (C). 35

5. The correct answer is (A). 26

6. The correct answer is (B). 148

7. The correct answer is (E). 131

8. The correct answer is (D). 184

9. The correct answer is (B). 97

10. The correct answer is (A). 224

11. The correct answer is (C). .03

12. The correct answer is (D). .04

13. The correct answer is (B). .07

14. The correct answer is (E). .05

15. The correct answer is (A). .04

16. The correct answer is (B). 8:21

17. The correct answer is (E). 8:16

18. The correct answer is (C). 8:53

19. The correct answer is (A). 8:27

20. The correct answer is (D). 8:30

21. The correct answer is (B). 930

22. The correct answer is (D). 880

23. The correct answer is (E). 445

24. The correct answer is (D). 2,810

25. The correct answer is (A). 2,050

26. The correct answer is (A). 3,200

27. The correct answer is (D). 760

28. The correct answer is (B). 550

29. The correct answer is (E). 2,450

30. The correct answer is (C). 1,600

31. The correct answer is (E). 36

32. The correct answer is (B). 35

33. The correct answer is (A). 31

34. The correct answer is (E). 48

35. The correct answer is (D). 34

36. The correct answer is (D). 31

37. The correct answer is (C). 24

38. The correct answer is (A). 41

39. The correct answer is (E). 26

40. The correct answer is (B). 23

Part 8: Aviation Information

1. C	5. A	9. B	13. D	17. C
2. C	6. C	10. D	14. B	18. E
3. D	7. B	11. A	15. D	19. A
4. A	8. E	12. E	16. E	20. B

1. **The correct answer is (C).** While the airplane is propelled through the air and sufficient lift is developed to sustain it in flight, four forces are acting on it: thrust, or forward force; lift, or upward force; drag, or rearward acting force; and weight, or downward force.

2. **The correct answer is (C).** The top of the wing is curved; the bottom is relatively flat. The air flowing over the top travels a little farther than the air flowing along the flat bottom. This means that the air above must travel more quickly. Hence, pressure decreases, resulting in a lower pressure on top of the wing than below it. The higher pressure then pushes (lifts) the wing up, toward the lower pressure area.

3. **The correct answer is (D).** The tachometer indicates the speed at which the engine crankshaft is rotating. The other answer choices are all flight instruments.

4. **The correct answer is (A).** In a steady flight condition, the always-present forces that oppose each other are also equal. That is, lift equals weight and thrust equals drag.

5. **The correct answer is (A).** A flashing green signal directed to an aircraft on the ground signals that the pilot is cleared to taxi.

6. **The correct answer is (C).** A steady red signal from the tower to an aircraft in flight means the aircraft must continue circling; a flashing red signal means that it is unsafe to land.

7. **The correct answer is (B).** The propeller blades, just like a wing, are curved on one side and straight on the other side. As the propeller is rotated by the engine, forces similar to those on the wing "lift" in a forward direction to produce thrust.

8. **The correct answer is (E).** When in the downward (extended) position, wing flaps pivot downward from the hinged points. This in effect increases the wing camber and angle of attack, thereby providing greater lift and more drag so that the airplane can descend or climb at a steeper angle or a slower airspeed.

9. **The correct answer is (B).** The lift acting upward and opposing weight is called the vertical lift component. The lift acting horizontally and opposing inertia or centrifugal force is called the horizontal lift component. The horizontal lift component is the sideward force that forces the airplane from straight flight and causes it to turn.

10. **The correct answer is (D).** Stability is the inherent ability of a

body, after its equilibrium is disturbed, to develop forces or moments that tend to return the body to its original position. The ability of the airplane to return, of its own accord, to its original condition of flight after it has been disturbed by some outside force (such as turbulent air) makes the airplane easier to fly and requires less effort to control.

11. **The correct answer is (A).** The elevator trim tab is a small auxiliary control surface hinged at the trailing edge of the elevators. The elevator trim tab acts on the elevators, which in turn act upon the entire airplane. A downward deflection of the trim tab will force the elevator upward, which will force the tail down and the nose up.

12. **The correct answer is (E).** The thrust required to maintain straight-and-level flight at a given airspeed is not sufficient to maintain the same airspeed in a climb. Climbing flight takes more power than straight and level flight. Consequently, the engine power control must be advanced to a higher power setting.

13. **The correct answer is (D).** Getting a feel for control pressures is very important in recognizing the approach of a stall. As speed is reduced, the "live" resistance to pressures on the controls becomes progressively lower. Pressures exerted on the controls tend to become movements of the control surfaces, and the lag between those movements and the response of the airplane increases. In a complete stall, all controls can be moved with almost no resistance and with little immediate effect on the airplane.

14. **The correct answer is (B).** Heavily loaded ships require a longer ground roll; consequently, they need much more space to develop the minimum lift necessary for takeoff. Similarly, takeoff in still air precludes a takeoff as nearly into the wind as possible to reduce ground roll. Accordingly, municipal airports have found it desirable to provide an unusually long flight strip to cope with adverse takeoff factors.

15. **The correct answer is (D).** Area A is a no-landing portion of the runway; however, takeoff is permitted. Area B is the threshold line and marks the start of the usable portion of the runway for landing. Area C is not available for takeoff or landing. Area E is an emergency over-run only; taxi, takeoff, and landing are not allowed in this area.

16. **The correct answer is (E).** Area A, the no-landing portion of the runway, may be used for taxi and takeoff. Area E may be used only as an emergency overrun; taxi, takeoff, and landing are not allowed in this area.

17. **The correct answer is (C).** Runway symbol X is a runway marker signifying that the runway is closed.

18. **The correct answer is (E).** 17–35 runs roughly north-south. 9–27 runs west-east. The traffic pattern indicators (⌐,⌐) show the direction of the turns when landing on the runways. A left turn is required to land on Runways 9 and 35. A right turn is required to land on Runways 17 and 27.

19. The correct answer is (A). Runway 27 runs due west. When the wind blows through the large end of the wind cone, it causes the small end to stand out and point downward.

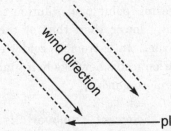

wind direction

plane movement

The sketch shows that the landing will be with a right-quartering headwind.

20. The correct answer is (B). Runways 35 and 27 are the two most desirable ones for landing, as both would be with a quartering headwind. Runway 35 takes left traffic; Runway 27 takes right traffic.

Part 9: Rotated Blocks

1. D	4. D	7. E	10. B	13. C
2. C	5. B	8. B	11. A	14. E
3. C	6. A	9. E	12. A	15. D

Note: Practicing with toy blocks or modeling clay will help you visualize how views change when blocks are rotated.

Part 10: General Science

1. C	5. B	9. A	13. D	17. E
2. E	6. B	10. C	14. E	18. D
3. C	7. C	11. B	15. A	19. A
4. B	8. D	12. A	16. E	20. D

1. The correct answer is (C). When organic matter decays, it decomposes into its constituent elements. These elements are returned to the soil, thus increasing its fertility.

2. The correct answer is (E). The cornea, a thin clear layer, forms the front part of the eyeball.

3. The correct answer is (C). The extinction of all sizes and varieties of dinosaurs all over the world can be explained neither by local phenomena nor on a one-by-one basis.

The most reasonable assumption is that the dinosaurs failed to adapt and were unable to survive as climatic conditions changed radically.

4. The correct answer is (B). Combustion is a chemical process.

5. The correct answer is (B). Salt contributes to high blood pressure. The critical element in the action of salt upon the blood pressure is sodium. Iodine or the lack of it plays no role in raising blood pressure.

answers practice test 1

6. **The correct answer is (B).** Protein is the chief nutrient of lean meat.

7. **The correct answer is (C).** All spiders have four pairs of legs. True insects have three pairs of legs.

8. **The correct answer is (D).** *Uranium* is present in pitchblende and other rare metals. *Hematite* is a source of iron; *chalcopyrite* is an ore of copper; *bauxite* is a source of aluminum; *feldspar* is a source of silicates.

9. **The correct answer is (A).** The atomic weight of hydrogen is 1.0080, that of helium is 4.003, and of oxygen is 16.00. Air is a mixture of gases, not an element. The atomic weight of nitrogen is 14.0067.

10. **The correct answer is (C).** Nitrogen constitutes about four-fifths of the atmosphere by volume. Oxygen is the most plentiful gas on Earth, but not in the air.

11. **The correct answer is (B).** Light travels at 186,300 miles per second. The sun is 92,900,000 miles from the earth, so its light arrives here in just over 8 minutes.

12. **The correct answer is (A).** *Cirrus clouds* occur at 20,000–40,000 feet and are composed of ice crystals. *Nimbus clouds* are gray rain clouds; *cumulus clouds* are fluffy white clouds; *stratus clouds* are long, low clouds, generally at altitudes of 2,000–7,000 feet; *altostratus clouds* occur at intermediate heights.

13. **The correct answer is (D).** Group B was the control group. If the condition of patients in Group A were to improve significantly more than that of patients in Group B, scientists might have reason to believe in the effectiveness of the drug.

14. **The correct answer is (E).** The freezing point of a solution is generally lower than that of the pure solvent. In extremely cold weather, salt on iced sidewalks helps melt the ice more quickly.

15. **The correct answer is (A).** Radiation cannot pass through lead.

16. **The correct answer is (E).** Ball-and-socket joints permit movement in almost all directions. The shoulder joint is a ball-and-socket joint.

17. **The correct answer is (E).** Scurvy is caused by a vitamin C deficiency. Limes are rich in vitamin C.

18. **The correct answer is (D).** The earth rotates 360 degrees in 24 hours; therefore, it rotates 45 degrees in 3 hours.

19. **The correct answer is (A).** Mercury is closest to the sun; therefore, it has the shortest revolutionary period around the sun of all the planets in the answer choices.

20. **The correct answer is (D).** An *electron* is a negative particle. A *proton* is positively charged; a *neutron* is neutral and without charge; a *meson* has both positive and negative charges. An *isotope* is an atom of the same element but with a different number of neutrons.

Part 11: Hidden Figures

1. A	4. D	7. E	10. B	13. E
2. A	5. C	8. B	11. B	14. C
3. E	6. D	9. A	12. A	15. D

1. The correct answer is (A).

4. The correct answer is (D).

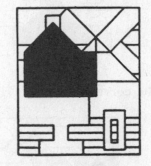

2. The correct answer is (A).

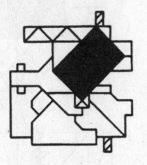

5. The correct answer is (C).

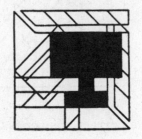

3. The correct answer is (E).

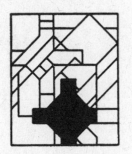

6. The correct answer is (D).

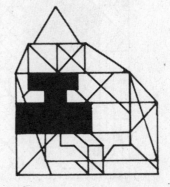

answers **practice test 1**

7. **The correct answer is (E).**

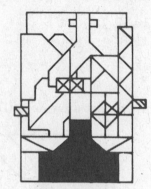

8. **The correct answer is (B).**

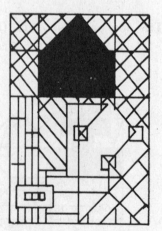

9. **The correct answer is (A).**

10. **The correct answer is (B).**

11. **The correct answer is (B).**

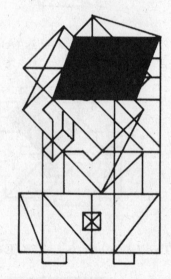

12. The correct answer is (A).

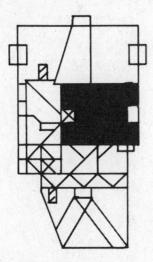

15. The correct answer is (D).

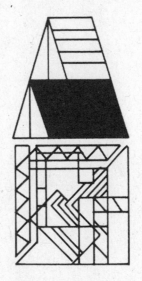

13. The correct answer is (E).

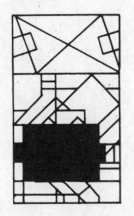

14. The correct answer is (C).

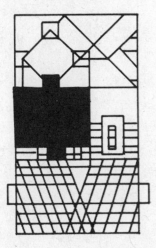

answers practice test 1

ANSWER SHEETS

Schematic Sample

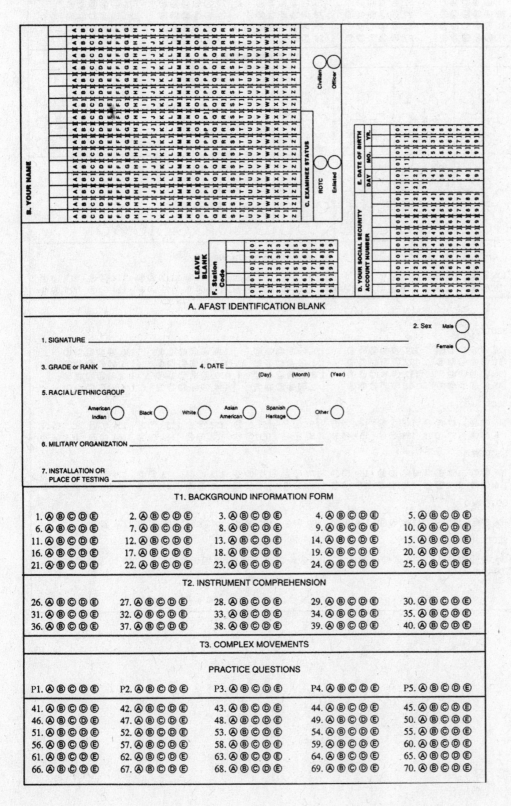

A. AFAST IDENTIFICATION BLANK

1. SIGNATURE _____

2. Sex Male ◯ Female ◯

3. GRADE or RANK _____ 4. DATE _____
(Day) (Month) (Year)

5. RACIAL/ETHNIC GROUP

American Indian ◯   Black ◯   White ◯   Asian American ◯   Spanish Heritage ◯   Other ◯

6. MILITARY ORGANIZATION _____

7. INSTALLATION OR PLACE OF TESTING _____

T1. BACKGROUND INFORMATION FORM

1. Ⓐ Ⓑ Ⓒ Ⓓ Ⓔ	2. Ⓐ Ⓑ Ⓒ Ⓓ Ⓔ	3. Ⓐ Ⓑ Ⓒ Ⓓ Ⓔ	4. Ⓐ Ⓑ Ⓒ Ⓓ Ⓔ	5. Ⓐ Ⓑ Ⓒ Ⓓ Ⓔ
6. Ⓐ Ⓑ Ⓒ Ⓓ Ⓔ	7. Ⓐ Ⓑ Ⓒ Ⓓ Ⓔ	8. Ⓐ Ⓑ Ⓒ Ⓓ Ⓔ	9. Ⓐ Ⓑ Ⓒ Ⓓ Ⓔ	10. Ⓐ Ⓑ Ⓒ Ⓓ Ⓔ
11. Ⓐ Ⓑ Ⓒ Ⓓ Ⓔ	12. Ⓐ Ⓑ Ⓒ Ⓓ Ⓔ	13. Ⓐ Ⓑ Ⓒ Ⓓ Ⓔ	14. Ⓐ Ⓑ Ⓒ Ⓓ Ⓔ	15. Ⓐ Ⓑ Ⓒ Ⓓ Ⓔ
16. Ⓐ Ⓑ Ⓒ Ⓓ Ⓔ	17. Ⓐ Ⓑ Ⓒ Ⓓ Ⓔ	18. Ⓐ Ⓑ Ⓒ Ⓓ Ⓔ	19. Ⓐ Ⓑ Ⓒ Ⓓ Ⓔ	20. Ⓐ Ⓑ Ⓒ Ⓓ Ⓔ
21. Ⓐ Ⓑ Ⓒ Ⓓ Ⓔ	22. Ⓐ Ⓑ Ⓒ Ⓓ Ⓔ	23. Ⓐ Ⓑ Ⓒ Ⓓ Ⓔ	24. Ⓐ Ⓑ Ⓒ Ⓓ Ⓔ	25. Ⓐ Ⓑ Ⓒ Ⓓ Ⓔ

T2. INSTRUMENT COMPREHENSION

26. Ⓐ Ⓑ Ⓒ Ⓓ Ⓔ	27. Ⓐ Ⓑ Ⓒ Ⓓ Ⓔ	28. Ⓐ Ⓑ Ⓒ Ⓓ Ⓔ	29. Ⓐ Ⓑ Ⓒ Ⓓ Ⓔ	30. Ⓐ Ⓑ Ⓒ Ⓓ Ⓔ
31. Ⓐ Ⓑ Ⓒ Ⓓ Ⓔ	32. Ⓐ Ⓑ Ⓒ Ⓓ Ⓔ	33. Ⓐ Ⓑ Ⓒ Ⓓ Ⓔ	34. Ⓐ Ⓑ Ⓒ Ⓓ Ⓔ	35. Ⓐ Ⓑ Ⓒ Ⓓ Ⓔ
36. Ⓐ Ⓑ Ⓒ Ⓓ Ⓔ	37. Ⓐ Ⓑ Ⓒ Ⓓ Ⓔ	38. Ⓐ Ⓑ Ⓒ Ⓓ Ⓔ	39. Ⓐ Ⓑ Ⓒ Ⓓ Ⓔ	40. Ⓐ Ⓑ Ⓒ Ⓓ Ⓔ

T3. COMPLEX MOVEMENTS

PRACTICE QUESTIONS

P1. Ⓐ Ⓑ Ⓒ Ⓓ Ⓔ	P2. Ⓐ Ⓑ Ⓒ Ⓓ Ⓔ	P3. Ⓐ Ⓑ Ⓒ Ⓓ Ⓔ	P4. Ⓐ Ⓑ Ⓒ Ⓓ Ⓔ	P5. Ⓐ Ⓑ Ⓒ Ⓓ Ⓔ

41. Ⓐ Ⓑ Ⓒ Ⓓ Ⓔ	42. Ⓐ Ⓑ Ⓒ Ⓓ Ⓔ	43. Ⓐ Ⓑ Ⓒ Ⓓ Ⓔ	44. Ⓐ Ⓑ Ⓒ Ⓓ Ⓔ	45. Ⓐ Ⓑ Ⓒ Ⓓ Ⓔ
46. Ⓐ Ⓑ Ⓒ Ⓓ Ⓔ	47. Ⓐ Ⓑ Ⓒ Ⓓ Ⓔ	48. Ⓐ Ⓑ Ⓒ Ⓓ Ⓔ	49. Ⓐ Ⓑ Ⓒ Ⓓ Ⓔ	50. Ⓐ Ⓑ Ⓒ Ⓓ Ⓔ
51. Ⓐ Ⓑ Ⓒ Ⓓ Ⓔ	52. Ⓐ Ⓑ Ⓒ Ⓓ Ⓔ	53. Ⓐ Ⓑ Ⓒ Ⓓ Ⓔ	54. Ⓐ Ⓑ Ⓒ Ⓓ Ⓔ	55. Ⓐ Ⓑ Ⓒ Ⓓ Ⓔ
56. Ⓐ Ⓑ Ⓒ Ⓓ Ⓔ	57. Ⓐ Ⓑ Ⓒ Ⓓ Ⓔ	58. Ⓐ Ⓑ Ⓒ Ⓓ Ⓔ	59. Ⓐ Ⓑ Ⓒ Ⓓ Ⓔ	60. Ⓐ Ⓑ Ⓒ Ⓓ Ⓔ
61. Ⓐ Ⓑ Ⓒ Ⓓ Ⓔ	62. Ⓐ Ⓑ Ⓒ Ⓓ Ⓔ	63. Ⓐ Ⓑ Ⓒ Ⓓ Ⓔ	64. Ⓐ Ⓑ Ⓒ Ⓓ Ⓔ	65. Ⓐ Ⓑ Ⓒ Ⓓ Ⓔ
66. Ⓐ Ⓑ Ⓒ Ⓓ Ⓔ	67. Ⓐ Ⓑ Ⓒ Ⓓ Ⓔ	68. Ⓐ Ⓑ Ⓒ Ⓓ Ⓔ	69. Ⓐ Ⓑ Ⓒ Ⓓ Ⓔ	70. Ⓐ Ⓑ Ⓒ Ⓓ Ⓔ

answer sheet

Schematic Sample (Continued)

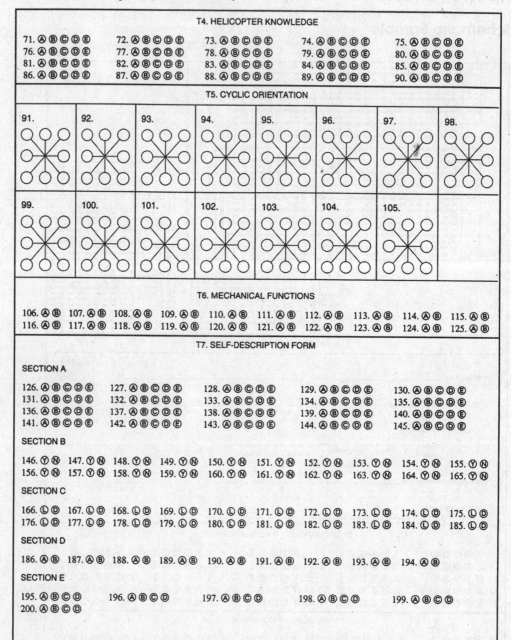

T4. HELICOPTER KNOWLEDGE

71. Ⓐ Ⓑ Ⓒ Ⓓ Ⓔ   72. Ⓐ Ⓑ Ⓒ Ⓓ Ⓔ   73. Ⓐ Ⓑ Ⓒ Ⓓ Ⓔ   74. Ⓐ Ⓑ Ⓒ Ⓓ Ⓔ   75. Ⓐ Ⓑ Ⓒ Ⓓ Ⓔ
76. Ⓐ Ⓑ Ⓒ Ⓓ Ⓔ   77. Ⓐ Ⓑ Ⓒ Ⓓ Ⓔ   78. Ⓐ Ⓑ Ⓒ Ⓓ Ⓔ   79. Ⓐ Ⓑ Ⓒ Ⓓ Ⓔ   80. Ⓐ Ⓑ Ⓒ Ⓓ Ⓔ
81. Ⓐ Ⓑ Ⓒ Ⓓ Ⓔ   82. Ⓐ Ⓑ Ⓒ Ⓓ Ⓔ   83. Ⓐ Ⓑ Ⓒ Ⓓ Ⓔ   84. Ⓐ Ⓑ Ⓒ Ⓓ Ⓔ   85. Ⓐ Ⓑ Ⓒ Ⓓ Ⓔ
86. Ⓐ Ⓑ Ⓒ Ⓓ Ⓔ   87. Ⓐ Ⓑ Ⓒ Ⓓ Ⓔ   88. Ⓐ Ⓑ Ⓒ Ⓓ Ⓔ   89. Ⓐ Ⓑ Ⓒ Ⓓ Ⓔ   90. Ⓐ Ⓑ Ⓒ Ⓓ Ⓔ

T5. CYCLIC ORIENTATION

91.   92.   93.   94.   95.   96.   97.   98.

99.   100.   101.   102.   103.   104.   105.

T6. MECHANICAL FUNCTIONS

106. Ⓐ Ⓑ   107. Ⓐ Ⓑ   108. Ⓐ Ⓑ   109. Ⓐ Ⓑ   110. Ⓐ Ⓑ   111. Ⓐ Ⓑ   112. Ⓐ Ⓑ   113. Ⓐ Ⓑ   114. Ⓐ Ⓑ   115. Ⓐ Ⓑ
116. Ⓐ Ⓑ   117. Ⓐ Ⓑ   118. Ⓐ Ⓑ   119. Ⓐ Ⓑ   120. Ⓐ Ⓑ   121. Ⓐ Ⓑ   122. Ⓐ Ⓑ   123. Ⓐ Ⓑ   124. Ⓐ Ⓑ   125. Ⓐ Ⓑ

T7. SELF-DESCRIPTION FORM

SECTION A

126. Ⓐ Ⓑ Ⓒ Ⓓ Ⓔ   127. Ⓐ Ⓑ Ⓒ Ⓓ Ⓔ   128. Ⓐ Ⓑ Ⓒ Ⓓ Ⓔ   129. Ⓐ Ⓑ Ⓒ Ⓓ Ⓔ   130. Ⓐ Ⓑ Ⓒ Ⓓ Ⓔ
131. Ⓐ Ⓑ Ⓒ Ⓓ Ⓔ   132. Ⓐ Ⓑ Ⓒ Ⓓ Ⓔ   133. Ⓐ Ⓑ Ⓒ Ⓓ Ⓔ   134. Ⓐ Ⓑ Ⓒ Ⓓ Ⓔ   135. Ⓐ Ⓑ Ⓒ Ⓓ Ⓔ
136. Ⓐ Ⓑ Ⓒ Ⓓ Ⓔ   137. Ⓐ Ⓑ Ⓒ Ⓓ Ⓔ   138. Ⓐ Ⓑ Ⓒ Ⓓ Ⓔ   139. Ⓐ Ⓑ Ⓒ Ⓓ Ⓔ   140. Ⓐ Ⓑ Ⓒ Ⓓ Ⓔ
141. Ⓐ Ⓑ Ⓒ Ⓓ Ⓔ   142. Ⓐ Ⓑ Ⓒ Ⓓ Ⓔ   143. Ⓐ Ⓑ Ⓒ Ⓓ Ⓔ   144. Ⓐ Ⓑ Ⓒ Ⓓ Ⓔ   145. Ⓐ Ⓑ Ⓒ Ⓓ Ⓔ

SECTION B

146. Ⓨ Ⓝ   147. Ⓨ Ⓝ   148. Ⓨ Ⓝ   149. Ⓨ Ⓝ   150. Ⓨ Ⓝ   151. Ⓨ Ⓝ   152. Ⓨ Ⓝ   153. Ⓨ Ⓝ   154. Ⓨ Ⓝ   155. Ⓨ Ⓝ
156. Ⓨ Ⓝ   157. Ⓨ Ⓝ   158. Ⓨ Ⓝ   159. Ⓨ Ⓝ   160. Ⓨ Ⓝ   161. Ⓨ Ⓝ   162. Ⓨ Ⓝ   163. Ⓨ Ⓝ   164. Ⓨ Ⓝ   165. Ⓨ Ⓝ

SECTION C

166. Ⓛ Ⓓ   167. Ⓛ Ⓓ   168. Ⓛ Ⓓ   169. Ⓛ Ⓓ   170. Ⓛ Ⓓ   171. Ⓛ Ⓓ   172. Ⓛ Ⓓ   173. Ⓛ Ⓓ   174. Ⓛ Ⓓ   175. Ⓛ Ⓓ
176. Ⓛ Ⓓ   177. Ⓛ Ⓓ   178. Ⓛ Ⓓ   179. Ⓛ Ⓓ   180. Ⓛ Ⓓ   181. Ⓛ Ⓓ   182. Ⓛ Ⓓ   183. Ⓛ Ⓓ   184. Ⓛ Ⓓ   185. Ⓛ Ⓓ

SECTION D

186. Ⓐ Ⓑ   187. Ⓐ Ⓑ   188. Ⓐ Ⓑ   189. Ⓐ Ⓑ   190. Ⓐ Ⓑ   191. Ⓐ Ⓑ   192. Ⓐ Ⓑ   193. Ⓐ Ⓑ   194. Ⓐ Ⓑ

SECTION E

195. Ⓐ Ⓑ Ⓒ Ⓓ   196. Ⓐ Ⓑ Ⓒ Ⓓ   197. Ⓐ Ⓑ Ⓒ Ⓓ   198. Ⓐ Ⓑ Ⓒ Ⓓ   199. Ⓐ Ⓑ Ⓒ Ⓓ
200. Ⓐ Ⓑ Ⓒ Ⓓ

SUBTEST 1: BACKGROUND INFORMATION

Directions: Answer each question as accurately as you can, to the best of your ability and recollection. Skip those questions that do not pertain to you. The 25 questions on this subtest are all five-option items.

Sample Item

1. What type of high school program did you take?

   (A) Academic
   (B) General
   (C) Technical
   (D) Vocational
   (E) High school equivalency

If you took the academic program and graduated, select choice (A). ● Ⓑ Ⓒ Ⓓ Ⓔ

If you took the general program and graduated, select choice (B). Ⓐ ● Ⓒ Ⓓ Ⓔ

If you took the technical program and graduated, select choice (C). Ⓐ Ⓑ ● Ⓓ Ⓔ

If you took the vocational program and graduated, select choice (D). Ⓐ Ⓑ Ⓒ ● Ⓔ

If you did not graduate from high school but earned the high school equivalency diploma, select choice (E). Ⓐ Ⓑ Ⓒ Ⓓ ●

When you begin, be sure to start with question number 1 on your test booklet and number 1 on your answer sheet.

STOP! DO NOT TURN THIS PAGE UNTIL TOLD TO DO SO.

practice test 2

25 Questions • 10 Minutes

Directons: The questions in this subtest are biographical and pertain to your general background. Answer each question to the best of your ability and recollection. Skip those questions that do not pertain to you.

1. What is your age?

   (A) Younger than 20 years
   (B) 20–23 years
   (C) 24–27 years
   (D) 28–31 years
   (E) 32 years or older

2. Where did you live most of the time before you were 20 years old?

   (A) The Northeast region of the United States
   (B) The Southern region of the United States
   (C) The Central region of the United States
   (D) The Western region of the United States
   (E) Outside the continental United States

3. If foreign born, when did you come to the United States permanently?

   (A) 0–5 years ago
   (B) 6–10 years ago
   (C) 11–15 years ago
   (D) 16–20 years ago
   (E) 21 or more years ago

4. If foreign born, in which geographical area were you born?

   (A) Asia
   (B) Africa
   (C) North or South America
   (D) Europe
   (E) Australia

5. What is your parents' citizenship status?

   (A) Both are native-born American citizens.
   (B) One is native-born; the other is naturalized.
   (C) Both are naturalized American citizens.
   (D) One is a naturalized citizen; the other is a permanent resident.
   (E) Both are legally admitted permanent residents.

6. How many years of schooling did your father complete?

   (A) College graduation
   (B) Some college training
   (C) High school graduation
   (D) Some high school training
   (E) Elementary school training

GO ON TO THE NEXT PAGE.

7. If your father served in the U.S. Armed Forces, in which branch did he serve?

   (A) Navy

   (B) Marines

   (C) Coast Guard

   (D) Army

   (E) Air Force

8. How many years of schooling did your mother complete?

   (A) College graduation

   (B) Some college training

   (C) High school graduation

   (D) Some high school training

   (E) Elementary school training

9. If your mother served in the U.S. Armed Forces, in which branch did she serve?

   (A) Navy

   (B) Marines

   (C) Coast Guard

   (D) Army

   (E) Air Force

10. How many siblings do you have in your family?

    (A) 0

    (B) 1

    (C) 2

    (D) 3

    (E) 4 or more

11. How were you raised?

    (A) In a two-parent household

    (B) In a single-parent household

    (C) By relatives

    (D) By foster parents

    (E) In an institution

12. Which one of the following best characterizes the behavior of your parents toward you?

    (A) They always were very strict with you.

    (B) They usually were very strict with you.

    (C) They often were very strict with you.

    (D) They seldom were very strict with you.

    (E) They never were very strict with you.

13. In what type of community did you live most of the time before you were 20 years old?

    (A) Large city (population of more than 250,000)

    (B) Small city (population of less than 250,000)

    (C) Suburb of the city

    (D) Town or village

    (E) Rural community

14. Which of the following types of high schools did you attend?

    (A) Public, academic

    (B) Public, vocational

    (C) Private, parochial

    (D) Private, non-parochial

    (E) Military

15. How old were you when you graduated from high school?

    (A) 16 years or younger

    (B) 17

    (C) 18

    (D) 19

    (E) 20 years or older

GO ON TO THE NEXT PAGE.

16. How many years of college have you completed?

(A) Less than one year

(B) 1 year

(C) 2 years

(D) 3 years

(E) 4 or more years

17. If you were employed on school days during the last four years of your schooling, how many hours did you work per week?

(A) 5 or fewer

(B) 6–10

(C) 11–15

(D) 16 or more

(E) Did not work on school days

18. How did you usually travel to and from school during the last four years of your schooling?

(A) Walking

(B) Bus

(C) Private car

(D) Taxi

(E) Train or subway

19. How many hours a week did you devote to volunteer work in the community during the last four years of your schooling?

(A) 5 or less

(B) 6–10

(C) 11–15

(D) 16 or more

(E) Did no volunteer work

20. If you were a volunteer, which of the following best describes the nature of the volunteer work?

(A) Religious

(B) Educational

(C) Civil or political

(D) Charitable

(E) Health-care related

21. If you took the Armed Services Vocational Aptitude Battery (ASVAB), in which of the following categories did your score fall?

(A) Category I 93rd–100th percentile range

(B) Category II 65th–92nd percentile range

(C) Category III 31st–64th percentile range

(D) Category IV 10th–30th percentile range

(E) Category V 9th percentile and below

22. If you are a college graduate, how old were you when you graduated?

(A) 20 years or younger

(B) 21 years

(C) 22 years

(D) 23 years

(E) 24 years or older

23. What was your standing in your college graduating class?

(A) Honor graduate

(B) Top third but not an honor graduate

(C) Middle third

(D) Bottom third

(E) Not a college graduate

STOP! DO NOT GO ON UNTIL TIME IS UP.

24. What is your present marital status?

    (A) Married

    (B) Divorced

    (C) Separated

    (D) Widowed

    (E) Never married

25. What is your current or most recent employment?

    (A) Employee of private company, business, or individual for wages, salary, or commission

    (B) Government employee

    (C) Self-employed in own business, professional practice, or farm

    (D) Working without pay in family business or farm

    (E) Never employed

practice test

SUBTEST 2: INSTRUMENT COMPREHENSION

Directons: Below are shown two sets of dials, labeled ARTIFICIAL HORIZON and COMPASS. The *heavy black line* on the ARTIFICIAL HORIZON represents the horizon line. If the airplane is *above* the horizon, it is climbing. If it is *below* the horizon, it is diving. The greater amount of climb or dive, the farther up or down the horizon line is seen. The ARTIFICIAL HORIZON dial also has a black arrowhead showing the degree of bank to left or right. If the airplane has *no* bank, the arrowhead points to *zero*. If it is banked to the *left*, the arrowhead points to the *right* of zero. If the airplane is banked to the *right*, the arrowhead points to the *left* of zero.

Examples of the Artificial Horizon

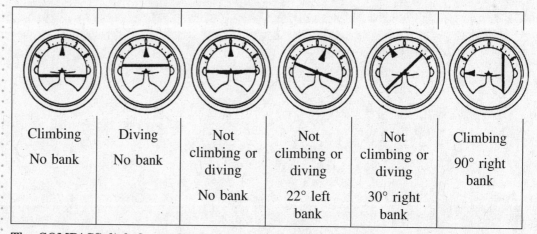

Climbing	Diving	Not climbing or diving	Not climbing or diving	Not climbing or diving	Climbing
No bank	No bank	No bank	22° left bank	30° right bank	90° right bank

The COMPASS dial shows the direction the airplane is headed at the moment.

Examples of the Compass Dial

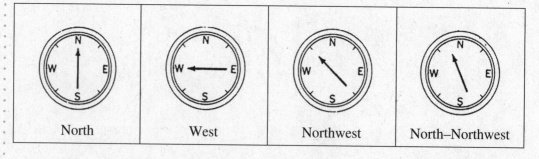

North	West	Northwest	North–Northwest

GO ON TO THE NEXT PAGE.

Now look at sample item X and decide which airplane is in the position indicated by the dials. You are always looking north at the same altitude as each of the planes. East is always to your right as you look at the page.

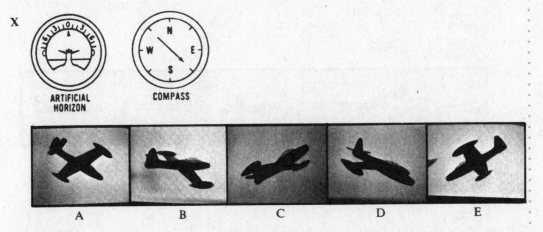

In sample item X, the dial labeled ARTIFICIAL HORIZON shows that the airplane is climbing but is not banked. The COMPASS shows that it is headed southeast. The only one of the five airplane silhouettes that meets these specifications is in the box lettered C, so the answer to sample item X is choice (C).

When you begin, be sure to start with question number 26 on Subtest 2 in your test booklet and number 26 on your answer form. Do not spend too much time on any one question.

practice test

STOP! DO NOT TURN THIS PAGE UNTIL TOLD TO DO SO.

15 Questions • 5 Minutes

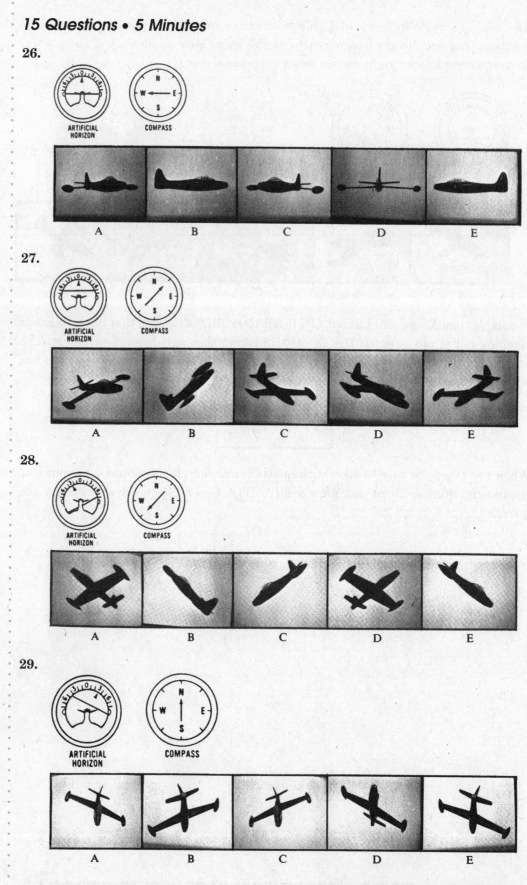

26.

27.

28.

29.

GO ON TO THE NEXT PAGE.

30.

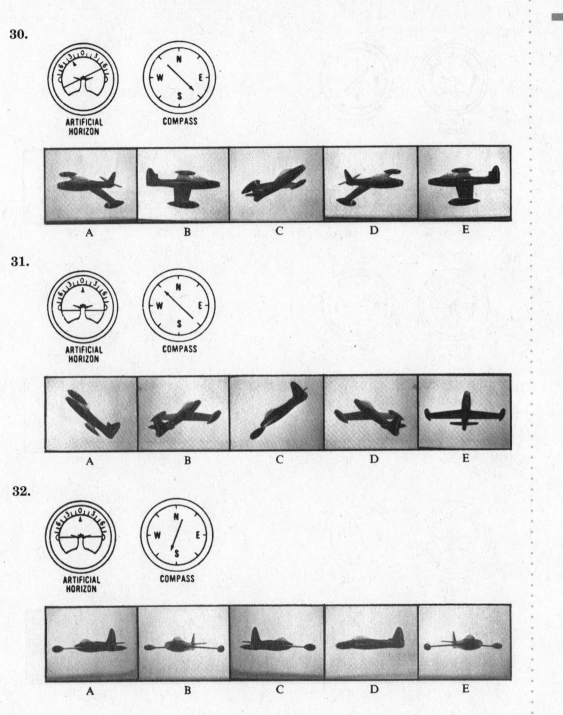

31.

32.

practice test

33.

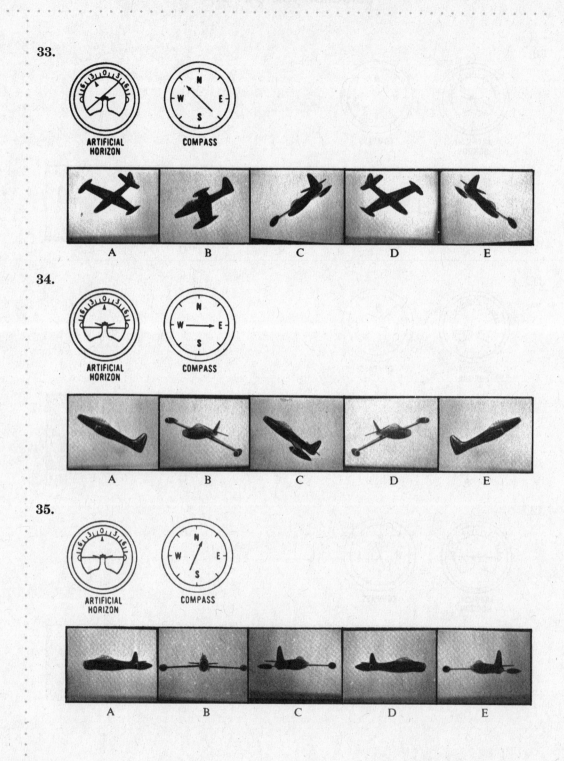

34.

35.

GO ON TO THE NEXT PAGE.

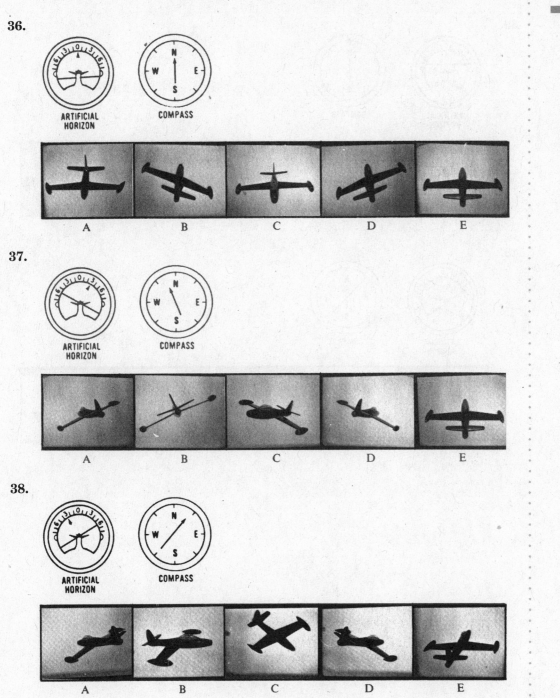

36.

ARTIFICIAL HORIZON   COMPASS

A   B   C   D   E

37.

ARTIFICIAL HORIZON   COMPASS

A   B   C   D   E

38.

ARTIFICIAL HORIZON   COMPASS

A   B   C   D   E

practice test

39.

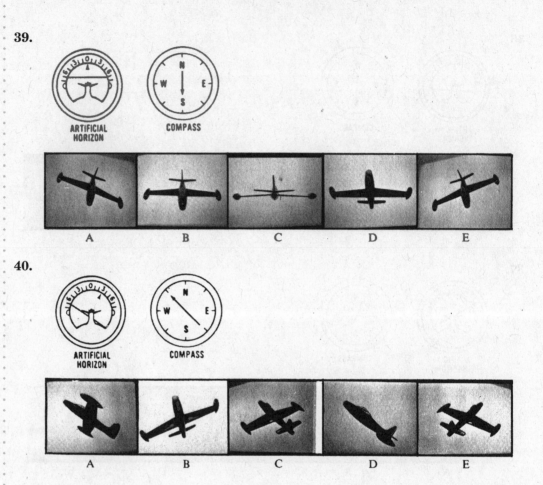

STOP! DO NOT GO ON UNTIL TIME IS UP.

SUBTEST 3: COMPLEX MOVEMENTS

Directions: Look at the heavy dark dot below the circle in sample question 1. Your task is to move this dot to the center of the circle. You will have to decide which *direction* or *directions* (right or left and up or down) the dot has to be moved and the *distance* in each direction moved to reach the center of the circle.

Look at the KEYS. These show the meaning of the symbols in the test. There is a *Direction Key,* which shows the meaning of the *top row of symbols* for movement *right* or *left* (horizontal movement) and the *bottom row of symbols* for movement *up* or *down* (vertical movement). Notice in each there is a symbol for no movement. The *Distance Key* shows the three line widths in which the arrows can be drawn. The thinnest line width represents movement of approximately $\frac{1}{8}$ inch. The medium-width line represents approximately $\frac{2}{8}$ inch, and the thickest line represents approximately $\frac{3}{8}$ inch.

Now decide which answer in sample question 1 is correct by looking at the arrows in the top row *and* the arrows in the bottom row and the width of the line in which the arrows are drawn. Only one pair of symbols is correct.

No horizontal movement is required as the heavy dark dot is directly below the circle. However, it must be moved up approximately $\frac{1}{8}$ inch. Choice (A) is the correct answer.

Look at the "T3. COMPLEX MOVEMENTS" section of your answer sheet labeled PRACTICE QUESTIONS. Notice that there are five answer spaces marked P1, P2, P3, P4, and P5. Now do practice questions P1–P5 by yourself using the DIRECTION KEY and the DISTANCE KEY. Find the correct answer to the practice question, then mark the space on your answer sheet that has the same letter as the answer you picked. Do this now.

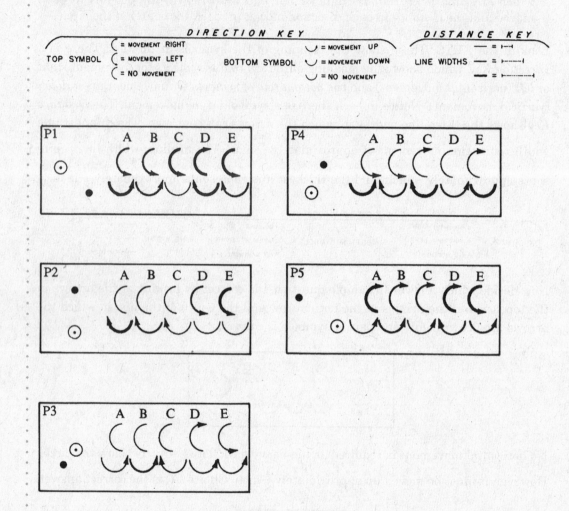

**Practice Test 2: Army Alternate Flight Aptitude
Selection Test (AFAST)**

257

You should have marked the practice questions as follows:

P1 (B) (2 left, 2 up)
P2 (A) (no horizontal movement, 3 down)
P3 (D) (1 right, 1 up)
P4 (B) (1 left, 2 down)
P5 (D) (3 right, 2 down)

If you made any mistakes, erase your mark carefully and blacken the correct answer space. Do this now.

Be sure to start with question number 41 of Subtest 3 of your test booklet and number 41 on your answer sheet. Do not spend too much time on any one question.

practice test

30 Questions • 5 Minutes

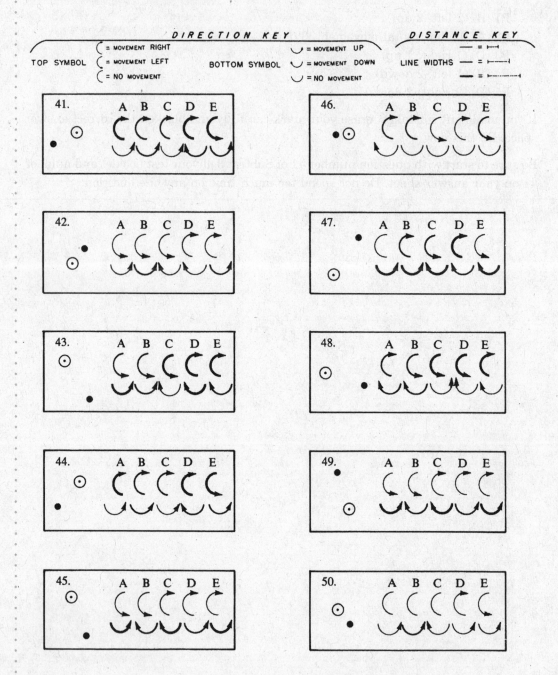

GO ON TO THE NEXT PAGE.

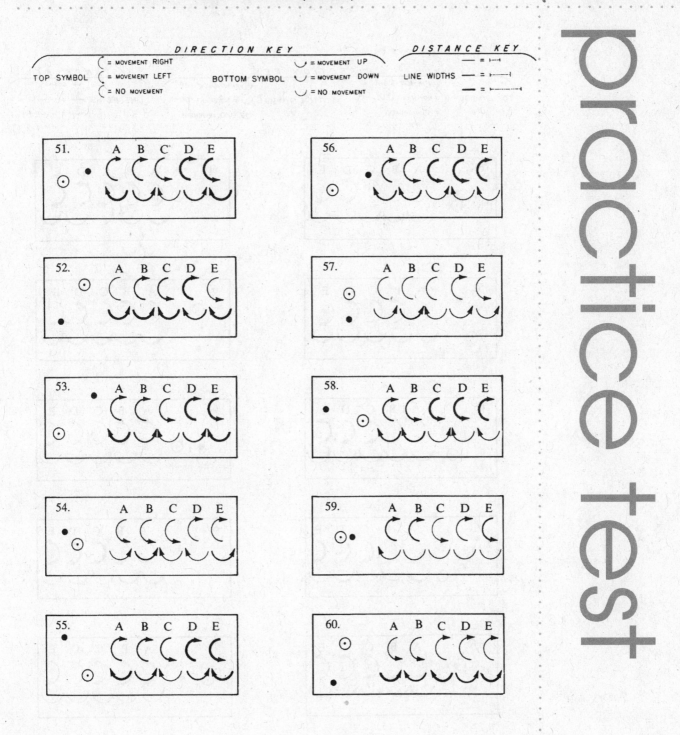

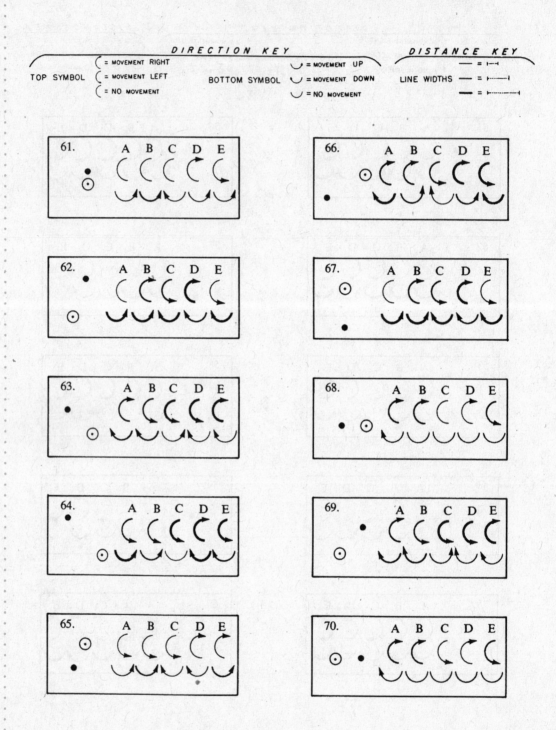

STOP! DO NOT GO ON UNTIL TIME IS UP.

SUBTEST 4: HELICOPTER KNOWLEDGE

Directions: The incomplete statement is followed by several choices. Decide which one of the choices *best* completes the statement. Then mark the space on your answer sheet that has the same number and letter as your choice.

Unless otherwise indicated, these questions are based on a helicopter that has the following characteristics:

- An unsupercharged reciprocating engine
- A single main rotor rotating in a counterclockwise direction (looking downward on the rotor)
- An antitorque (tail) rotor
- Kid-type landing gear

Now look at the following sample question.

1. You are in a helicopter in straight and level flight with a constant power setting. When the nose of the helicopter is pulled up, the altitude will

   (A) remain the same.
   (B) initially increase.
   (C) initially decrease.
   (D) initially decrease and then remain the same.
   (E) None of the above

When the nose of the helicopter is pulled up, the altitude will initially increase. Choice (B) is the correct answer.

When you begin, be sure to start with question number 71 of Subtest 4 of your test booklet and number 71 on your answer sheet.

STOP! DO NOT TURN THIS PAGE UNTIL TOLD TO DO SO.

20 Questions • 10 Minutes

71. A lighted heliport may be identified by

    (A) a flashing yellow light.
    (B) a blue lighted square landing area.
    (C) white and red lights.
    (D) a green, yellow, and white rotating beacon.
    (E) blue and red alternating flashes.

72. The primary purpose of the tail rotor system is to

    (A) assist in making a coordinated turn.
    (B) maintain heading during forward flight.
    (C) counteract the torque effect of the main rotor.
    (D) provide additional thrust and lift.
    (E) increase maximum speed.

73. During a hover, a helicopter tends to drift in the direction of tail rotor thrust. This movement is called

    (A) flapping.
    (B) gyroscopic precession.
    (C) transverse flow effect.
    (D) translating tendency.
    (E) Coriolis force.

74. The upward bending of the rotor blades resulting from the combined forces of lift and centrifugal force is known as

    (A) translational lift.
    (B) blade flapping.
    (C) Coriolis effect.
    (D) dissymmetry of lift.
    (E) coning.

75. In a helicopter, the center of gravity (CG) range is usually located

    (A) in front of the main rotor mast.
    (B) in the rear of the main rotor mast.
    (C) directly above the main fuel tank.
    (D) directly below the main fuel tank.
    (E) a short distance fore and aft of the main rotor mast.

76. The lift differential that exists between the advancing main rotor blade and the retreating main rotor blade is known as

    (A) Coriolis effect.
    (B) dissymmetry of lift.
    (C) translating tendency.
    (D) translational lift.
    (E) lift vector.

77. Ground resonance is most likely to develop when

    (A) there is a sudden change in blade velocity in the plane of rotation.
    (B) a series of shocks causes the rotor system to become unbalanced.
    (C) there is a combination of a decrease in the angle of attack on the advancing blade and an increase in the angle of attack on the retreating blade.
    (D) initial ground contact is made with a combination of high gross weight and low RPM.
    (E) there is a defective clutch or missing or bent fan blades in the helicopter engine.

GO ON TO THE NEXT PAGE.

78. The proper action to initiate a quick stop is to

(A) increase the RPM.

(B) decrease the RPM.

(C) raise the collective pitch.

(D) lower collective pitch and apply forward cyclic.

(E) lower collective pitch and apply aft cyclic.

79. Takeoff from a slope in a helicopter with skid-type landing gear is normally accomplished by

(A) simultaneously applying collective pitch and downslope cyclic control.

(B) bringing the helicopter to a level attitude before completely leaving the ground.

(C) making a downslope running takeoff if the surface is smooth.

(D) rapidly increasing collective pitch and upslope cyclic controls to avoid sliding downslope.

(E) turning the tail upslope, when moving away from the slope, to reduce the danger of the tail rotor striking the surface.

80. The proper procedure for a slope landing in a helicopter with skid-type landing gear is

(A) to use maximum RPM and maximum manifold pressure.

(B) when parallel to the slope, slowly lower the downslope skid to the ground prior to lowering the upslope skid.

(C) if the slope is 10 degrees or less, the landing should be made perpendicular to the slope.

(D) when parallel to the slope, slowly lower the upslope skid to the ground prior to lowering the downslope skid.

(E) if the slope is 10 degrees or less, the landing should be downslope or downhill.

81. Density altitude refers to a theoretical air density that exists under standard conditions at a given altitude. Standard conditions at sea level are

(A) 29.92 inHg (inches of mercury) and 15°C.

(B) 29.92 inHg (inches of mercury) and 20°C.

(C) 29.92 inHg (inches of mercury) and 30°C.

(D) 14.96 inHg (inches of mercury) and 15°C.

(E) 14.96 inHg (inches of mercury) and 30°C.

practice test

GO ON TO THE NEXT PAGE.

82. A helicopter pilot should consider using a running takeoff

(A) if the helicopter cannot be lifted vertically.

(B) when a normal climb speed is assured between 10 and 20 feet.

(C) when power is insufficient to hover at a very low altitude.

(D) when the additional airspeed can be quickly converted to altitude.

(E) when gross weight or density altitude prevents a sustained hover at normal hovering altitude.

83. Foot pedals in the helicopter cockpit enable the pilot to

(A) control torque effect.

(B) regulate flight speed.

(C) regulate rate of climb.

(D) regulate rate of descent.

(E) stabilize rotor RPM.

84. If the helicopter is moving forward, the advancing blade will be in the

(A) forward half of the rotor disc.

(B) left half of the rotor disc.

(C) rear half of the rotor disc.

(D) right half of the rotor disc.

(E) It cannot be estimated.

85. The method of control by which the pitch of all main rotor blades is varied equally and simultaneously is the

(A) auxiliary rotor control.

(B) collective pitch control.

(C) cyclic pitch control.

(D) tail rotor control.

(E) throttle control.

86. The combination of factors that will reduce helicopter performance the most is

(A) low altitude, low temperature, and low humidity.

(B) low altitude, high temperature, and low humidity.

(C) low altitude, low temperature, and high humidity.

(D) high altitude, low temperature, and low humidity.

(E) high altitude, high temperature, and high humidity.

87. The most favorable conditions for helicopter performance are the combination of

(A) low-density altitude, light gross weight, and moderate-to-strong winds.

(B) high-density altitude, heavy gross weight, and calm or no wind.

(C) low-density altitude, light gross weight, and calm or no wind.

(D) high-density altitude, light gross weight, and moderate-to-strong winds.

(E) low-density altitude, heavy gross weight, and moderate-to-strong winds.

88. Refer to the figure below. The acute angle A is the angle of

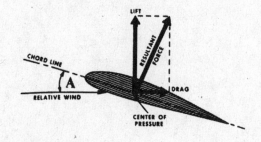

(A) dihedral.

(B) attack.

(C) camber.

(D) incidence.

(E) pitch.

GO ON TO THE NEXT PAGE.

89. During surface taxiing, the helicopter pilot should use the pedals to maintain heading and the cyclic to maintain

    (A) ground track.
    (B) proper RPM.
    (C) starting.
    (D) stopping.
    (E) All of the above

90. The thinner air of higher altitudes causes the airspeed indicator to read "too low." An indicated airspeed of 80 mph at 5,000 feet is actually a true airspeed of approximately

    (A) 72 mph.
    (B) 88 mph.
    (C) 96 mph.
    (D) 104 mph.
    (E) 112 mph.

practice test

STOP! DO NOT GO ON UNTIL TIME IS UP.

SUBTEST 5: CYCLIC ORIENTATION

Directions: You are the pilot of a helicopter with a constant power setting going through a maneuver as shown in the pictures on the next page. The helicopter can be climbing, diving, banking (turning) to the right or left, or in a climbing or diving bank. Look at the pictures from *top* to *bottom* and decide what maneuver it is doing. Then decide which position the cyclic (stick) would be in to perform the maneuver.

For items in this test, the cyclic is moved as follows:

- *For banks*
  To bank left, move the cyclic stick to the left. To bank right, move the cyclic to the right.
- *For climbs and dives*
  To dive, push the cyclic forward. To climb, pull the cyclic back.

EXAMPLE OF CYCLIC MOVEMENT

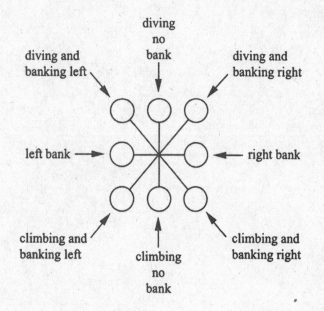

GO ON TO THE NEXT PAGE.

Now look at the set of pictures below in sample item 1 and decide the cyclic position for the maneuver shown.

Now look at the set of pictures below in sample item 2 and decide the cyclic position for the maneuver shown.

1.

2.

1.

Climbing; no bank

2.

Diving and banking right

When you begin, be sure to start with question number 91 on Subtest 5 in your test booklet and number 91 on your answer sheet. Do not spend too much time on any one question.

STOP! DO NOT TURN THIS PAGE UNTIL TOLD TO DO SO.

practice test

15 Questions • 5 Minutes

Directions: Each of the following questions consists of a series of three sequential pictures that represents the pilot's view out of a helicopter windshield. The three pictures change from top to bottom showing a view from an aircraft in a climb, dive, bank to the left or right, or a combination of these maneuvers. Determine which position the cyclic would be in to perform the maneuver indicated by the pictures and blacken the appropriate cyclic circle on your answer sheet.

91.   92.

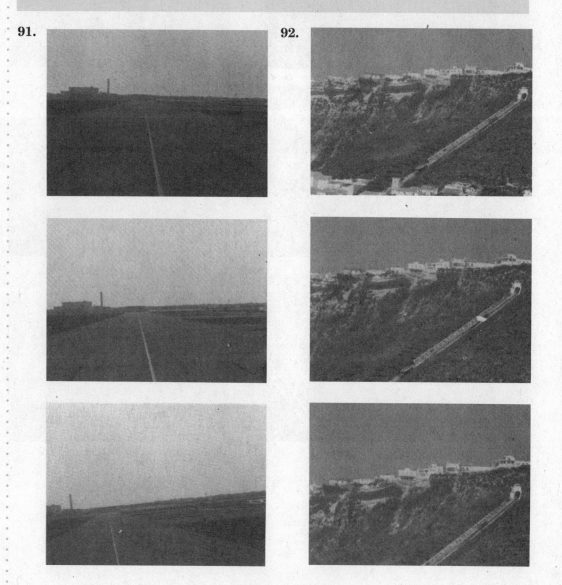

GO ON TO THE NEXT PAGE.

93.

94.

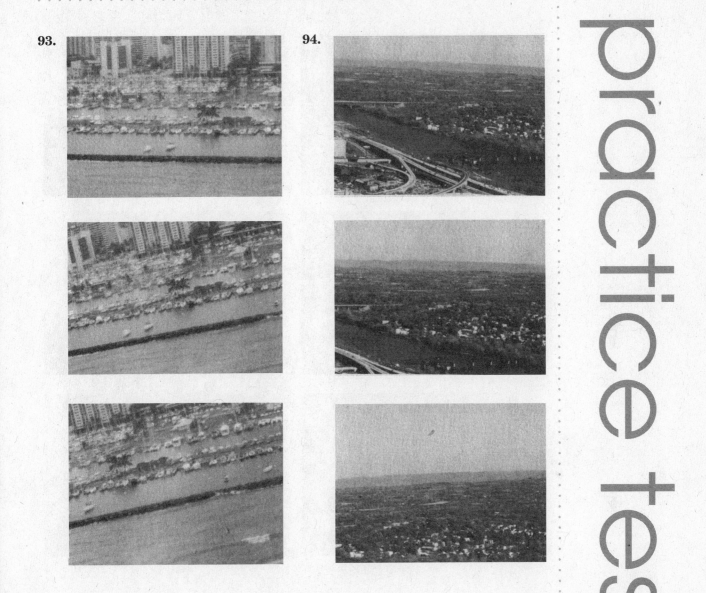

GO ON TO THE NEXT PAGE.

practice test

95.

96.

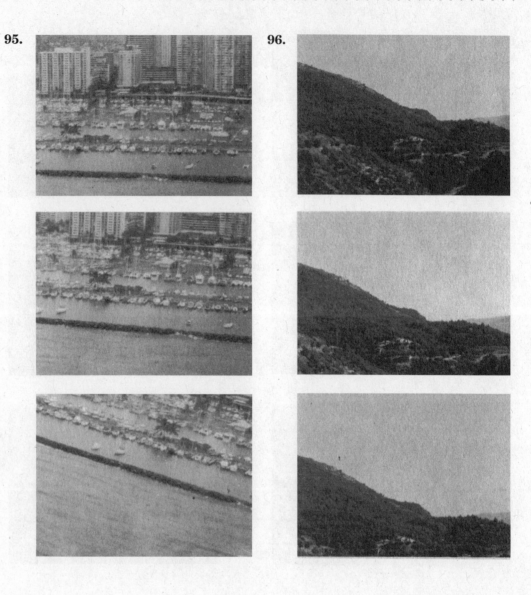

GO ON TO THE NEXT PAGE.

97.

98.

practice test

99.   **100.**

GO ON TO THE NEXT PAGE.

101. 102.

103.

104.

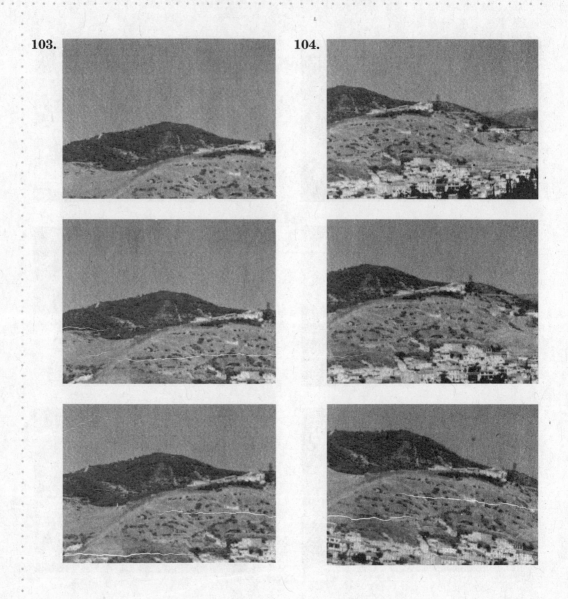

GO ON TO THE NEXT PAGE.

105.

practice test

SUBTEST 6: MECHANICAL FUNCTIONS

Directions: Decide which mechanical principle is illustrated in each picture. Pick the best answer. There is only one correct answer.

Now look at the sample question below.

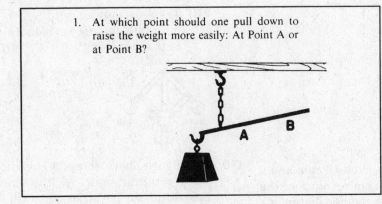

1. At which point should one pull down to raise the weight more easily: At Point A or at Point B?

Pulling down at B gives a longer lever arm, which results in raising the weight more easily. Choice (B) is the correct answer.

1. (A) ●

When you begin, be sure to start with question number 106 of Subtest 6 of your test booklet and number 106 on your answer sheet.

STOP! DO NOT TURN THIS PAGE UNTIL TOLD TO DO SO.

20 Questions • 10 Minutes

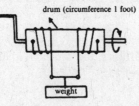

drum (circumference 1 foot)

weight

106. In the figure shown above, one complete revolution of the windlass drum will move the weight up

(A) 6 inches.

(B) 12 inches.

Valve

Cam

x
y

107. The figure above shows a cam and a valve. For each cam revolution, the vertical valve rise equals distance

(A) Y

(B) X

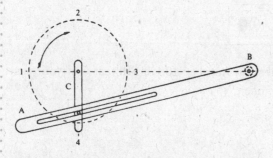

108. In the diagram above, crank arm C revolves at a constant speed of 400 RPM and drives the lever AB. When lever AB is moving the fastest, arm C will be in positions

(A) 1 and 3

(B) 2 and 4

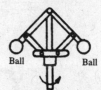

A
B

109. What is the function of A and B in the crankshaft shown in the drawing above?

(A) They strengthen the crankshaft by increasing its weight.

(B) They are necessary to maintain the proper balance of the crankshaft.

Ball   Ball

110. The figure above shows a governor on a rotating shaft. As the shaft speeds up, the governor balls will

(A) move down.

(B) move upward.

Brass

Iron

111. The figure above shows a brass and an iron strip continuously riveted together. High temperatures would probably

(A) have no effect at all.

(B) bend the strips.

GO ON TO THE NEXT PAGE.

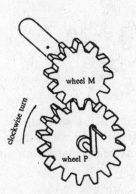

112. Study the gear wheels in the figure above, then determine which of the following statements is true.

(A) It will take less time for a tooth of wheel P to make a full turn than it will take a tooth of wheel M.

(B) It will take more time for a tooth of wheel P to make a full turn than it will for a tooth of wheel M.

113. Which hydraulic press requires the least force to lift the weight?

(A) A

(B) B

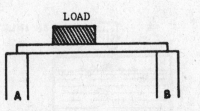

114. In the figure above, which upright supports the greater part of the load?

(A) Upright A

(B) Upright B

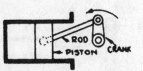

115. The figure above shows a crank and piston. The piston moves from mid-position to the extreme right if the crank

(A) makes a $\frac{3}{4}$ turn.

(B) makes one turn.

116. When the 100-pound weight is being slowly hoisted up by the pulley, as shown in the figure above, the downward pull on the ceiling to which the pulley is attached is

(A) 100 pounds.

(B) 150 pounds.

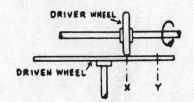

117. When the driver wheel is moved from location X to location Y, the driven wheel will

(A) turn slower.

(B) turn faster.

GO ON TO THE NEXT PAGE.

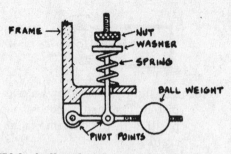

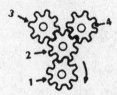

118. If the ball and spring mechanism are balanced in the position shown above, the ball will move upward if

  (A) the nut is loosened.

  (B) the nut is tightened.

119. Neglecting friction, what is the mechanical advantage in using the single fixed pulley shown above?

  (A) 1

  (B) 2

120. Four gears are shown in the figure above. If gear 1 turns as shown, then the gears turning in the same direction are

  (A) 2 and 3

  (B) 3 and 4

121. If both cyclists pedal at the same rate on the same surface, the cyclist in front will

  (A) travel at the same speed as the cyclist behind.

  (B) move faster than the cyclist behind.

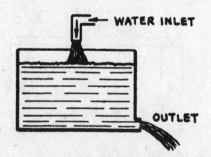

122. If water is flowing into the tank at the rate of 120 gallons per hour and flowing out of the tank at a constant rate of one gallon per minute, the water level in the tank will

  (A) rise 1 gallon per minute.

  (B) rise 2 gallons per minute.

GO ON TO THE NEXT PAGE.

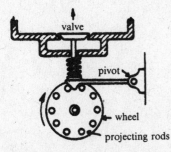

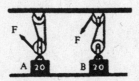

123. In order to open the valve in the figure above once every second, the wheel must rotate at

(A) 6 rpm.

(B) 10 rpm.

125. Which pulley arrangement requires less force at F in order to lift the weight?

(A) A

(B) B

124. In the figure above, a 150-pound individual jumps off a 500-pound raft to a point in the water 10 feet away. Theoretically, the raft will move

(A) 1 foot in the opposite direction.

(B) 3 feet in the opposite direction.

practice test

SUBTEST 7: SELF-DESCRIPTION

Directions: On this subtest you will read the question, then pick the one answer that applies best to you. Be honest in responding to these questions. Answer them as accurately as you can, to the best of your ability and recollection.

Now look at the sample question below.

1. From each pair, select the one activity you would prefer.

   (A) Keep a set of office files in order

   (B) Keep a piece of machinery in order

If you would prefer to keep a set of office files rather than a piece of machinery in order, select choice (A) and mark it in the appropriate space.

If you would prefer to keep a piece of machinery rather than a set of office files in order, select choice (B) and mark it in the appropriate space.

The 75 questions on this subtest are divided into five sections, as follows:

Section A: Questions 126–145 (5-option items)
Section B: Questions 146–165 (2-option items)
Section C: Questions 166–185 (2-option items)
Section D: Questions 186–194 (2-option items)
Section E: Questions 195–200 (4-option items)

When you begin, be sure to start with question number 126 in Section A of your test booklet and number 126 in Section A on your answer sheet.

STOP! DO NOT TURN THIS PAGE UNTIL TOLD TO DO SO.

75 Questions • 25 Minutes

Section A: Questions 126–145

The questions in this section consist of sets of five descriptive words from which you are to select the choice that MOST accurately describes you or the choice that LEAST describes you.

126. Which of the following MOST accurately describes you?

    (A) Adventurous
    (B) Energetic
    (C) Impetuous
    (D) Impulsive
    (E) Restless

127. Which one of the following LEAST describes you?

    (A) Adventurous
    (B) Energetic
    (C) Impetuous
    (D) Impulsive
    (E) Restless

128. Which one of the following MOST accurately describes you?

    (A) Ambitious
    (B) Emotional
    (C) Logical
    (D) Resourceful
    (E) Sentimental

129. Which one of the following LEAST describes you?

    (A) Ambitious
    (B) Emotional
    (C) Logical
    (D) Resourceful
    (E) Sentimental

130. Which one of the following MOST accurately describes you?

    (A) Cautious
    (B) Deliberate
    (C) Impatient
    (D) Impulsive
    (E) Patient

131. Which one of the following LEAST describes you?

    (A) Cautious
    (B) Deliberate
    (C) Impatient
    (D) Impulsive
    (E) Patient

132. Which one of the following MOST accurately describes you?

    (A) Competent
    (B) Gifted
    (C) Intelligent
    (D) Quick-witted
    (E) Skillful

133. Which one of the following LEAST describes you?

    (A) Competent
    (B) Gifted
    (C) Intelligent
    (D) Quick-witted
    (E) Skillful

134. Which one of the following MOST accurately describes you?

    (A) Compromising
    (B) Dependable
    (C) Independent
    (D) Sincere
    (E) Studious

GO ON TO THE NEXT PAGE.

135. Which one of the following LEAST describes you?

    (A) Compromising
    (B) Dependable
    (C) Independent
    (D) Sincere
    (E) Studious

136. Which one of the following MOST accurately describes you?

    (A) Condescending
    (B) Friendly
    (C) Pleasant
    (D) Polite
    (E) Reserved

137. Which one of the following LEAST describes you?

    (A) Condescending
    (B) Friendly
    (C) Pleasant
    (D) Polite
    (E) Reserved

138. Which one of the following MOST accurately describes you?

    (A) Courteous
    (B) Curious
    (C) Patronizing
    (D) Studious
    (E) Thoughtful

139. Which one of the following LEAST describes you?

    (A) Courteous
    (B) Curious
    (C) Patronizing
    (D) Studious
    (E) Thoughtful

140. Which one of the following MOST accurately describes you?

    (A) Discreet
    (B) Jealous
    (C) Loyal
    (D) Open-minded
    (E) Suspicious

141. Which one of the following LEAST describes you?

    (A) Discreet
    (B) Jealous
    (C) Loyal
    (D) Open-minded
    (E) Suspicious

142. Which one of the following MOST accurately describes you?

    (A) Economical
    (B) Extravagant
    (C) Lavish
    (D) Sensible
    (E) Thrifty

143. Which one of the following LEAST describes you?

    (A) Economical
    (B) Extravagant
    (C) Lavish
    (D) Sensible
    (E) Thrifty

144. Which one of the following MOST accurately describes you?

    (A) Generous
    (B) Intolerant
    (C) Judgmental
    (D) Opportunistic
    (E) Sensitive

practice test

GO ON TO THE NEXT PAGE.

145. Which one of the following LEAST describes you?

   (A) Generous

   (B) Intolerant

   (C) Judgmental

   (D) Opportunistic

   (E) Sensitive

Section B: Questions 146–165

The items in this section consist of questions that you must answer either with "Yes" or "No."

146. Did you generally start each new school year with a great deal of enthusiasm?

   (Y) Yes

   (N) No

147. Do you readily trust people?

   (Y) Yes

   (N) No

148. Do you generally have a strong opinion on most matters?

   (Y) Yes

   (N) No

149. Do you tend to speak rapidly?

   (Y) Yes

   (N) No

150. Do you like sports?

   (Y) Yes

   (N) No

151. Are you often in low spirits?

   (Y) Yes

   (N) No

152. Do you find off-color language offensive?

   (Y) Yes

   (N) No

153. Do you often find yourself finishing sentences for other people?

   (Y) Yes

   (N) No

154. Do you like to visit museums?

   (Y) Yes

   (N) No

155. Are you frequently in a hurry?

   (Y) Yes

   (N) No

156. Do you get much time to keep up with the things you like to do?

   (Y) Yes

   (N) No

157. When under pressure, do you tend to lose your temper?

   (Y) Yes

   (N) No

158. Did you enjoy going to school dances?

   (Y) Yes

   (N) No

159. Do you become upset when you think something is taking too long?

   (Y) Yes

   (N) No

160. Do you have trouble going to sleep at night?

   (Y) Yes

   (N) No

161. Do you wish you could do over some of the things you have done?

   (Y) Yes

   (N) No

162. Did you ever build a model airplane?

   (Y) Yes

   (N) No

GO ON TO THE NEXT PAGE.

163. Did you ever build a model airplane that could fly?

(Y) Yes

(N) No

164. Did you ever fly in a helicopter?

(Y) Yes

(N) No

165. Did you ever fly in a glider or pilot a hang glider?

(Y) Yes

(N) No

Section C: Questions 166–185

The items in this section consist of a listing of many occupations. Some may appeal to you; others may not. For each of the listed occupations you would like for a life career, answer by selecting "Like." For each of the listed occupations you would *not* like for a life career, answer by selecting "Dislike."

166. Artist

(L) Like

(D) Dislike

167. Author

(L) Like

(D) Dislike

168. Bank Teller

(L) Like

(D) Dislike

169. Clothing Designer

(L) Like

(D) Dislike

170. Electrician

(L) Like

(D) Dislike

171. Explorer

(L) Like

(D) Dislike

172. Inventor

(L) Like

(D) Dislike

173. Investigator

(L) Like

(D) Dislike

174. Lawyer

(L) Like

(D) Dislike

175. Musician

(L) Like

(D) Dislike

176. Nurse

(L) Like

(D) Dislike

177. Politician

(L) Like

(D) Dislike

178. Professional Ballplayer

(L) Like

(D) Dislike

179. Prison Warden

(L) Like

(D) Dislike

180. Research Scientist

(L) Like

(D) Dislike

181. Sales Manager

(L) Like

(D) Dislike

182. School Principal

(L) Like

(D) Dislike

183. Singer

(L) Like

(D) Dislike

GO ON TO THE NEXT PAGE.

practice test

184. Social Worker

    (L) Like

    (D) Dislike

185. Teacher

    (L) Like

    (D) Dislike

Section D: Questions 186–194

The questions in this section consist of pairs of statements describing personal characteristics and preferences. For each question, select the statement that describes you better.

186. **(A)** I feel happy most of the time.

    (B) I rarely see the bright side of life.

187. **(A)** I have a great deal of self-confidence.

    (B) I try to avoid getting together with people.

188. **(A)** I prefer working with people.

    (B) I prefer working with equipment or my hands.

189. **(A)** New and different experiences excite me.

    (B) New and different experiences frighten me.

190. **(A)** I prefer to work with competent coworkers.

    (B) I prefer to work with congenial coworkers.

191. **(A)** I enjoy engaging actively in athletic sports.

    (B) I enjoy watching athletic events.

192. **(A)** One of my most important career goals is security.

    (B) One of my most important career goals is high income.

193. **(A)** I rarely worry about what other people think of me.

    (B) It bothers me that people have wrong ideas about me.

194. **(A)** I prefer having a few close friends.

    (B) I prefer having many friends.

Section E: Questions 195–200

Each question in this section consists of a statement that may be considered somewhat controversial. Select one of the following choices that best describes the extent to which you agree or disagree with each statement:

    (A) Strongly agree

    (B) Tend to agree

    (C) Tend to disagree

    (D) Strongly disagree

195. Generally speaking, people get the recognition they deserve.

    (A) Strongly agree

    (B) Tend to agree

    (C) Tend to disagree

    (D) Strongly disagree

196. There is too much power concentrated in the hands of labor union officials.

    (A) Strongly agree

    (B) Tend to agree

    (C) Tend to disagree

    (D) Strongly disagree

197. Global warming is one of the most serious environmental problems facing us today.

    (A) Strongly agree

    (B) Tend to agree

    (C) Tend to disagree

    (D) Strongly disagree

GO ON TO THE NEXT PAGE.

198. Success at work depends on hard work; luck has very little to do with it.

(A) Strongly agree

(B) Tend to agree

(C) Tend to disagree

(D) Strongly disagree

199. Most people use politeness to cover up what is actually ruthless competition.

(A) Strongly agree

(B) Tend to agree

(C) Tend to disagree

(D) Strongly disagree

200. Breaking the law is hardly ever justified.

(A) Strongly agree

(B) Tend to agree

(C) Tend to disagree

(D) Strongly disagree

STOP! END OF TEST.

ANSWER KEY AND EXPLANATIONS

Subtest 1: Background Information Form

There are no "correct" answers to these 25 questions.

Subtest 2: Instrument Comprehension

26. E	29. B	32. B	35. C	38. D
27. C	30. D	33. A	36. E	39. B
28. A	31. D	34. E	37. A	40. C

26. The correct answer is (E). Not climbing or diving; no bank; heading 270° (west).

27. The correct answer is (C). Diving; no bank; heading 45° (northeast).

28. The correct answer is (A). Climbing; 30° right bank; heading 225° (southwest).

29. The correct answer is (B). Diving; 30° left bank; heading 360° (north).

30. The correct answer is (D). Not climbing or diving; 30° right bank; heading 135° (southeast).

31. The correct answer is (D). Climbing; no bank; heading 315° (northwest).

32. The correct answer is (B). Not climbing or diving; no bank; heading (south-southwest).

33. The correct answer is (A). Diving; 30° right bank; heading 315° (northwest).

34. The correct answer is (E). Climbing; no bank; heading 90° (east).

35. The correct answer is (C). Not climbing or diving; no bank; heading (north-northeast).

36. The correct answer is (E). Climbing; no bank; heading 360° (north).

37. The correct answer is (A). Not climbing or diving; 30° left bank; heading (north-northwest).

38. The correct answer is (D). Not climbing or diving; 30° right bank; heading 45° (northeast).

39. The correct answer is (B). Diving; no bank; heading 180° (south).

40. The correct answer is (C). Climbing; 30° left bank; heading 315° (northwest).

Subtest 3: Complex Movements

41. C	47. C	53. E	59. C	65. E
42. C	48. C	54. D	60. E	66. D
43. A	49. C	55. A	61. C	67. A
44. B	50. E	56. D	62. E	68. B
45. A	51. C	57. B	63. A	69. B
46. D	52. B	58. E	64. D	70. E

41. **The correct answer is (C).** (2 right, 1 up).

42. **The correct answer is (C).** (1 left, 1 down).

43. **The correct answer is (A).** (2 left, 3 up).

44. **The correct answer is (B).** (2 right, 2 up).

45. **The correct answer is (A).** (1 left, 3 up).

46. **The correct answer is (D).** (1 right, no vertical movement)

47. **The correct answer is (C).** (2 left, 3 down).

48. **The correct answer is (C).** (3 left, 1 up).

49. **The correct answer is (C).** (1 right, 3 down).

50. **The correct answer is (E).** (1 left, 1 up).

51. **The correct answer is (C).** (2 left, 1 down).

52. **The correct answer is (B).** (2 right, 3 up).

53. **The correct answer is (E).** (3 left, 3 down).

54. **The correct answer is (D).** (1 right, 1 down).

55. **The correct answer is (A).** (2 right, 3 down).

56. **The correct answer is (D).** (3 left, 1 down).

57. **The correct answer is (B).** (no horizontal movement, 2 up).

58. **The correct answer is (E).** (3 right, 1 down).

59. **The correct answer is (C).** (1 left, no vertical movement)

60. **The correct answer is (E).** (1 right, 3 up).

61. **The correct answer is (C).** (no horizontal movement, 1 down).

62. **The correct answer is (E).** (1 left, 3 down).

63. **The correct answer is (A).** (2 right, 2 down).

64. **The correct answer is (D).** (3 right, 3 down).

65. **The correct answer is (E).** (1 right, 2 up).

66. **The correct answer is (D).** (3 right, 2 up).

answers practice test 2

67. The correct answer is (A). (no horizontal movement, 3 up).

68. The correct answer is (B). (2 right, no vertical movement).

69. The correct answer is (B). (2 left, 2 down).

70. The correct answer is (E). (2 left, no vertical movement).

Subtest 4: Helicopter Knowledge

71. D	75. E	79. B	83. A	87. A
72. C	76. B	80. D	84. D	88. B
73. D	77. B	81. A	85. B	89. A
74. E	78. E	82. E	86. E	90. B

71. The correct answer is (D). The color combination of green, yellow, and white flashed by beacons indicates a lighted heliport.

72. The correct answer is (C). The auxiliary or tail rotor is the anti-torque rotor that produces thrust in the direction opposite to the torque reaction developed by the main rotor.

73. The correct answer is (D). The entire helicopter has a tendency to move in the direction of tail rotor thrust when hovering. This movement is generally referred to as translating tendency or drift.

74. The correct answer is (E). The upward bending of the rotor blades caused by the combined forces of lift and centrifugal force is called coning.

75. The correct answer is (E). The exact location and length of the CG range is specified for each helicopter, but it usually extends a short distance fore and aft of the main rotor mast.

76. The correct answer is (B). Dissymmetry of lift is created by horizontal flight or by wind during hovering flight. It is the difference in lift (unequal lift) across the rotor disc resulting from the difference in the velocity of air over the advancing blade half of the disc area and retreating blade half of the disc area.

77. The correct answer is (B). Ground resonance may develop when a series of shocks causes the rotor head to become unbalanced. When one landing gear of the helicopter strikes the surface first, a shock is transmitted through the fuselage to the rotor. When one of the other landing gears strikes, the unbalance can be aggravated and become even greater. This establishes a resonance, which sets up a pendulum-like oscillation of the fuselage—a severe wobbling or shaking.

78. The correct answer is (E). Rapid deceleration or quick stop is initiated by applying aft cyclic to reduce forward speed and lowering the collective pitch to counteract climbing.

79. The correct answer is (B). For slope takeoff, first obtain takeoff RPM and move the cyclic stick so that the rotor rotation is parallel to the true horizon rather than the slope. Apply up-collective pitch and apply pedal to maintain heading. As the downslope skid rises and the helicopter approaches a level altitude, move the cyclic stick back to the neutral position and take the helicopter straight up to a hover before moving away from the slope. The tail should not be turned upslope because of the danger of the tail rotor striking the surface.

80. **The correct answer is (D).** The helicopter should be landed on a cross-slope rather than on either an upslope or downslope. As the upslope skid touches the ground, the pilot should apply the cyclic stick in the direction of the slope. This will hold the skid against the slope while the downslope skid continues to be let down with the collective pitch.

81. **The correct answer is (A).** Standard conditions at sea level are: Atmospheric pressure: 29.92 inHg (inches of mercury); Temperature: 59°F. (15°C.)

82. **The correct answer is (E).** A running takeoff is used when conditions of load and/or density altitude prevent a sustained hover at normal hovering altitude. It is often referred to as a high-altitude takeoff. A running takeoff may be accomplished safely only if surface area of sufficient length and smoothness is available and if no barriers exist in the flight-path to interfere with a shallow climb.

83. **The correct answer is (A).** Foot pedals in the cockpit permit the pilot to increase or decrease tail-rotor thrust, as needed, to neutralize torque effect.

84. **The correct answer is (D).** With a single main rotor rotating in a counterclockwise direction, the advancing blade will be in the right half of the rotor disc during forward flight.

85. **The correct answer is (B).** The collective pitch control lever changes the pitch angle of the main rotor blades simultaneously and equally.

86. **The correct answer is (E).** High altitude, high temperature, and high moisture content contribute to a high density altitude condition that lessens helicopter performance.

87. **The correct answer is (A).** The most favorable conditions for helicopter performance are the combination of a low-density altitude, light gross weight, and moderate-to-strong winds. The most adverse conditions are the combination of a high-density altitude, heavy gross weight, and calm or no wind.

88. **The correct answer is (B).** The acute angle between the chord line of an airfoil and the relative wind is called the angle of attack.

89. **The correct answer is (A).** The collective pitch controls starting, stopping, and rate of speed. Pedals are used to maintain heading and the cyclic is used to maintain ground track.

90. **The correct answer is (B).** True airspeed may be roughly computed by adding to the indicated airspeed, 2 percent of the indicated airspeed for each 1,000 feet of altitude above sea level.

answers practice test 2

Subtest 5: Cyclic Orientation

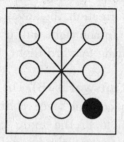

91. Climbing and banking right

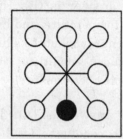

92. Climbing; no bank

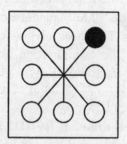

93. Diving and banking right

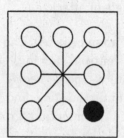

94. Climbing and banking right

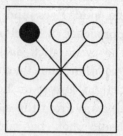

95. Diving and banking left

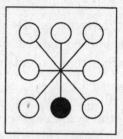

96. Climbing; no bank

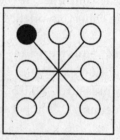

97. Diving and banking left

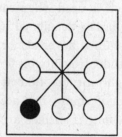

98. Climbing and banking left

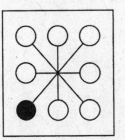

99. Climbing and banking left

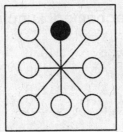

103. Diving; no bank

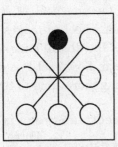

100. Diving; no bank

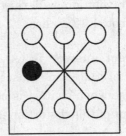

104. Left bank

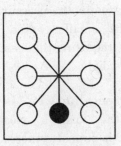

101. Climbing; no bank

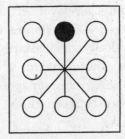

105. Diving; no bank

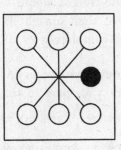

102. Right bank

answers practice test 2

Subtest 6: Mechanical Functions

106. B	110. B	114. A	118. B	122. A
107. A	111. B	115. A	119. A	123. A
108. A	112. B	116. B	120. B	124. B
109. B	113. A	117. A	121. B	125. A

106. The correct answer is (B). One complete revolution will raise the weight 1 foot or 12 inches.

107. The correct answer is (A). The distortion of the cam causes the valve to rise when contact is made. The amount of this distortion is the length Y.

108. The correct answer is (A). The slowest points for lever AB are 2 and 4, where the direction reverses and the velocity momentarily becomes zero. The midpoint, 1 or 3, represents the maximum speed, as it is halfway between these minimum points.

109. The correct answer is (B). The function of A and B in the crankshaft is to counterbalance the weight for smooth piston motion.

110. The correct answer is (B). The centrifugal force acts to pull the balls outward. Since the two balls are connected to a yolk around the center bar, this outward motion pulls the balls upward.

111. The correct answer is (B). The figure shown is a bimetallic strip that works like the wire in a thermostat. High temperatures will cause the metals to heat unevenly. The rivets will keep the strips together, so the only thing that they can do is bend.

112. The correct answer is (B). Wheel P has 16 teeth; wheel M has 12 teeth. When wheel M makes a full turn, wheel P will still have 4 more teeth to turn. So wheel P is slower and will take more time to turn.

113. The correct answer is (A). Pressure is defined as $\frac{\text{Force}}{\text{Area}}$. For a given force, 20 lbs., the smaller the area, the greater the pressure produced. The smallest area is at position A, requiring the least force to lift the weight.

114. The correct answer is (A). Because the load is closer to upright A, it supports more of the load. If the load were directly over A, all of the weight would be supported by A; then upright B could be removed completely.

115. The correct answer is (A). The piston is now in part of the compression stroke; $\frac{1}{4}$ turn will move it to full compression; $\frac{1}{2}$ more turn will move it to the end of the power stroke. Adding $\frac{1}{4} + \frac{1}{2} = \frac{3}{4}$ turn.

116. The correct answer is (B). The downward pull of the 100-lb. weight being hoisted plus the 50-lb. effort = 150 lbs.

117. The correct answer is (A). Imagine the driven wheel as a record. For one rotation of the record, point Y travels much farther than point X. It takes more turns of the driver wheel to turn point Y one complete revolution.

118. The correct answer is (B). The ball will move up if the arm holding it is pulled up. This will happen when the nut is tightened.

119. The correct answer is (A). A single fixed pulley is actually a first-class lever with equal arms. The mechanical advantage, neglecting friction, is 1.

120. The correct answer is (B). Gear 1 turns clockwise; gear 2 turns counterclockwise; gears 3 and 4 turn clockwise.

121. The correct answer is (B). The formula for circumference of a wheel is $C = 2\pi r$. The wheel radius of the bike in front is larger. One revolution of the larger wheel will cover a greater linear distance along the road in a given period of time.

122. The correct answer is (A). The water is filling up in the tank at a rate of 120 gallons per hour, or 2 gallons per minute $\left(\dfrac{120}{60} = 2\right)$. The tank is also emptying at a rate of 1 gallon per minute. The net flow is increasing by 1 gallon per minute, since 2 gal./min input − 1 gal./min output = 1 gal./min increase.

Note: The easiest way to find the answer is to change all measurements to gallons per minute.

123. The correct answer is (A). Once every second = 60 times a minute. With 10 projection rods on the wheel, the wheel must rotate at 6 rpm to make 60 rod contacts per minute.

124. The correct answer is (B). The raft will move in the opposite direction. Let x = theoretical distance moved.

$$10 \times 150 = x \times 500$$
$$500x = 1500$$
$$x = \frac{1500}{500} = 3 \text{ feet}$$

125. The correct answer is (A). The mechanical advantage is calculated by the number of strands supporting the weight. A has 3 strands, B has 2.

Subtest 7: Self-Description Form

There are no correct answers to these questions.

ANSWER SHEET

SIDE 1

ANSWER SHEET
for
NAVY and MARINE CORPS
AVIATION SELECTION TEST BATTERY

NAME _____
       Last   First   MI.

TEST
DATE ____ / ____ / ____
     Month   Day   Year

INSTALLATION OR
PLACE OF TESTING _____

SCHEMATIC SAMPLE

STATUS
- ○ Civilian
- ○ Officer, Navy
- ○ Officer, Marine Corps
- ○ Officer, Coast Guard
- ○ Enlisted, Navy
- ○ Enlisted, Marine Corps
- ○ Enlisted, Coast Guard
- ○ Officer Candidate–ROTC
- ○ Naval Academy
- ○ Other

EDUCATION LEVEL	RACE/ETHNIC GROUP	SEX
○ High School Graduate	○ American Indian	○ Male
○ College Freshman	○ Hispanic	○ Female
○ College Sophomore	○ Asian	
○ College Junior	○ Black	
○ College Senior	○ White	
○ College Graduate	○ Other	
○ Graduate Student		
○ Other		

SOCIAL SECURITY NUMBER

DATE OF BIRTH — MO. DAY YR.

(grid of bubbles 0–9)

Math Skills Test

1. Ⓐ Ⓑ Ⓒ Ⓓ	7. Ⓐ Ⓑ Ⓒ Ⓓ	13. Ⓐ Ⓑ Ⓒ Ⓓ	19. Ⓐ Ⓑ Ⓒ Ⓓ	25. Ⓐ Ⓑ Ⓒ Ⓓ
2. Ⓐ Ⓑ Ⓒ Ⓓ	8. Ⓐ Ⓑ Ⓒ Ⓓ	14. Ⓐ Ⓑ Ⓒ Ⓓ	20. Ⓐ Ⓑ Ⓒ Ⓓ	26. Ⓐ Ⓑ Ⓒ Ⓓ
3. Ⓐ Ⓑ Ⓒ Ⓓ	9. Ⓐ Ⓑ Ⓒ Ⓓ	15. Ⓐ Ⓑ Ⓒ Ⓓ	21. Ⓐ Ⓑ Ⓒ Ⓓ	27. Ⓐ Ⓑ Ⓒ Ⓓ
4. Ⓐ Ⓑ Ⓒ Ⓓ	10. Ⓐ Ⓑ Ⓒ Ⓓ	16. Ⓐ Ⓑ Ⓒ Ⓓ	22. Ⓐ Ⓑ Ⓒ Ⓓ	28. Ⓐ Ⓑ Ⓒ Ⓓ
5. Ⓐ Ⓑ Ⓒ Ⓓ	11. Ⓐ Ⓑ Ⓒ Ⓓ	17. Ⓐ Ⓑ Ⓒ Ⓓ	23. Ⓐ Ⓑ Ⓒ Ⓓ	29. Ⓐ Ⓑ Ⓒ Ⓓ
6. Ⓐ Ⓑ Ⓒ Ⓓ	12. Ⓐ Ⓑ Ⓒ Ⓓ	18. Ⓐ Ⓑ Ⓒ Ⓓ	24. Ⓐ Ⓑ Ⓒ Ⓓ	30. Ⓐ Ⓑ Ⓒ Ⓓ

Reading Skills Test

1. Ⓐ Ⓑ Ⓒ Ⓓ	7. Ⓐ Ⓑ Ⓒ Ⓓ	13. Ⓐ Ⓑ Ⓒ Ⓓ	18. Ⓐ Ⓑ Ⓒ Ⓓ	23. Ⓐ Ⓑ Ⓒ Ⓓ
2. Ⓐ Ⓑ Ⓒ Ⓓ	8. Ⓐ Ⓑ Ⓒ Ⓓ	14. Ⓐ Ⓑ Ⓒ Ⓓ	19. Ⓐ Ⓑ Ⓒ Ⓓ	24. Ⓐ Ⓑ Ⓒ Ⓓ
3. Ⓐ Ⓑ Ⓒ Ⓓ	9. Ⓐ Ⓑ Ⓒ Ⓓ	15. Ⓐ Ⓑ Ⓒ Ⓓ	20. Ⓐ Ⓑ Ⓒ Ⓓ	25. Ⓐ Ⓑ Ⓒ Ⓓ
4. Ⓐ Ⓑ Ⓒ Ⓓ	10. Ⓐ Ⓑ Ⓒ Ⓓ	16. Ⓐ Ⓑ Ⓒ Ⓓ	21. Ⓐ Ⓑ Ⓒ Ⓓ	26. Ⓐ Ⓑ Ⓒ Ⓓ
5. Ⓐ Ⓑ Ⓒ Ⓓ	11. Ⓐ Ⓑ Ⓒ Ⓓ	17. Ⓐ Ⓑ Ⓒ Ⓓ	22. Ⓐ Ⓑ Ⓒ Ⓓ	27. Ⓐ Ⓑ Ⓒ Ⓓ
6. Ⓐ Ⓑ Ⓒ Ⓓ	12. Ⓐ Ⓑ Ⓒ Ⓓ			

Mechanical Comprehension Test

1. Ⓐ Ⓑ Ⓒ	7. Ⓐ Ⓑ Ⓒ	13. Ⓐ Ⓑ Ⓒ	19. Ⓐ Ⓑ Ⓒ	25. Ⓐ Ⓑ Ⓒ
2. Ⓐ Ⓑ Ⓒ	8. Ⓐ Ⓑ Ⓒ	14. Ⓐ Ⓑ Ⓒ	20. Ⓐ Ⓑ Ⓒ	26. Ⓐ Ⓑ Ⓒ
3. Ⓐ Ⓑ Ⓒ	9. Ⓐ Ⓑ Ⓒ	15. Ⓐ Ⓑ Ⓒ	21. Ⓐ Ⓑ Ⓒ	27. Ⓐ Ⓑ Ⓒ
4. Ⓐ Ⓑ Ⓒ	10. Ⓐ Ⓑ Ⓒ	16. Ⓐ Ⓑ Ⓒ	22. Ⓐ Ⓑ Ⓒ	28. Ⓐ Ⓑ Ⓒ
5. Ⓐ Ⓑ Ⓒ	11. Ⓐ Ⓑ Ⓒ	17. Ⓐ Ⓑ Ⓒ	23. Ⓐ Ⓑ Ⓒ	29. Ⓐ Ⓑ Ⓒ
6. Ⓐ Ⓑ Ⓒ	12. Ⓐ Ⓑ Ⓒ	18. Ⓐ Ⓑ Ⓒ	24. Ⓐ Ⓑ Ⓒ	30. Ⓐ Ⓑ Ⓒ

answer sheet

SIDE 2

ANSWER SHEET
for
NAVY and MARINE CORPS
AVIATION SELECTION TEST BATTERY

SCHEMATIC SAMPLE

Spatial Apperception Test

1. Ⓐ Ⓑ Ⓒ Ⓓ Ⓔ	6. Ⓐ Ⓑ Ⓒ Ⓓ Ⓔ	11. Ⓐ Ⓑ Ⓒ Ⓓ Ⓔ	16. Ⓐ Ⓑ Ⓒ Ⓓ Ⓔ	21. Ⓐ Ⓑ Ⓒ Ⓓ Ⓔ
2. Ⓐ Ⓑ Ⓒ Ⓓ Ⓔ	7. Ⓐ Ⓑ Ⓒ Ⓓ Ⓔ	12. Ⓐ Ⓑ Ⓒ Ⓓ Ⓔ	17. Ⓐ Ⓑ Ⓒ Ⓓ Ⓔ	22. Ⓐ Ⓑ Ⓒ Ⓓ Ⓔ
3. Ⓐ Ⓑ Ⓒ Ⓓ Ⓔ	8. Ⓐ Ⓑ Ⓒ Ⓓ Ⓔ	13. Ⓐ Ⓑ Ⓒ Ⓓ Ⓔ	18. Ⓐ Ⓑ Ⓒ Ⓓ Ⓔ	23. Ⓐ Ⓑ Ⓒ Ⓓ Ⓔ
4. Ⓐ Ⓑ Ⓒ Ⓓ Ⓔ	9. Ⓐ Ⓑ Ⓒ Ⓓ Ⓔ	14. Ⓐ Ⓑ Ⓒ Ⓓ Ⓔ	19. Ⓐ Ⓑ Ⓒ Ⓓ Ⓔ	24. Ⓐ Ⓑ Ⓒ Ⓓ Ⓔ
5. Ⓐ Ⓑ Ⓒ Ⓓ Ⓔ	10. Ⓐ Ⓑ Ⓒ Ⓓ Ⓔ	15. Ⓐ Ⓑ Ⓒ Ⓓ Ⓔ	20. Ⓐ Ⓑ Ⓒ Ⓓ Ⓔ	25. Ⓐ Ⓑ Ⓒ Ⓓ Ⓔ

Aviation and Nautical Information Test

1. Ⓐ Ⓑ Ⓒ Ⓓ Ⓔ	7. Ⓐ Ⓑ Ⓒ Ⓓ Ⓔ	13. Ⓐ Ⓑ Ⓒ Ⓓ Ⓔ	19. Ⓐ Ⓑ Ⓒ Ⓓ Ⓔ	25. Ⓐ Ⓑ Ⓒ Ⓓ Ⓔ
2. Ⓐ Ⓑ Ⓒ Ⓓ Ⓔ	8. Ⓐ Ⓑ Ⓒ Ⓓ Ⓔ	14. Ⓐ Ⓑ Ⓒ Ⓓ Ⓔ	20. Ⓐ Ⓑ Ⓒ Ⓓ Ⓔ	26. Ⓐ Ⓑ Ⓒ Ⓓ Ⓔ
3. Ⓐ Ⓑ Ⓒ Ⓓ Ⓔ	9. Ⓐ Ⓑ Ⓒ Ⓓ Ⓔ	15. Ⓐ Ⓑ Ⓒ Ⓓ Ⓔ	21. Ⓐ Ⓑ Ⓒ Ⓓ Ⓔ	27. Ⓐ Ⓑ Ⓒ Ⓓ Ⓔ
4. Ⓐ Ⓑ Ⓒ Ⓓ Ⓔ	10. Ⓐ Ⓑ Ⓒ Ⓓ Ⓔ	16. Ⓐ Ⓑ Ⓒ Ⓓ Ⓔ	22. Ⓐ Ⓑ Ⓒ Ⓓ Ⓔ	28. Ⓐ Ⓑ Ⓒ Ⓓ Ⓔ
5. Ⓐ Ⓑ Ⓒ Ⓓ Ⓔ	11. Ⓐ Ⓑ Ⓒ Ⓓ Ⓔ	17. Ⓐ Ⓑ Ⓒ Ⓓ Ⓔ	23. Ⓐ Ⓑ Ⓒ Ⓓ Ⓔ	29. Ⓐ Ⓑ Ⓒ Ⓓ Ⓔ
6. Ⓐ Ⓑ Ⓒ Ⓓ Ⓔ	12. Ⓐ Ⓑ Ⓒ Ⓓ Ⓔ	18. Ⓐ Ⓑ Ⓒ Ⓓ Ⓔ	24. Ⓐ Ⓑ Ⓒ Ⓓ Ⓔ	30. Ⓐ Ⓑ Ⓒ Ⓓ Ⓔ

Aviation Supplemental Test

1. Ⓐ Ⓑ Ⓒ Ⓓ	8. Ⓐ Ⓑ Ⓒ	15. Ⓐ Ⓑ Ⓒ Ⓓ	22. Ⓐ Ⓑ Ⓒ Ⓓ	29. Ⓐ Ⓑ Ⓒ Ⓓ Ⓔ
2. Ⓐ Ⓑ Ⓒ Ⓓ	9. Ⓐ Ⓑ Ⓒ	16. Ⓐ Ⓑ Ⓒ Ⓓ	23. Ⓐ Ⓑ Ⓒ Ⓓ	30. Ⓐ Ⓑ Ⓒ Ⓓ Ⓔ
3. Ⓐ Ⓑ Ⓒ Ⓓ	10. Ⓐ Ⓑ Ⓒ	17. Ⓐ Ⓑ Ⓒ Ⓓ	24. Ⓐ Ⓑ Ⓒ Ⓓ	31. Ⓐ Ⓑ Ⓒ Ⓓ Ⓔ
4. Ⓐ Ⓑ Ⓒ Ⓓ	11. Ⓐ Ⓑ Ⓒ	18. Ⓐ Ⓑ Ⓒ Ⓓ	25. Ⓐ Ⓑ Ⓒ Ⓓ	32. Ⓐ Ⓑ Ⓒ Ⓓ Ⓔ
5. Ⓐ Ⓑ Ⓒ Ⓓ	12. Ⓐ Ⓑ Ⓒ	19. Ⓐ Ⓑ Ⓒ Ⓓ	26. Ⓐ Ⓑ Ⓒ Ⓓ Ⓔ	33. Ⓐ Ⓑ Ⓒ Ⓓ Ⓔ
6. Ⓐ Ⓑ Ⓒ Ⓓ	13. Ⓐ Ⓑ Ⓒ Ⓓ	20. Ⓐ Ⓑ Ⓒ Ⓓ	27. Ⓐ Ⓑ Ⓒ Ⓓ Ⓔ	34. Ⓐ Ⓑ Ⓒ Ⓓ Ⓔ
7. Ⓐ Ⓑ Ⓒ Ⓓ	14. Ⓐ Ⓑ Ⓒ Ⓓ	21. Ⓐ Ⓑ Ⓒ Ⓓ	28. Ⓐ Ⓑ Ⓒ Ⓓ Ⓔ	

TEST 1: MATH SKILLS TEST

30 Questions • 25 Minutes

Directions: The following questions consist of a math problem followed by four possible answers. Decide which one of the four choices is the correct answer.

1. Two trains running on the same track travel at the rates of 30 and 35 mph, respectively. If the slower train starts out an hour earlier, how long will it take the faster train to catch up with it?

   (A) 4 hours
   (B) 5 hours
   (C) 6 hours
   (D) 7 hours

2. A naval detachment has enough rations to feed sixteen people for 10 days. If four more people join the detachment, for how many fewer days will the rations last?

   (A) 1
   (B) 2
   (C) 3
   (D) 4

3. A field can be plowed by 9 machines in 5 hours. If 3 machines are broken and cannot be used, how many hours will it take to plow the field?

   (A) $7\frac{1}{2}$ hours

   (B) $8\frac{1}{2}$ hours

   (C) $9\frac{1}{2}$ hours

   (D) $10\frac{1}{2}$ hours

4. What is the square root of 9 raised to the fourth power?

   (A) 12
   (B) 27
   (C) 49
   (D) 81

5. If $2^{n-2} = 32$, then n equals

   (A) 5
   (B) 7
   (C) 8
   (D) 12

6. If the sum of the edges of a cube is 48 inches, what is the volume of the cube?

   (A) 4 cubic inches
   (B) 8 cubic inches
   (C) 16 cubic inches
   (D) 64 cubic inches

7. How much pure acid must be added to 12 ounces of a 40% acid solution in order to produce a 60% acid solution?

   (A) 5 ounces
   (B) 6 ounces
   (C) 7 ounces
   (D) 8 ounces

8. A farmer who is 6 feet tall wants to determine the height of his barn. He notices that his shadow is 10 feet long and that his barn casts a shadow 75 feet long. How high is the barn?

   (A) 30 feet
   (B) 35 feet
   (C) 40 feet
   (D) 45 feet

9. If $(x - y)^2 = 40$ and $x^2 + y^2 = 60$, then $xy =$

   (A) 40
   (B) 20
   (C) 12
   (D) 10

GO ON TO THE NEXT PAGE.

10. In the figure shown below, what is the measure of angle x?

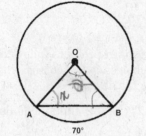

(A) 35°

(B) 45°

(C) 55°

(D) 70°

11. Jane received grades of 90, 88, and 75 on three tests. What grade must she receive on the next test so that her average for these four tests is 86?

(A) 88

(B) 89

(C) 90

(D) 91

12. A family drove from New York to San Francisco, a distance of 3000 miles. They drove $\frac{1}{10}$ of the distance the first day and $\frac{1}{9}$ of the remaining distance the second day. How many miles were left to be driven?

(A) 2200 miles

(B) 2300 miles

(C) 2400 miles

(D) 2500 miles

13. In a 3-hour examination of 320 questions, there are 40 mathematics problems. If twice as much time should be allowed for each mathematics problem as for each of the other questions, how many minutes should be spent on the mathematics problems?

(A) 40 minutes

(B) 45 minutes

(C) 50 minutes

(D) 55 minutes

14. 100,000 may be represented as

(A) 10^4

(B) 10^5

(C) 10^6

(D) 10^7

15. If $a = 3b$ and $6b = 12c$, then $a =$

(A) $6c$

(B) $9c$

(C) $12c$

(D) $15c$

16. A cash box contains a certain number of coins, of which 53 are dimes and 19 are nickels. The rest of the coins in the box are quarters. If the probability of selecting a quarter from this bank is 1/4, how many quarters does the bank contain?

(A) 24

(B) 27

(C) 30

(D) 35

17. A CD system originally priced at $500 is first discounted by 10%, then later by another 10%. If a 20% tax is added to the purchase price, how much would a customer buying the system at its lowest price pay for it to the nearest dollar, including tax?

(A) $413

(B) $480

(C) $486

(D) $500

GO ON TO THE NEXT PAGE.

18. A closed rectangular box with a square base is 5 inches high. If the volume of the box is 45 square inches, what is the box's surface area in square inches?

    (A) 66
    (B) 78
    (C) 81
    (D) 90

19. If x varies directly as y^2 and if $x = 9$ when $y = 2$, what is the value of x when $y = 8$?

    (A) 32
    (B) 130
    (C) 144
    (D) 168

20. An island is defended by a battery of coastal guns placed at the easternmost point of the island and having a maximum range of 10 miles. A ship, sailing due north at 24 mph along a course that will bring it within 8 miles of these guns, is approaching the position where it will be 10 miles from these guns. Assuming that the ship will maintain a straight course and the same speed, for approximately how long will the ship be within range of the coastal guns?

    (A) 15 minutes
    (B) 20 minutes
    (C) 25 minutes
    (D) 30 minutes

21. A tank that holds 450 gallons of water can be filled by one pipe in 15 minutes and emptied by another in 30 minutes. How long would it take to fill the tank if both pipes are open?

    (A) 30 minutes
    (B) 31 minutes
    (C) 32 minutes
    (D) 33 minutes

22. A class of 204 recruits consists of three racial and ethnic groups. If $\frac{1}{3}$ are black, $\frac{1}{4}$ are Hispanic, and the remaining recruits are white, how many of the recruits in the class are white?

    (A) 94
    (B) 85
    (C) 75
    (D) 68

23. If a driver completes a trip of 120 miles at the rate of 30 mph, at what rate would the driver have to travel on the return trip in order to average 40 mph for the round trip?

    (A) 50 mph
    (B) 55 mph
    (C) 60 mph
    (D) 65 mph

24. If x is less than 0 and y is less than 0, then

    (A) x is greater than y.
    (B) y is greater than x.
    (C) xy is less than 0.
    (D) xy is greater than 0.

25. Angle E is 30° larger than its complement. The number of degrees in angle E is

    (A) 30°
    (B) 45°
    (C) 60°
    (D) 90°

26. Two ships are 1,800 miles apart and sailing toward each other. One sails at the rate of 95 miles per day and the other at the rate of 75 miles per day. How far apart will they be at the end of 8 days?

    (A) 364 miles
    (B) 380 miles
    (C) 440 miles
    (D) 500 miles

GO ON TO THE NEXT PAGE.

27. Successive discounts of 20 percent and 15 percent are equivalent to a single discount of

    (A) 32 percent.
    (B) 33 percent.
    (C) 34 percent.
    (D) 35 percent.

28. A bridge crosses a river that is 1520 feet wide. One bank of the river holds $\frac{1}{5}$ of the bridge, while the other holds $\frac{1}{6}$ of it. How long is the bridge?

    (A) 2200 feet
    (B) 2300 feet
    (C) 2400 feet
    (D) 2500 feet

29. What is the perimeter of a right triangle whose legs are 6 and 8 feet?

    (A) 10 feet
    (B) 14 feet
    (C) 20 feet
    (D) 24 feet

30. The fourth root of 16 is

    (A) 2
    (B) 3
    (C) 4
    (D) 8

STOP! DO NOT GO ON UNTIL TIME IS UP.

TEST 2: READING SKILLS TEST

27 Questions • 25 Minutes

Directions: Each item consists of a passage which you should assume to be true, followed by four possible answer choices. For each item, select the choice that can be inferred *only* from the passage itself. Some or all of the choices following each passage may be true and reasonable, but only one of them can be derived solely from the information in the passage.

1. "In a pole-vaulting competition, the judge decides on the minimum height to be jumped. The vaulter may attempt to jump any height above the minimum. Using flexible fiberglass poles, vaulters have jumped as high as 18 feet, 8¼ inches."

   This passage means most nearly that

   (A) pole vaulters may attempt to jump any height in competition.

   (B) pole vaulters must jump higher than 18 feet, 8¼ inches to win.

   (C) pole vaulters must jump higher than the height set by the judge.

   (D) pole vaulters must use fiberglass poles.

2. "Only about one-tenth of an iceberg is visible above water. Eight to nine times as much ice is hidden below the waterline. In the Antarctic Ocean, near the South Pole, there are icebergs that rise as high as 300 feet above the water."

   The passage best supports the statement that icebergs in the Antarctic Ocean

   (A) are usually 300 feet high.

   (B) can be as much as 3,000 feet high.

   (C) are difficult to spot.

   (D) are hazards to navigation.

3. "You can tell a frog from a toad by its skin. In general, a frog's skin is moist, smooth, and shiny, but a toad's skin is dry, dull, and rough or covered with warts. Frogs are also better at jumping than toads are."

   The passage best supports the statement that

   (A) you can recognize a toad by its great jumping ability.

   (B) you can recognize a toad by its smooth, shiny skin.

   (C) you can recognize a toad by its lack of warts.

   (D) you can recognize a toad by its dry, rough skin.

4. "Thomas Edison was responsible for more than 1,000 inventions in his 84-year lifespan. Among the most famous of his inventions are the phonograph, the electric light bulb, motion picture film, the electric generator, and the battery."

   This passage means most nearly that

   (A) Thomas Edison was the most famous inventor.

   (B) Thomas Edison was responsible for 84 inventions.

   (C) Thomas Edison invented many things in his short life.

   (D) Thomas Edison invented the phonograph and motion picture film.

GO ON TO THE NEXT PAGE.

5. "Amateur sportsmen and sportswomen are those who take part in sports purely for enjoyment, not for financial reward. Professional sportsmen and sportswomen are people who are paid to participate in sports. Most athletes who compete in the Olympic Games are amateurs."

The passage best supports the statement that an amateur sportsperson might be

(A) an Olympic champion.

(B) a member of the Pittsburgh Steelers.

(C) the holder of the heavyweight boxing crown.

(D) a participant in the World Series.

6. "A year—the time it takes Earth to go exactly once around the sun—is not 365 days. It is actually 365 days, 6 hours, 9 minutes, 9½ seconds—or 365¼ days. Leap years make up for this discrepancy by adding an extra day to the calendar once every four years."

This passage means most nearly that

(A) the purpose of leap years is to adjust for the fact that it takes 365¼ days for Earth to circle the sun.

(B) the purpose of leap years is to make up for time lost in the work year.

(C) the purpose of leap years is to occur every four years.

(D) the purpose of leap years is to allow for differences in the length of a year in each time zone.

7. "Scientists are taking a closer look at the recent boom in the use of wood for heating. Wood burning, it seems, releases high-level pollutants. It is believed that burning wood produces a thousand times more CO—carbon monoxide—than natural gas does when it burns."

The passage best supports the statement that CO is

(A) natural gas.

(B) wood.

(C) carbon monoxide.

(D) heat.

8. "The average American family makes a move every ten years. This means that family history becomes scattered. In some cases, a person searching for his or her family's past must hire a professional researcher to track down ancestors."

This passage means most nearly that every few years,

(A) somebody tries to trace his or her family's history.

(B) the average American family moves.

(C) family history becomes scattered.

(D) professional researchers are hired to track down ancestors.

9. "When gas is leaking, any spark or sudden flame can ignite it. This can create a 'flashback,' which burns off the gas in a quick puff of smoke and flame. But the real danger is a large leak, which can cause an explosion."

The passage best supports the statement that the real danger from leaking gas is

(A) a flashback.

(B) a puff of smoke and flame.

(C) an explosion.

(D) a spark.

GO ON TO THE NEXT PAGE.

10. "With the exception of Earth, all of the planets in our solar system are named for gods and goddesses in Greek or Roman mythology. This is because other planets were thought to be in heaven, like the gods, and our planet lay beneath, like the earth."

The passage best supports the statement that all the planets except Earth

(A) were part of Greek and Roman mythology.

(B) were thought to be in heaven.

(C) are part of the same solar system.

(D) were worshipped as gods.

11. "The Supreme Court was established by Article 3 of the Constitution. Since 1869, it has been made up of nine members—the Chief Justice and eight associate justices—who are appointed for life. Supreme Court justices are named by the President and must be confirmed by the Senate."

This passage means most nearly that the Supreme Court

(A) was established in 1869.

(B) consists of nine judges.

(C) consists of judges appointed by the Senate.

(D) changes with each presidential election.

12. "The sport of automobile racing originated in France in 1894. There are five basic types of competition: (1) the grand prix, a series of races that leads to a world championship; (2) stock car racing, which uses specially equipped standard cars; (3) midget car racing; (4) sports car racing; and (5) drag racing. The best-known U.S. race is the Indianapolis 500, first held in 1911."

The passage best supports the statement that the sport of auto racing

(A) started with the Indianapolis 500 in 1911.

(B) uses only standard cars, which are specially equipped.

(C) holds its championship race in France.

(D) includes five different types of competition.

13. "The brain controls both voluntary behavior such as walking and talking, and most involuntary behavior such as the beating of the heart and breathing. In higher animals, the brain is also the site of emotions, memory, self-awareness, and thought."

The passage best supports the statement that in higher animals, the brain controls

(A) emotion, memory, and thought.

(B) voluntary behavior.

(C) most involuntary behavior.

(D) all of the above.

14. "The speed of a boat is measured in knots. One knot is equal to a speed of one nautical mile per hour. A nautical mile is equal to 6,080 feet, while an ordinary mile is 5,280 feet."

This passage means most nearly that

(A) a nautical mile is longer than an ordinary mile.

(B) a speed of 2 knots is the same as 2 miles per hour.

(C) a knot is the same as a mile.

(D) the distance a boat travels is measured in knots.

15. "It is recommended that the net be held by not more than 14 persons nor less than 10 persons, although under certain conditions it may become necessary to use fewer persons."

According to this passage, it is

(A) best to use between 10 and 14 persons on the net.

(B) better to use 10 persons on the net rather than 14.

(C) impossible to use a net unless at least 10 persons are available to hold it.

(D) sometimes advisable to use more than 14 persons on the net.

16. "The overuse of antibiotics today represents a growing danger, according to many medical authorities. Patients everywhere, stimulated by reports of new wonder drugs, continue to ask their doctors for a shot to relieve a cold, flu, or any other viral infections that occur during the course of a bad winter. But, for the common cold and many other viral infections, antibiotics have no effect."

The passage best supports the statement that

(A) the use of antibiotics is becoming a health hazard.

(B) antibiotics are of no value in treating many viral infections.

(C) patients should ask their doctors for a shot of one of the new wonder drugs to relieve the symptoms of the flu.

(D) the treatment of colds and other viral infections by antibiotics will lessen their severity.

17. "In examining the scene of a homicide, one should not only look for the usual, standard traces—fingerprints, footprints, etc.—but also take notice of details that at first glance may not seem to have any connection to the crime."

One may conclude from the above statement that at the scene of a homicide,

(A) one cannot tell in advance what will be important.

(B) only the usual, standard traces are important.

(C) sometimes one should not look for footprints.

(D) standard traces are not generally available.

GO ON TO THE NEXT PAGE.

18. "Alertness and attentiveness are essential qualities for success as a telephone operator. The work the operator performs often requires careful attention under conditions of stress."

The passage best supports the statement that a telephone operator

(A) always works under stress.

(B) cannot be successful unless he or she memorizes many telephone numbers.

(C) must be trained before he or she can render good service.

(D) must be able to work under difficult conditions.

19. "To prevent industrial accidents, safety devices must be used to guard exposed machinery, the light in the plant must be adequate, and mechanics should be instructed in safety rules that they must follow for their own protection."

The passage best supports the statement that industrial accidents

(A) are always avoidable.

(B) may be due to ignorance.

(C) usually result from inadequate machinery.

(D) cannot be entirely overcome.

20. "The leader of an industrial enterprise has two principal functions. He or she must manufacture and distribute a product at a profit, and he or she must keep individuals and groups of individuals working effectively."

The passage best supports the statement that an industrial leader should

(A) increase the distribution of his or her plant's products.

(B) introduce large-scale production methods.

(C) coordinate the activities of employees.

(D) profit by the experience of other leaders.

21. "Genuine coins have an even and distinct corrugated outer edge; the corrugated outer edges of counterfeit coins are usually uneven, crooked, or missing."

According to this statement,

(A) counterfeit coins can rarely be distinguished from genuine coins.

(B) counterfeit coins never lose their corrugated outer edge.

(C) genuine coins never lose their uneven, corrugated outer edge.

(D) the quality of the outer edge of a coin may show that it is counterfeit.

22. "In most U.S. states, no crime is considered to have occurred unless there is a written law forbidding the act, and even though an act may not be exactly in harmony with public policy, such act is not a crime unless it is expressly forbidden by legislative enactment."

Which of the following statements is most nearly in keeping with the above passage?

(A) A crime is committed only with reference to a particular law.

(B) All acts not in harmony with public policy should be expressly forbidden by law.

(C) Legislative enactments frequently forbid actions that are exactly in harmony with public policy.

(D) Nothing contrary to public policy can be done without legislative authority.

GO ON TO THE NEXT PAGE.

23. "Only one measure, but a quite obvious measure, of the merits of the personnel policies of an organization and of the adequacy and fairness of the wages and other conditions of employment prevailing in it is the rate at which replacements must be made in order to maintain the work force."

This statement means most nearly that

(A) maximum effectiveness in personnel management has been achieved when there is no employee turnover.

(B) organization policies should be based on both social and economic considerations.

(C) rate of employee turnover is one indicator of the effectiveness of personnel management.

(D) wages and working conditions are of prime importance to both union leaders and managers.

24. "Education should not stop when the individual has been prepared to make a livelihood and to live in modern society; living would be mere existence were there no appreciation and enjoyment of the riches of art, literature, and science."

This passage best supports the statement that true education

(A) deals chiefly with art, literature, and science.

(B) disregards practical goals.

(C) should continue throughout the duration of one's life.

(D) teaches a person to focus on the routine problems of life.

25. "Just as the procedure of a collection department must be clear-cut and definite, the steps being taken with the sureness of a skilled chess player, so the various paragraphs of a collection letter must show clear organization, giving evidence of mind that, from the beginning, has had a specific end in view."

The passage means most nearly that a collection letter should always

(A) be carefully planned.

(B) be courteous but brief.

(C) be divided into several long paragraphs.

(D) show a spirit of sportsmanship.

26. "Although manufacturers exercise, through advertising, a high degree of control over consumers' desires, the manufacturer assumes enormous risks in attempting to predict what consumers will want and in producing goods in quantity and distributing them in advance of final selection by the consumers."

The quotation best supports the statement that manufacturers

(A) can predict with great accuracy the success of any product they put on the market.

(B) must depend upon the final selection by consumers for the success of their undertakings.

(C) must distribute goods directly to the consumers.

(D) must eliminate the risk of overproduction by advertising.

GO ON TO THE NEXT PAGE.

27. "In almost every community, fortunately, there are certain people known to be public spirited; others, however, may be selfish and act only as their private interests seem to require."

This quotation means most nearly that those citizens who disregard others are

(A) community minded.
(B) fortunate.
(C) not public spirited.
(D) unknown.

TEST 3: MECHANICAL COMPREHENSION TEST

30 Questions • 15 Minutes

Directions: This test has 30 questions designed to measure your ability to learn and reason with mechanical terms. Each diagram is followed with a question or an incomplete statement. Study the diagram carefully and select the choice that best answers the question or completes the statement. Then, mark the space on your answer form that has the same number and letter as your choice.

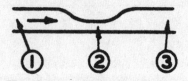

1. The figure above represents a pipe through which water is flowing in the direction of the arrow. There is a constriction in the pipe at the point indicated by the number 2. Water is being pumped into the pipe at a constant rate of 350 gallons per minute. Of the following, the most accurate statement is that

   (A) the velocity of the water at point 2 is the same as the velocity of the water at point 3.

   (B) a greater volume of water is flowing past point 1 in a minute than is flowing past point 2.

   (C) the volume of water flowing past point 2 in a minute is the same as the volume of water flowing past point 1 in a minute.

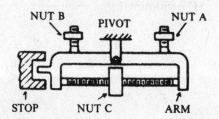

2. The arm in the figure above is exactly balanced as shown. If nut A is removed entirely, then, in order to rebalance the arm, it will be necessary to move nut

   (A) C toward the right.

   (B) C toward the left.

   (C) B up.

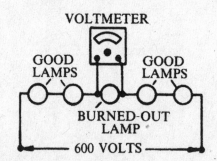

3. The reading of the voltmeter should be

   (A) 600

   (B) 120

   (C) 0

GO ON TO THE NEXT PAGE.

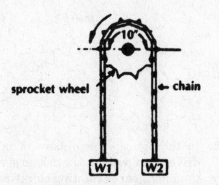

4. In the figure shown above, one complete revolution of the sprocket wheel will bring weight W2 higher than weight W1 by

(A) 24 inches.

(B) 36 inches.

(C) 48 inches.

7. A 150-pound person jumps off a 600-pound raft to a point in the water 10 feet away. Theoretically, the raft would move in the opposite direction a distance of

(A) $2\frac{1}{2}$ feet.

(B) 3 feet.

(C) $3\frac{1}{2}$ feet.

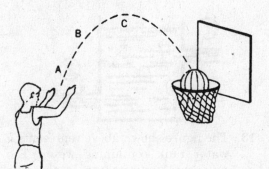

5. At which point was the basketball moving slowest?

(A) A

(B) B

(C) C

8. If cam A makes 120 complete turns per minute, the setscrew will hit the contact point

(A) once each second.

(B) twice each second.

(C) four times each second.

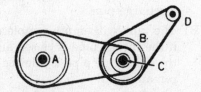

6. If pulley D is the driver in the arrangement of pulleys shown above, the pulley that turns slowest is

(A) A

(B) B

(C) C

GO ON TO THE NEXT PAGE.

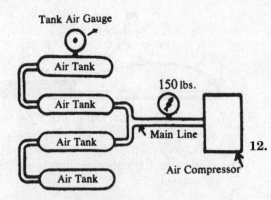

Tank Air Gauge

Air Tank

Air Tank

150 lbs.

Air Tank

Main Line

Air Tank

Air Compressor

9. As shown in the figure above, four air reservoirs have been filled with air by the air compressor. If the main gauge reads 150 pounds, then the tank air gauge will read

(A) 50 pounds.

(B) 75 pounds.

(C) 150 pounds.

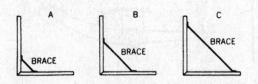

A   B   C

BRACE   BRACE   BRACE

10. Which of the angles is braced most securely?

(A) A

(B) B

(C) C

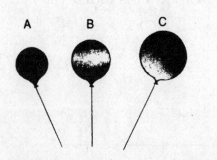

A   B   C

11. The amount of gas in the balloons is equal. The atmospheric pressure outside the balloons is lowest on which balloon?

(A) A

(B) B

(C) C

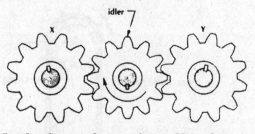

idler

X   Y

12. In the figure shown above, X is the driver gear and Y is the driven gear. If the idler gear is rotating clockwise,

(A) gear X and gear Y are rotating clockwise.

(B) gear X and gear Y are rotating counterclockwise.

(C) gear X is rotating clockwise, while gear Y is rotating counterclockwise.

① ②

13. The figure shown above represents a water tank containing water. The number 1 indicates an intake pipe and 2 indicates a discharge pipe. Which of the following statements is correct?

(A) The tank will eventually overflow if water flows through the intake pipe at a slower rate than it flows out through the discharge pipe.

(B) The tank will empty completely if the intake pipe is closed and the discharge pipe is allowed to remain open.

(C) The water in the tank will remain at a constant level if the rate of intake is equal to the rate of discharge.

GO ON TO THE NEXT PAGE.

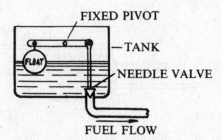

14. If the float in the tank develops a bad leak, then the

  (A) flow of fuel will stop.

  (B) float will stay in the position shown.

  (C) needle value will remain in the open position.

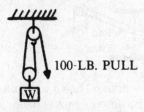

15. The maximum weight, W, that can be lifted as shown with a pull of 100 pounds is

  (A) 100 pounds.

  (B) 200 pounds.

  (C) 300 pounds.

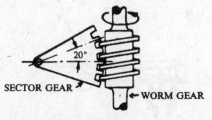

16. One revolution of the worm gear will turn the sector gear through an angle of

  (A) 5 degrees.

  (B) 10 degrees.

  (C) 15 degrees.

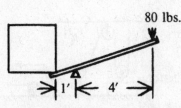

17. A pry bar is used to move a concrete block. A force of 80 lbs. applied as shown will produce a tipping force on the edge of the block of

  (A) 80 lbs.

  (B) 240 lbs.

  (C) 320 lbs.

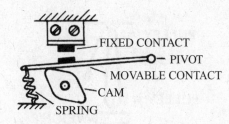

18. If the contacts come together once every second, the cam is rotating at

  (A) 30 rpm.

  (B) 45 rpm.

  (C) 60 rpm.

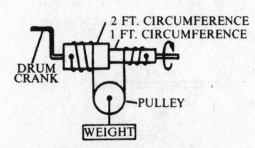

19. One complete turn of the drum crank will move the weight vertically upward a distance of

  (A) 3 feet.

  (B) $2\frac{1}{2}$ feet.

  (C) $1\frac{1}{2}$ feet.

GO ON TO THE NEXT PAGE.

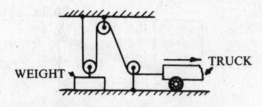

20. The weight is to be raised by means of the rope attached to the truck. If the truck moves forward 30 feet, then the weight will rise

(A) 20 feet.

(B) 15 feet.

(C) 10 feet.

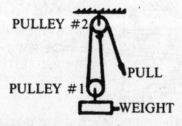

21. The block and tackle shown has two pulleys of equal diameter. While the weight is being raised, pulley 2 will rotate at

(A) twice the speed of pulley 1.

(B) the same speed as pulley 1.

(C) one-half the speed of pulley 1.

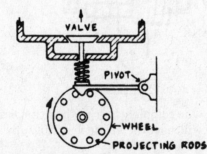

22. In order to open the valve twice every second, the wheel must rotate at

(A) 6 rpm.

(B) 9 rpm.

(C) 12 rpm.

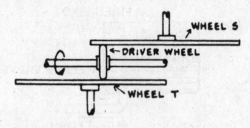

23. With the wheels in the position shown,

(A) wheel S will rotate at a faster speed than wheel T.

(B) wheels S and T will rotate at the same speed.

(C) wheel S will rotate at a slower speed than wheel T.

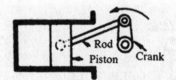

24. The figure above shows a crank and piston. The piston moves from mid-position to the extreme left and then back to the midposition if the crank makes a

(A) $\frac{1}{4}$ turn.

(B) $\frac{1}{2}$ turn.

(C) $\frac{3}{4}$ turn.

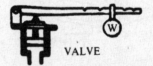

25. The figure above shows a lever-type safety valve. It will blow off at a higher pressure if weight W is

(A) decreased.

(B) moved to the left.

(C) moved to the right.

GO ON TO THE NEXT PAGE.

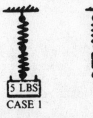

26. In the figure above, all four springs are identical. In Case 1, with the springs end to end, the stretch of each spring due to the 5-pound weight is

(A) $\frac{1}{2}$ as much as in Case 2.

(B) the same as in Case 2.

(C) twice as much as in Case 2.

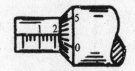

27. In the figure above, the micrometer reads

(A) .2270

(B) .2250

(C) .2120

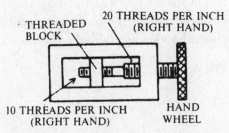

28. In the figure above, the threaded block can slide in the slot but cannot revolve. If the hand wheel is turned 20 revolutions clockwise, the threaded block will move

(A) 1 inch to the left.

(B) $\frac{1}{2}$ inch to the left.

(C) 1 inch to the right.

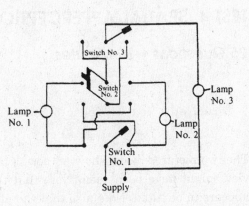

Answer questions 29 and 30 on the basis of the wiring diagram with three switches and three lamps shown above. (Symbol ⌒ indicates that wires cross but are not connected.)

29. If all three switches are closed to the left, the following lamp condition results:

(A) No. 1 and No. 3 light

(B) No. 2 and No. 3 light

(C) Only No. 3 lights

30. If switches No. 1 and No. 2 are closed to the right and switch No. 3 is closed to the left, the following lamp condition results:

(A) No. 1 and No. 3 light

(B) No. 2 and No. 3 light

(C) Only No. 3 lights

STOP! DO NOT GO ON UNTIL TIME IS UP.

TEST 4: SPATIAL APPERCEPTION TEST

25 Questions • 10 Minutes

Directions: You will have 5 minutes to read these instructions; read them carefully.

The two pictures below show an aerial view and a picture of a plane from which the view might have been seen. Note that the view is out at sea and that the horizon appears to be tilted. Note also that the plane is shown flying out to sea and that it is banked. You can determine the position of a plane by the view that the pilot has when he or she looks directly ahead through the windshield of the cockpit.

Each problem in this test consists of six pictures: an aerial view at the upper left and five pictured choices below labeled A, B, C, D, and E. Each pictured choice shows a plane in flight. The picture at the upper left shows the view that the pilot would have looking straight ahead from the cockpit of one of the five pictured planes. Determine which of the five lettered sketches most nearly represents the position or attitude of the plane and the direction of flight from which the view would have been seen.

Try the two sample problems on the following page.

GO ON TO THE NEXT PAGE.

1.

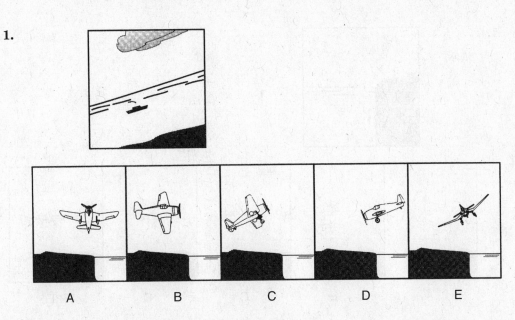

The correct answer is (B). The plane is shown in the position from which the pilot would have seen through the windshield of the cockpit—the view shown in the upper left aerial view. The plane is shown on a level flight, banking right, and flying out to sea.

2.

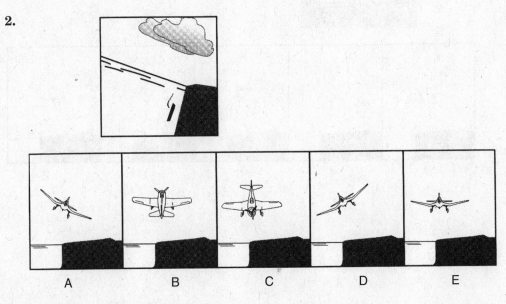

The correct answer is (D). The plane is shown on a level flight, banking left, and flying up the coastline.

You will have 10 minutes to answer the 25 questions on the test.

STOP! DO NOT TURN THIS PAGE UNTIL TOLD TO DO SO.

practice test

1.

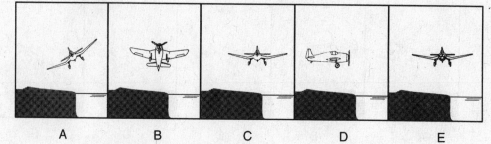

A   B   C   D   E

2.

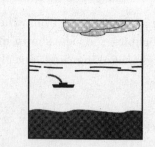

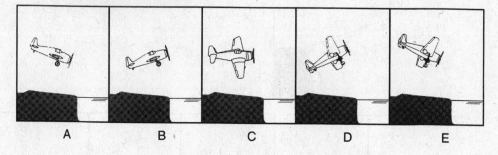

A   B   C   D   E

GO ON TO THE NEXT PAGE.

3.

4.

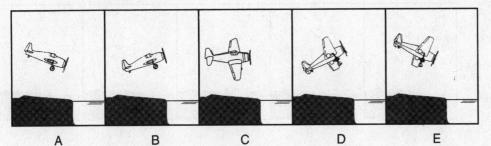

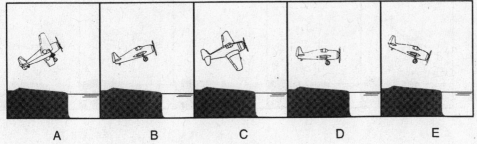

practice test

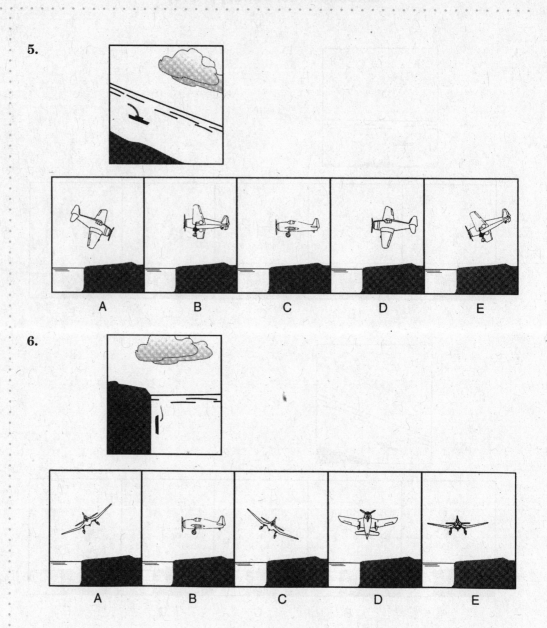

5.

   A   B   C   D   E

6.

   A   B   C   D   E

GO ON TO THE NEXT PAGE.

7.

A   B   C   D   E

8.

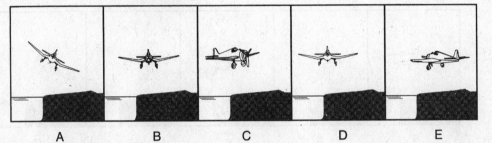

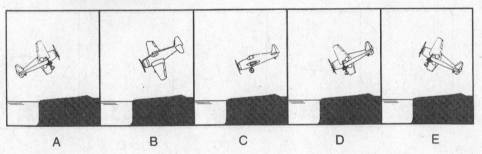

A   B   C   D   E

practice test

GO ON TO THE NEXT PAGE.

9.

10.

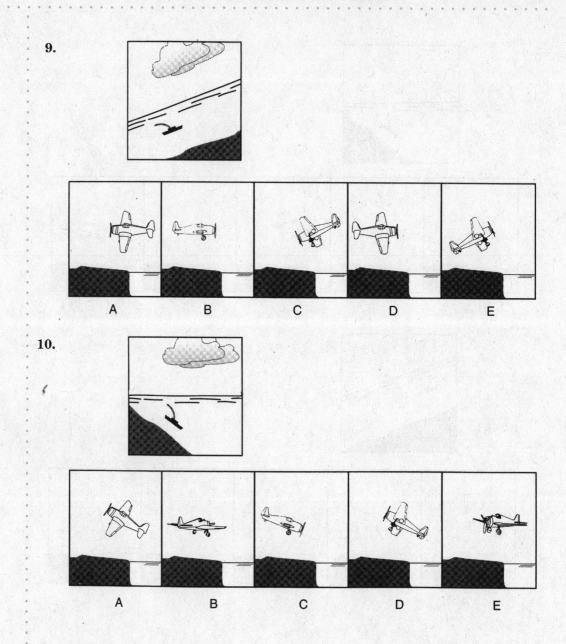

GO ON TO THE NEXT PAGE.

11.

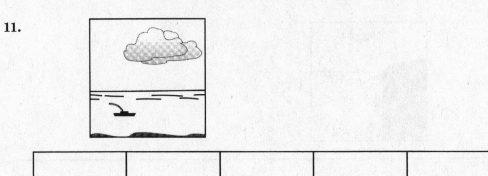

12.

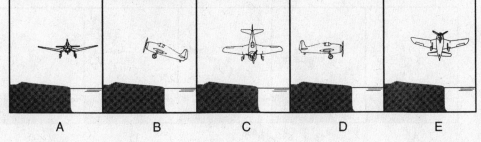

practice test

13.

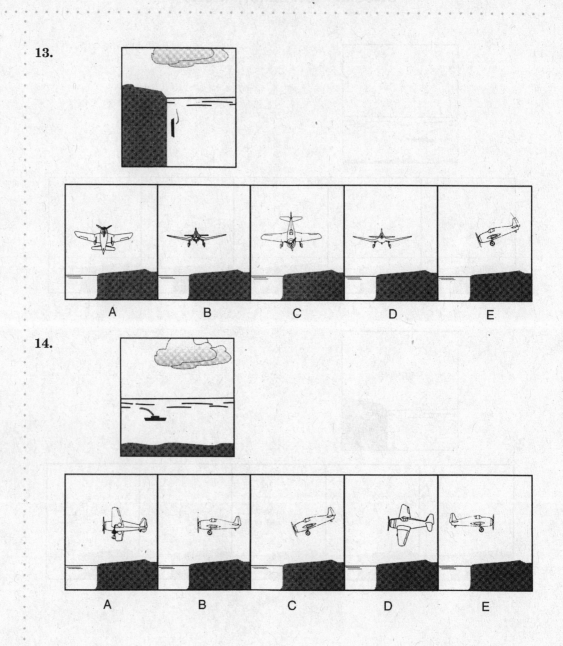

A   B   C   D   E

14.

A   B   C   D   E

GO ON TO THE NEXT PAGE.

15.

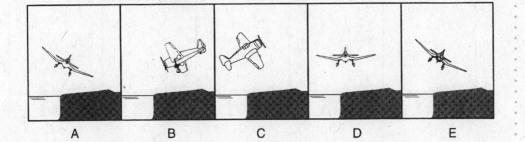

A   B   C   D   E

16.

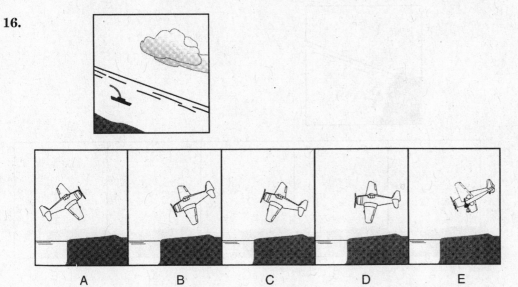

A   B   C   D   E

practice test

17.

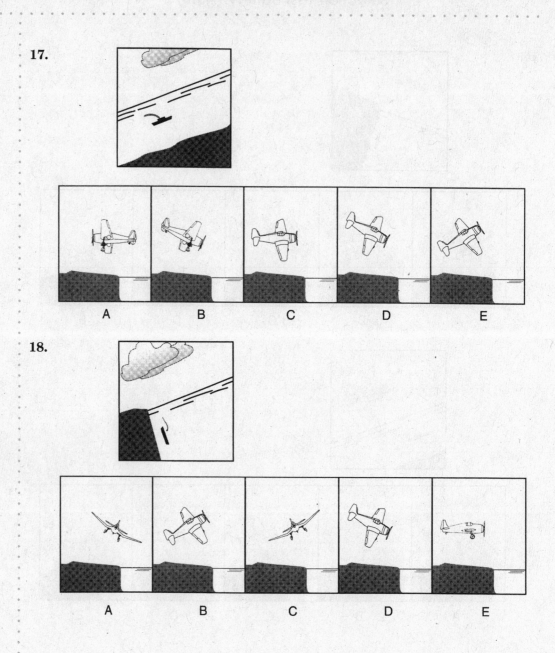

A   B   C   D   E

18.

A   B   C   D   E

GO ON TO THE NEXT PAGE.

19.

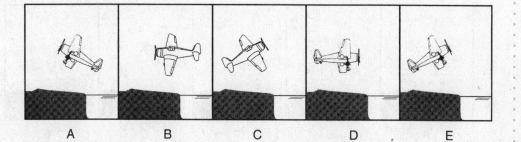

A   B   C   D   E

20.

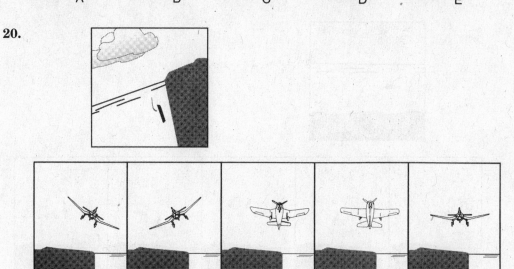

A   B   C   D   E

GO ON TO THE NEXT PAGE.

21.

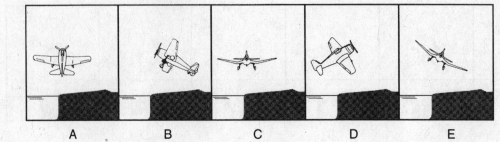

A   B   C   D   E

22.

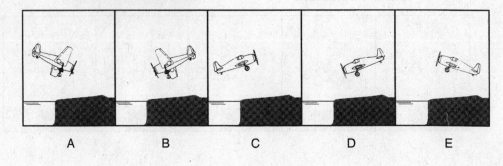

A   B   C   D   E

GO ON TO THE NEXT PAGE.

23.

24.

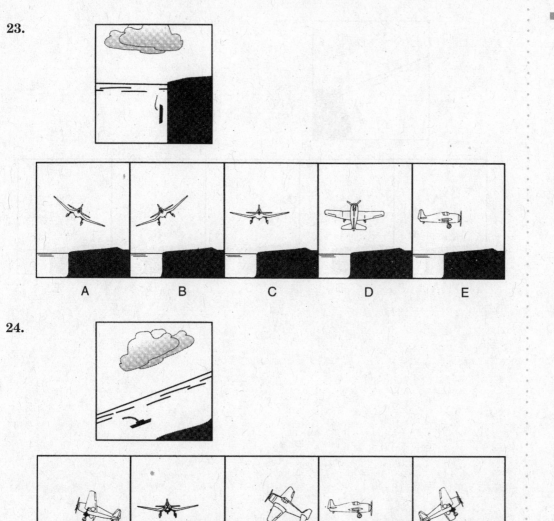

practice test

25.

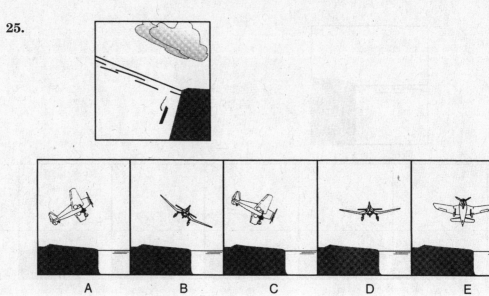

A   B   C   D   E

STOP! DO NOT GO ON UNTIL TIME IS UP.

TEST 5: AVIATION AND NAUTICAL INFORMATION TEST

30 Questions • 15 Minutes

Questions 1–15 pertain to aviation information.

1. The wing shape shown below is best described as a(n)

    (A) delta wing.

    (B) elliptical wing.

    (C) rectangular wing.

    (D) rotary wing.

    (E) sweptback wing.

2. The wing span is the distance from

    (A) leading edge to trailing edge.

    (B) top to bottom of airfoil.

    (C) wing root to wing tip.

    (D) wing tip to center of the fuselage.

    (E) wing tip to wing tip.

3. The pilot banks the airplane by using the

    (A) ailerons.

    (B) brakes.

    (C) elevators.

    (D) flaps.

    (E) rudder.

4. The airplane is controlled around its vertical axis by means of the

    (A) ailerons.

    (B) elevators.

    (C) pilot.

    (D) rudder.

    (E) wing flaps.

5. There are several forces acting on an aircraft in straight-and-level flight. The backward or retarding force produced by air resistance is termed

    (A) drag.

    (B) gravity.

    (C) lift.

    (D) thrust.

    (E) weight.

6. The angle between the chord line of the airfoil and the direction of the relative wind is termed

    (A) angle of attack.

    (B) angle of bank.

    (C) angle of deflection.

    (D) angle of incidence.

    (E) pitch angle.

7. In a steady flight condition,

    (A) lift equals drag; weight equals thrust.

    (B) lift equals gravity; weight equals drag.

    (C) lift equals thrust; weight equals drag.

    (D) lift equals weight; gravity equals drag.

    (E) lift equals weight; thrust equals drag.

8. If a hard-surfaced runway is numbered 22, the opposite direction of the same runway would be numbered

    (A) 4

    (B) 12

    (C) 22

    (D) 26

    (E) 40

GO ON TO THE NEXT PAGE.

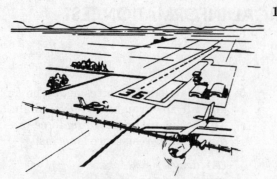

9. In the illustration above, the runway is aligned in a

(A) North-South direction.
(B) East-West direction.
(C) NE-SW direction.
(D) NW-SE direction.
(E) NNE-SSW direction.

10. The hand signal that directs an airplane to make an emergency stop is

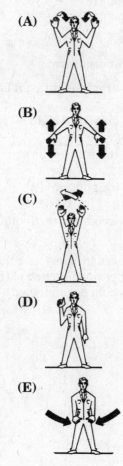

(A)

(B)

(C)

(D)

(E)

11. What was the name of the space vehicle that carried the American astronauts who first landed on the moon?

(A) Apollo 11
(B) Aurora 7
(C) Gemini 11
(D) Faith 7
(E) Skylab 1

12. If an astronaut weighed 60 kilograms on Earth, his or her weight on the moon would be

(A) more than 60 kilograms.
(B) less than 60 kilograms.
(C) the same.
(D) more or less, depending on location on lunar surface.
(E) more or less, depending on the earth's season.

13. Which of the following engines can operate outside the earth's atmosphere?

(A) Four-stroke diesel engine
(B) Four-stroke gasoline engine
(C) Jet engine
(D) Rocket engine
(E) Steam turbine

14. Which of the following is an important performance deficiency of an overloaded airplane?

(A) Higher landing speed
(B) Higher maximum altitude
(C) Increased rate and angle of climb
(D) Increased cruising speed
(E) Shorter takeoff run

GO ON TO THE NEXT PAGE.

15. During takeoff, a headwind will

(A) increase both the takeoff run and the angle of climb.

(B) increase the takeoff run and decrease the angle of climb.

(C) shorten the takeoff run and increase the angle of climb.

(D) shorten the takeoff run and decrease the angle of climb.

(E) have the same effect on airplane performance as a tailwind.

Questions 16–30 pertain to nautical information.

16. The outer walls of a ship are called the

(A) bulkhead.

(B) frame.

(C) hull.

(D) keel.

(E) trim.

17. A ship's windlass is designed primarily for

(A) cargo handling.

(B) fueling at sea.

(C) handling anchor chain.

(D) propulsion.

(E) steering.

18. A nautical mile is approximately

(A) 5,280 feet.

(B) 6,076 feet.

(C) 7,076 feet.

(D) 7,400 feet.

(E) 8,000 feet.

19. The coordinates latitude and longitude are generally used by the navigator to express

(A) direction.

(B) distance.

(C) position.

(D) speed.

(E) time.

20. Using the 24-hour basis in navigation, 9:05 p.m. would be written as

(A) 9.05

(B) 905

(C) 0905

(D) 21.05

(E) 2105

21. At sea, the time zones are generally bands of longitude

(A) $7\frac{1}{2}°$ in width.

(B) 15° in width.

(C) 24° in width.

(D) 30° in width.

(E) 45° in width.

22. A ship is at a latitude of 25°N and a longitude of 90°W. It is sailing in the

(A) Adriatic Sea.

(B) Black Sea.

(C) Gulf of Mexico.

(D) Hudson Bay.

(E) Red Sea.

23. A line drawn from a fix in the direction in which a ship is moving is called a

(A) course line.

(B) date line.

(C) line of position.

(D) line of sights.

(E) parallel line.

24. In marine navigation, soundings are used to measure

(A) depth of water.

(B) direction.

(C) Greenwich time.

(D) position of stars.

(E) standard time.

GO ON TO THE NEXT PAGE.

25. As the weight of the load carried by a ship increases,

   (A) both the freeboard and draft decrease.

   (B) both the freeboard and draft increase.

   (C) freeboard increases and draft decreases.

   (D) freeboard decreases and draft increases.

   (E) None of the above

26. Which of the following is NOT considered to be an "aid to navigation"?

   (A) Buoys

   (B) Fog signals

   (C) Lightships

   (D) Loran

   (E) Mountain peaks

27. Fog is generally formed when

   (A) cold air moves over cold water.

   (B) cold air moves over hot water.

   (C) colder air moves over warmer water.

   (D) warm air moves over warm water.

   (E) warmer air moves over colder water.

28. The navigation light associated with "starboard" is colored

   (A) green.

   (B) red.

   (C) white.

   (D) yellow.

   (E) None of the above

29. An unlighted buoy, used to mark the right side of a channel when facing inland, is called a

   (A) bell buoy.

   (B) can buoy.

   (C) gong buoy.

   (D) nun buoy.

   (E) spar.

30. Ships or boats are steered by one or more rudders at the stern. The faster the vessel is moving,

   (A) the greater the pressure against the rudder and the quicker the turning effect.

   (B) the greater the pressure against the rudder and the slower the turning effect.

   (C) the less the pressure against the rudder and the quicker the turning effect.

   (D) the less the pressure against the rudder and the slower the turning effect.

   (E) None of the above

STOP! DO NOT GO ON UNTIL TIME IS UP.

TEST 6: AVIATION SUPPLEMENTAL TEST

34 Questions • 25 Minutes

NOTE: Number of items in this subtest may vary.

The Aviation Supplemental Test (AST) is the final subtest of the ASTB. Typically, it contains a variety of items similar in format and content to those in the preceding subtests.

Directions: Questions 1–7 each consists of a problem followed by four possible answer choices. For each question, determine the answer choice that best answers the question.

1. $(0.1)^2 =$
   (A) 0.01
   (B) 0.02
   (C) 0.1
   (D) 0.2

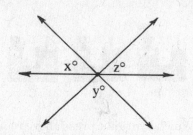

2. A punch recipe calls for $2\frac{1}{4}$ quarts of ginger ale. How many quarts of ginger ale would be needed to make $\frac{1}{3}$ of the recipe?

   (A) $\frac{2}{3}$
   (B) $\frac{3}{4}$
   (C) $1\frac{1}{4}$
   (D) $1\frac{1}{3}$

3. The average marksmanship score on four targets is 93. If the scores on the first three targets are 92, 98, and 96, what is the score on the fourth target?
   (A) 86
   (B) 88
   (C) 90
   (D) 93

4. The figure above shows three lines that intersect in a point. What is the value of $x + y + z$?
   (A) 90
   (B) 180
   (C) 240
   (D) 360

5. If 2 times r exceeds one-half of t by 5, which of the following represents the relationship between r and t?
   (A) $4r - t = 10$
   (B) $4r + t = 10$
   (C) $2r - t = 5$
   (D) $2r + t = -5$

GO ON TO THE NEXT PAGE.

6. Sam left his home at 11 a.m. traveling along Rt. 9 at 30 mph. At 1 p.m., his sister Jenna left home and started after him on the same road at 45 mph. At what time did Jenna catch up to Sam?

(A) 3:00 p.m.

(B) 3:30 p.m.

(C) 4:15 p.m.

(D) 5:00 p.m.

7. The length of a rectangle with area 12 is three times the rectangle's width. What is the perimeter of the rectangle?

(A) 12

(B) 14

(C) 16

(D) 18

Directions: For Questions 8–12, each question consists of a problem followed by three possible answer choices. For each question, determine the answer choice that best answers the question.

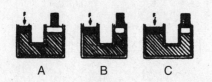

8. Which hydraulic press above requires the least force to lift the weight?

(A) A

(B) B

(C) C

9. In the case of the standard flanged pipe shown above, the maximum angle through which it would be necessary to rotate the pipe in order to line up the holes is

(A) 30°

(B) 45°

(C) 60°

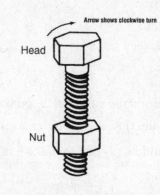

10. Referring to the figure above, which one of the following statements is true?

(A) If the nut is held stationary and the head turned clockwise, the bolt will move down.

(B) If the head of the bolt is held stationary and the nut is turned clockwise, the nut will move down.

(C) If the head of the bolt is held stationary and the nut is turned clockwise, the nut will move up.

GO ON TO THE NEXT PAGE.

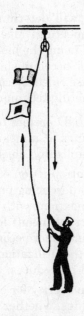

12. If the block on which the lever is resting is moved closer to the brick in the figure above, the brick will be

(A) easier to lift and will be lifted higher.

(B) harder to lift and will be lifted higher.

(C) easier to lift but will not be lifted as high.

11. Neglecting friction, what is the mechanical advantage in using a single fixed pulley shown above?

(A) 1

(B) 2

(C) 3

Directions: For questions 13–17, each item consists of a passage which you should assume to be true followed by four possible answer choices. For each question, select the choice that can be inferred *only* from the passage itself. Some or all of the choices following the passage may be true and reasonable, but only one of them can be derived solely from the information in the passage.

13. A storm must pass through different stages before becoming a hurricane. The onset of this process occurs when low pressure air spins inward cyclonically to form the eye of the building storm. During the intermediate stages of development, the storm is first referred to as a tropical depression, later as a tropical storm before increasing in intensity to become a hurricane.

(A) During the tropical depression stage of hurricane development, the eye is formed by winds moving in a clockwise direction.

(B) A hurricane is the most violent of all natural phenomena because the eye of the storm is composed of cyclonic air movement.

(C) Tropical storms do not contain eyes because they develop from high pressure air systems.

(D) Cyclonic air movement plays a central role in the creation of hurricane force winds.

GO ON TO THE NEXT PAGE.

14. Paper clips may be constructed of metal or of plastic. Some metal clips are covered in rubber to prevent damage to documents caused by rust.

(A) Paper clips tend to rust.

(B) Modern paper clips are covered in rubber.

(C) Rust can damage documents.

(D) Plastic paper clips tend to damage documents.

15. There was a barely detectable string dangling from his right sleeve. He was sure no one would notice it, but it still occupied his mind for the better part of the morning. On the other hand, the large ketchup stain he later got on his chest didn't bother him a bit.

(A) There were two problems with his shirt that caused him some concern.

(B) The two problems with his shirt did not occur at the same time.

(C) The ketchup stain didn't bother him because it was barely detectable.

(D) He worried more about the ketchup stain than about the dangling string.

16. The CNO will determine the venue for each meeting. Meetings will be conducted using the most economical method for accomplishing objectives and may use video teleconferencing or formal meeting techniques.

(A) The CNO prefers to use formal meetings as a means for accomplishing objectives.

(B) The introduction of video teleconferencing provided organizations with an important means for conducting meetings more economically than the utilization of traditional procedures.

(C) The authority for establishing meetings, whether through the utilization of teleconferencing or formal meetings, is the responsibility of the CNO.

(D) There is an ongoing debate surrounding the use of video teleconferencing and its effectiveness in accomplishing objectives.

17. Human DNA is composed of approximately 3 billion components. Each piece is described using one of four letters—A, C, G, or T. Each component is arranged in a unique and specific order, dictating each human's physical development.

(A) Parents and their children have identical DNA.

(B) Each human being has approximately 3 billion T components in his or her genetic makeup.

(C) A different arrangement of the pieces of a person's DNA would change his or her physical makeup.

(D) Adults' DNA is composed of more A, C, G, and T components than children's DNA.

GO ON TO THE NEXT PAGE.

Directions: For Questions 18–24, each question consists of a problem followed by four possible answer choices. For each question, determine the answer choice that best answers the question.

18. Who is known as the father of the U.S. Navy?

    (A) George Dewey
    (B) David G. Farragut
    (C) Stephen Decatur
    (D) John Paul Jones

19. What color is the starboard running light?

    (A) Green
    (B) Red
    (C) White
    (D) Yellow

20. What is the primary reason for dumping fuel from a jet transport aircraft before attempting an emergency landing?

    (A) Eliminate fire hazard
    (B) Reduce landing weight
    (C) Move the center of gravity
    (D) Obtain a steeper glide slope

21. Latitude is measured from the _____.

    (A) Equator
    (B) North Pole
    (C) South Pole
    (D) Prime meridian

22. How are runways numbered?

    (A) According to the types of aircraft that use the runway
    (B) By the first two digits of their compass direction
    (C) According to their lengths
    (D) In clockwise sequence, beginning with 1 at the north

23. Which was the first conflict in which helicopters were widely used?

    (A) World War I
    (B) World War II
    (C) Korean War
    (D) Vietnam War

24. The first person to break the sound barrier was

    (A) Alan Shepard.
    (B) Chuck Yeager.
    (C) Yuri Gagarin.
    (D) Ed White.

practice test

GO ON TO THE NEXT PAGE.

Directions: For Questions 25–34, each problem consists of six pictures: an aerial view of the horizon and five choices below that, labeled A, B, C, D, and E. Each picture shows a plane in flight. The picture at the upper left shows the view a pilot would have looking straight ahead from the cockpit of one of the five pictured planes. Determine which of the five lettered sketches most nearly represents the position or attitude of the plane and the direction of flight from which the view would have been seen.

25.

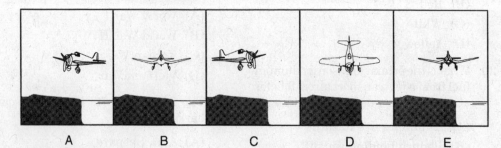

A   B   C   D   E

26.

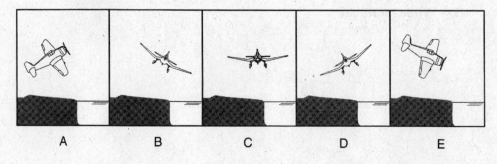

A   B   C   D   E

GO ON TO THE NEXT PAGE.

27.

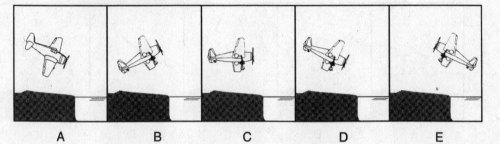

A   B   C   D   E

28.

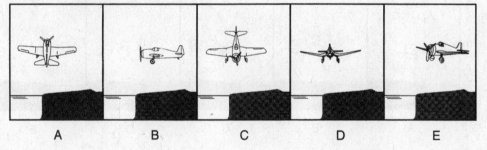

A   B   C   D   E

GO ON TO THE NEXT PAGE.

practice test

29.

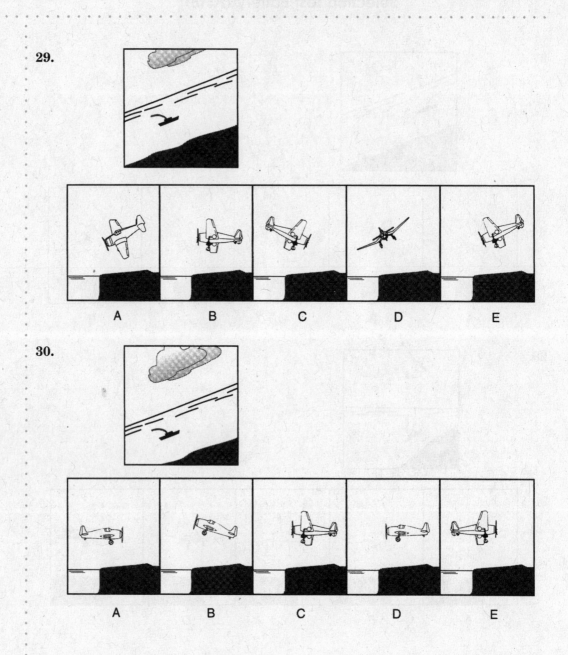

30.

GO ON TO THE NEXT PAGE.

31.

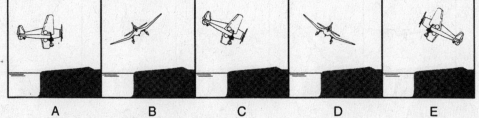

| A | B | C | D | E |

32.

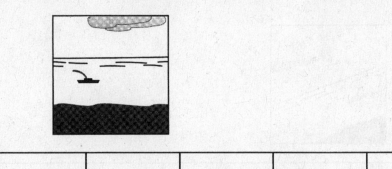

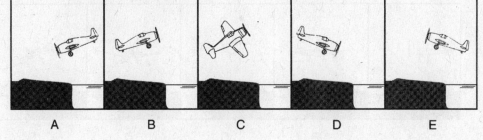

| A | B | C | D | E |

practice test

346

PART IV: Three Practice Tests

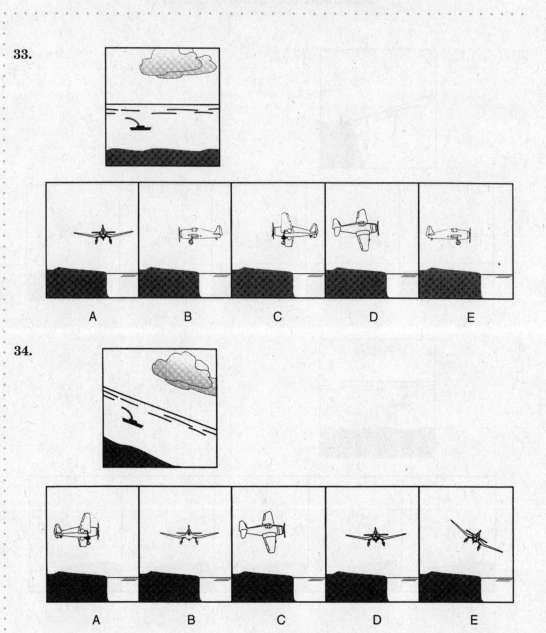

STOP! END OF TEST.

www.petersons.com

ANSWER KEY AND EXPLANATIONS

Use the answer keys to determine the number of questions you answered correctly on each test and to note those you answered incorrectly or of which you were unsure.

Be certain to review carefully the explanations and rationales for arriving at the correct answer for all items you answered incorrectly and those you answered correctly but were unsure of. This will help you score as high as possible on the real ASTB.

Test 1: Math Skills Test

1. C	7. B	13. A	19. C	25. C
2. B	8. D	14. B	20. D	26. C
3. A	9. D	15. A	21. A	27. A
4. D	10. C	16. A	22. B	28. C
5. B	11. D	17. C	23. C	29. D
6. D	12. C	18. B	24. D	30. A

1. **The correct answer is (C).** Slower train is 30 miles ahead in one hour. Difference in rate is 5 mph. $\frac{30}{5} = 6$ hours.

2. **The correct answer is (B).** Let $x =$ number ration days for 20 persons. $16 \times 10 = 20 \times x$; $20x = 160$; $x = \frac{160}{20} = 8$ ration days for 20 persons. 10 days − 8 days = 2 days fewer.

3. **The correct answer is (A).** Let $x =$ number of hours to plow with 6 machines.

$$9 \times 5 = 6 \times x$$
$$6x = 45$$
$$x = \frac{45}{8} = 7\frac{1}{2} \text{ hours}$$

4. **The correct answer is (D).** $\sqrt{9} = 3$; $3^4 = 3 \times 3 \times 3 \times 3 = 81$.

5. **The correct answer is (B).** $2^{n-2} = 32$; $2^5 = 32$; $n - 2 = 5$; $n = 7$.

6. **The correct answer is (D).** A cube has 12 edges.
$\frac{48}{12} = 4$ inches
(Volume = length × width × height)
4 inches × 4 inches × 4 inches = 64 cubic inches

7. The correct answer is (B).

	No. of Ounces	Parts Pure Acid	No. of Ounces of Pure Acid
Pure Acid	x	100	$100x$
40% Acid Solution	12	40	480
60% Acid Solution	$12 + x$	60	$60(12 + x)$

$$100x + 480 = 60(12 + x)$$
$$100x + 480 = 720 + 60x$$
$$40x = 240$$
$$x = 6$$

8. The correct answer is (D).

$$6 : 10 = x : 75$$
$$10x = 75 \times 6$$
$$10x = 450$$
$$x = 45$$

9. The correct answer is (D).

$$(x - y)^2 = 2xy + y^2$$
$$40 = 60 - 2xy$$
$$2xy = 20$$
$$xy = 10$$

10. The correct answer is (C). Arc AB $= 70°$; therefore, AOB $= 70°$. The two radii are equal. Angle $x = \frac{1}{2}(180° - 70°) = \frac{1}{2}(110°) = 55°$.

11. The correct answer is (D). $86 \times 4 = 344$; $90 + 88 + 75 = 253$; $344 - 253 = 91$.

12. The correct answer is (C). $\frac{1}{10}$ of $3000 = 300$; $3000 - 300 = 2700$; $\frac{1}{9}$ of $2700 = 300$; $2700 - 300 = 2400$ miles still to be driven.

13. The correct answer is (A). Let $x =$ minutes to be spent on each math problem, $x \times 40 + \frac{x}{2} \times 280 = 180$;

$40x + 140x = 180$; $180x = 180$; $x = 1$; $40x = 40$ minutes to be spent on the 40 math problems.

14. The correct answer is (B). $10 \times 10 \times 10 \times 10 \times 10 = 100,000$ or 10 raised to the 5th power.

15. The correct answer is (A). $a = 3b$; $2a = 6b = 12c$; $2a = 12c$; $a = 6c$.

16. The correct answer is (A). Let $x =$ the number of quarters in the cash box (the numerator of the formula's fraction), and let $x + 72 =$ the total number of coins (the fraction's denominator). Then solve for x:

$$\frac{1}{4} = \frac{x}{x} + 72$$
$$4x = x + 72$$
$$3x = 72$$
$$x = 24$$

17. The correct answer is (C). After the first 10% discount, the price was $450 ($500 minus 10% of $500). After the second discount, which is calculated based on the $450 price, the price of the CD system is $405 ($450 minus 10% of $450). A 20% tax on $405 is $81. Thus, the customer has paid $405 + $81 = $486.

18. **The correct answer is (B).** First, determine the dimensions of the square base. The box's height is given as 5. Accordingly, the box's volume (45) = $5lw$, and $lw = 9$. Since the base is square, the base is 3 inches long on each side. Now you can calculate the total surface area: $2lw + 2wh + 2lw = (2)(9) + (2)(15) + (2)(15) = 78$.

19. **The correct answer is (C).**

$$9 : 4 = x : 64$$
$$4x = 64 \times 9$$
$$x = 64 \times \frac{9}{4}$$
$$x = 144$$

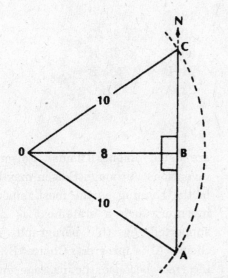

20. **The correct answer is (D).** Referring to the sketch above, the ship will be within range of the coastal guns from point A to point C. Triangle OBA and triangle OBC are right triangles with one leg of 8 miles and a hypotenuse of 10 miles.

The time for the ship to travel from point A to point C must be determined. Let x = the distance from A to B; $2x$ = distance from A to C.

$$8^2 + x^2 = 10^2$$
$$64 + x^2 = 100$$
$$x^2 = 36$$
$$x = 6 \text{ miles}; 2x = 12 \text{ miles}$$

Let t = time required to travel from A to C (in minutes)

$$\frac{24}{60} = \frac{12}{t} = 720$$
$$t = 30 \text{ minutes}$$

21. **The correct answer is (A).** $\frac{450}{15} = 30$ gallons/minute, filling rate. $\frac{450}{30} = 15$ gallons/minute, emptying rate.

$$30 - 15$$
$$= 15 \text{ gallons added per minute}$$
$$\text{with both pipes open}$$
$$\frac{450}{15} = 30 \text{ minutes}$$

22. **The correct answer is (B).**

$$\frac{1}{3} \times 204 = 68 \text{ blacks}$$
$$\frac{1}{4} \times 204 = 51 \text{ Hispanics}$$
$$68 + 51 = 119$$
$$204 - 119 = 85 \text{ whites}$$

23. **The correct answer is (C).** 30 mph for 4 hours = 120 miles; round trip = 240 miles; 240 miles at 40 mph would take 6 hours; if the first 120 miles took 4 hours, the return 120 miles must be covered in 2 hours, which equals a speed of 60 mph.

24. **The correct answer is (D).** When two negative numbers are multiplied, the product is positive.

25. **The correct answer is (C).** Let x = number of degrees in angle E; $x + x - 30 = 90$; $2x = 90 + 30$; $2x = 120$; $x = 60°$.

26. The correct answer is (C). $95 \times 8 = 760$; $75 \times 8 = 600$; $760 + 600 = 1,360$; $1,800 - 1,360 = 440$ miles.

27. The correct answer is (A). $100 \times .20 = 20$; $100 - 20 = 80$; $80 \times .15 = 12$; $80 - 12 = 68$; $100 - 68 = 32$.

28. The correct answer is (C).

$$\frac{1}{5}x + \frac{1}{6}x + 1,520 = x$$
$$6x + 5x + 45,600 = 30x$$
$$45,600 = 19x$$
$$2,400 = x$$

29. The correct answer is (D). The hypotenuse of the right triangle = 10 (Pythagorean theorem). $6' + 8' + 10' = 24'$.

30. The correct answer is (A). $2 \times 2 \times 2 \times 2 = 16$.

Test 2: Reading Skills Test

1. C	7. C	13. D	18. D	23. C
2. B	8. B	14. A	19. B	24. C
3. D	9. C	15. A	20. C	25. A
4. D	10. B	16. B	21. D	26. B
5. A	11. B	17. A	22. A	27. C
6. A	12. D			

1. The correct answer is (C). The judge decides on the minimum height to be jumped, so pole vaulters must jump higher than the height set by the judge.

2. The correct answer is (B). Because some icebergs in the Antarctic Ocean rise as high as 300 feet above the water, and because only one-tenth of an iceberg is visible above the waterline, some icebergs in the Antarctic Ocean are as high as 3,000 feet.

3. The correct answer is (D). A toad's skin is dry, dull, and rough, or covered with warts.

4. The correct answer is (D). The phonograph and motion picture film are listed among Thomas Edison's inventions. Although Edison may be in the running as the most famous inventor, such a statement is not supported by the paragraph, so choice (A) is incorrect. Choice (B) is incorrect because the passage specifically states that he was responsible for more than 1,000 inventions. Edison lived 84 years; his was not a short life, so choice (C) is incorrect.

5. The correct answer is (A). Because the other three answer choices involve monetary gain for the athlete, choice (A) can be the only correct answer.

6. The correct answer is (A). This is a restatement of the paragraph. The other answer choices are not relevant to the paragraph.

7. The correct answer is (C). This answer is stated in the last sentence of the passage.

8. The correct answer is (B). Although all four answer choices are somewhat supported by the passage, the one that *best* supports it is the statement that the average American family moves every few years.

9. The correct answer is (C). See the last sentence of the passage.

10. The correct answer is (B). This answer choice restates the last sentence of the passage.

11. The correct answer is (B). The other three answer choices are incorrect statements. The date 1869 refers to the establishment of the current nine-member court, so answer choice (A) is incorrect. Justices are appointed by the president, so answer choice (C) is incorrect. And justices serve for life, so choice (D) is incorrect.

12. The correct answer is (D). Most of the passage is devoted to describing the five different types of competition.

13. The correct answer is (D). The word *also* in the last sentence is the key to the fact that in higher animals the brain controls voluntary behavior, involuntary behavior, emotions, memory, and thought.

14. The correct answer is (A). Because 6,080 feet is greater than 5,280 feet, choice (A) is correct.

15. The correct answer is (A). The recommendation to use not more than 14 persons nor less than 10 persons means that it is best to use between 10 and 14 persons on the net, even if fewer can be used.

16. The correct answer is (B). The paragraph may open by mentioning that there is a growing danger in the overuse of antibiotics; however, the paragraph does not expand on this theme. The passage mainly focuses on the ineffectiveness of antibiotics against viral infections. Because more than twice as much of the paragraph is devoted to the second theme, choice (B) is the best answer.

17. The correct answer is (A). Choices (B), (C), and (D) are not valid options. To take notice of details that at first glance may not seem to have any connection to the crime implies that one cannot tell in advance what will be important.

18. The correct answer is (D). The passage states that the work of the operator often requires careful attention under stress. This means that the operator must be able to work under difficult conditions. The passage does not state that the work must *always* be performed under stress.

19. The correct answer is (B). The answer to this question is implied in the statement that "mechanics be instructed in safety rules that they must follow for their own protection." If the mechanics must be instructed, then we can infer that accidents may occur if they have not been instructed (that is, if they are ignorant of the rules).

20. **The correct answer is (C).** Keeping individuals and groups of individuals working effectively is coordinating the activities of employees. This answer choice is stated in the passage. The other choices require more interpretation. Introduction of large-scale production methods and increasing distribution of products may very well increase profits, but not necessarily.

21. **The correct answer is (D).** There is nothing in the passage to support answer choices (A), (B), or (C); only choice (D) summarizes the data given in the passage.

22. **The correct answer is (A).** There is nothing in the passage to support answer choices (B), (C), or (D). Choice (A) is supported by the excerpt "no crime is considered to occur unless there is a written law forbidding the act" at the beginning of the sentence.

23. **The correct answer is (C).** There is nothing in the passage to support answer choices (A), (B), or (D). Choice (C) is supported by this section: "Only one measure . . . is the

rate at which replacements must be made in order to maintain the work force."

24. **The correct answer is (C).** There is nothing in the passage to support answer choices (A), (B), or (D). Choice (C) summarizes the ideas expressed in the quotation.

25. **The correct answer is (A).** There is nothing in the passage to support answer choices (B), (C), or (D). Choice (A) is clearly implied from the ideas expressed in the passage.

26. **The correct answer is (B).** There is nothing in the quotation to support choices (A), (C), or (D). Choice (B) is supported by ". . . the manufacturer assumes enormous risks in attempting to predict what consumers will want and in providing goods in quantity and distributing them in advance of final selection by the consumers."

27. **The correct answer is (C).** According to the quotation, citizens who are selfish and act only as their private interests seem to require are not public spirited. Those who disregard others are concerned principally with their own selfish interests. Choice (C) is therefore the correct answer.

Test 3: Mechanical Comprehension Test

1. C	7. A	13. C	19. C	25. C
2. A	8. B	14. C	20. B	26. C
3. A	9. C	15. B	21. A	27. A
4. C	10. C	16. B	22. C	28. C
5. C	11. C	17. C	23. C	29. A
6. A	12. B	18. A	24. B	30. B

1. **The correct answer is (C).** The volume of water flowing at points 1, 2, and 3 must be the same because of the conservation of mass: mass in = mass out. Also, since no water is added or removed after point 1, there cannot be any change of volume.

2. **The correct answer is (A).** If nut A were removed, it would be necessary to move nut C to the right to counterbalance the loss of the weight of nut A.

3. **The correct answer is (A).** No electricity flows through a burned-out bulb. However, the voltmeter acts as a bypass around the burned-out bulb and is therefore connected in series. It measures all of the voltage in the circuit. The voltage is 600 volts.

4. **The correct answer is (C).** The circumference of the wheel is 24″. One complete revolution will raise W2 24″ and lower W1 24″, a difference of 48″.

5. **The correct answer is (C).** The vertical component of the momentum of the ball is zero only at position C.

6. **The correct answer is (A).** Pulley A has the largest circumference. In the arrangement shown, pulley A turns slowest.

7. **The correct answer is (A).** Let x = theoretical distance moved in the opposite direction. $10 \times 150 = x \times 600$; $600x = 1,500$; $x = \dfrac{1,500}{600} = 2\dfrac{1}{2}$ feet.

8. **The correct answer is (B).** Note that with each complete turn of the cam, the setscrew will hit the contact point once.

9. **The correct answer is (C).** The pressure is uniform in the system given. If the main line air gauge reads 150 pounds, the tank air gauge will also read 150 pounds.

10. **The correct answer is (C).** As brace C has the greatest area support, it is the most secure.

11. **The correct answer is (C).** The greater the pressure outside the balloon, the less expansion within the balloon; the less pressure, the greater the expansion.

12. **The correct answer is (B).** When two external gears mesh, they rotate in opposite directions. To avoid this, an idler gear is put between the driver gear and the driven gear.

13. **The correct answer is (C).** The tank would overflow only if water flows through the intake pipe at a faster, not slower, rate. The water in

the tank would remain at a constant level if rate of intake is equal to rate of discharge. The tank cannot empty completely, as the discharge pipe is not located at the tank's bottom.

14. **The correct answer is (C).** If the float in the tank develops a bad leak, it will fill with water and submerge. This will elevate the needle valve causing it to remain in an open position.

15. **The correct answer is (B).** The number of parts of the rope going to and from the movable block indicates a mechanical advantage of 2. Accordingly, a 100-lb. pull can lift, theoretically, a 200-lb. weight.

16. **The correct answer is (B).** Note that 2 revolutions of the worm gear will turn the sector gear 20 degrees. Accordingly, one revolution of the worm gear will turn the sector gear through an angle of 10 degrees.

17. **The correct answer is (C).** Let $x =$ tipping force produced on the edge of the block.
$$80 \times 4 = 1 \times x; x = 320 \text{ lbs.}$$

18. **The correct answer is (A).** Note that with each complete turn of the cam, the contacts come together twice. If the contacts come together 60 times a minute, the cam must be rotating at 30 rpm.

19. **The correct answer is (C).** One complete turn of the drum crank will raise the rope 2′ on the 2′ portion of the drum and 1′ on the 1′ portion of the drum. The net result is vertical movement upward a distance of $1\frac{1}{2}'$.

20. **The correct answer is (B).** The TMA of the pulley system is 2.
$$TMA = \frac{d_e}{d_R}$$
$$2 = \frac{30}{d_R} = 2d_R = 30$$
$$d_R = \frac{30}{2} = 15 \text{ feet}$$

21. **The correct answer is (A).** Pulley 2 is a fixed pulley; pulley 1 is a movable one. Both are of equal diameter. If the rope is pulled a distance equal to the circumference of pulley 2 (one full turn), pulley 1 would move up only half that distance making only a half turn.

22. **The correct answer is (C).** Twice per second = 120 times a minute. With 10 projection rods on the wheel, the wheel must rotate at 12 rpm (120/10 = 12) to make 120 rod contacts per minute.

23. **The correct answer is (C).** Both wheels S and T have the same diameter. However, the driver wheel makes contact with wheel T close to its center and makes contact with wheel S very near its edge. Accordingly, wheel T will rotate at a much faster speed than wheel S.

24. **The correct answer is (B).** A $\frac{1}{4}$ turn is needed to get to the extreme left position and another $\frac{1}{4}$ turn is required to return to the midposition.
$$\frac{1}{4} + \frac{1}{4} = \frac{1}{2}$$

25. **The correct answer is (C).** By increasing the length of the level arm, the effort is increased enabling

the valve to blow off at a higher pressure.

26. **The correct answer is (C).** In case 2, each spring is supporting $2\frac{1}{2}$ pounds ($\frac{1}{2}$ of 5 pounds) and would extend a certain distance. In case 1, each spring is supporting 5 pounds (the full weight) and would extend twice the distance of that for case 2.

27. **The correct answer is (A).** The reading is obtained as follows:

    .2 (on the sleeve scale)
    .025 (on the sleeve scale)
$$\frac{.002}{.227}$$ (on the thimble scale)

28. **The correct answer is (C).** The hand wheel tightens to the left when rotated clockwise since it has a right-handed thread. If the hand wheel is turned 20 revolutions, it moves one inch to the left, pulling the threaded block one inch in the opposite direction (to the right).

29. **The correct answer is (A).** If all three switches are closed to the left, the closed circuit would not include Lamp No. 2.

30. **The correct answer is (B).** If switches No. 1 and No. 2 are closed to the right, and switch No. 3 is closed to the left, the closed circuit would not include Lamp No. 1.

Test 4: Spatial Apperception Test

1. C	6. E	11. A	16. C	21. A
2. A	7. E	12. E	17. D	22. D
3. B	8. B	13. C	18. A	23. C
4. C	9. D	14. B	19. E	24. A
5. D	10. B	15. A	20. B	25. B

1. **The correct answer is (C).**

Straight-and-level; flying up the coastline.

2. **The correct answer is (A).**

Diving; no bank; flying out to sea.

3. **The correct answer is (B).**

Climbing; no bank; flying out to sea.

4. **The correct answer is (C).**

Climbing and banking right; flying out to sea.

5. The correct answer is (D).

Level flight; left bank; flying out to sea.

6. The correct answer is (E).

Straight-and-level; flying down the coastline.

7. The correct answer is (E).

Straight-and-level; heading 45° left of coastline.

8. The correct answer is (B).

Diving; banking left; flying out to sea.

9. The correct answer is (D).

Level flight; right bank; flying out to sea.

10. The correct answer is (B).

Straight-and-level; heading 45° right of coastline.

11. The correct answer is (A).

Climbing; no bank; flying out to sea.

12. The correct answer is (E).

Climbing; no bank; flying down the coastline.

13. The correct answer is (C).

Diving; no bank; flying down the coastline.

14. The correct answer is (B).

Straight-and-level; flying out to sea.

15. The correct answer is (A).

Level flight; right bank; flying up the coastline.

16. The correct answer is (C).

Climbing and banking left; flying out to sea.

17. The correct answer is (D).

Diving and banking right; flying out to sea.

18. The correct answer is (A).

Level flight; right bank; flying up the coastline.

19. The correct answer is (E).

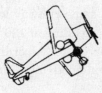

Climbing and banking left; flying out to sea.

20. The correct answer is (B).

Level flight; right bank; flying down the coastline.

21. The correct answer is (A).

Climbing; no bank; flying up the coastline.

22. The correct answer is (D).

Diving; no bank; flying out to sea.

23. The correct answer is (C).

Straight-and-level; flying up the coastline.

24. The correct answer is (A).

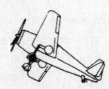

Climbing and banking right; flying out to sea.

answers practice test 3

25. The correct answer is (B).

Level flight; left bank; flying down
the coastline.

Test 5: Aviation and Nautical Information

1. E	7. E	13. D	19. C	25. D
2. E	8. A	14. A	20. E	26. E
3. A	9. A	15. C	21. B	27. E
4. D	10. C	16. C	22. C	28. A
5. A	11. A	17. C	23. A	29. D
6. A	12. B	18. B	24. A	30. A

1. The correct answer is (E). Note the sweptback wings.

2. The correct answer is (E). The maximum distance from wing tip to wing tip is called the wing span.

3. The correct answer is (A). Ailerons are used to bank the airplane.

4. The correct answer is (D). The rudder is used by the pilot to control the direction of yaw about the airplane's vertical axis.

5. The correct answer is (A). Drag is the resistance created by air particles striking and flowing around the airplane when it is moving through the air.

6. The correct answer is (A). The angle at which the wing meets the relative wind is called the angle of attack.

7. The correct answer is (E). In a steady flight condition, the forces that oppose each other are also equal to each other. Lift equals weight; thrust equals drag.

8. The correct answer is (A). Hard-surfaced runways are numbered by their magnetic headings. Runway 22 means a magnetic heading of 220° when taking off or landing. The opposite direction of the same runway would have a magnetic heading of approximately 40° and would be numbered 4.

9. The correct answer is (A). Runway 36 means a magnetic heading of 360°. The opposite direction of the same runway would have a magnetic heading of 180° and would be numbered 18. Accordingly, the runway is aligned in a North-South direction.

10. **The correct answer is (C).** The hand signals shown here are:
    (A) Come ahead
    (B) Slow down
    (C) Emergency stop
    (D) All clear
    (E) Insert chocks

11. **The correct answer is (A).** The space vehicle Apollo 11 carried Neil A. Armstrong, Edwin E. Aldrin Jr., and Michael Collins, who landed on the moon in 1969.

12. **The correct answer is (B).** The force of gravity on the surface of the moon is $\frac{1}{6}$ the force of gravity on the surface of the earth. Although the mass remains the same, the weight would be about 10 kilograms on the moon.

13. **The correct answer is (D).** Because the rocket carries its own oxidizer, it is able to travel into outer space where there is no oxygen.

14. **The correct answer is (A).** A higher landing speed is an important performance deficiency of an overloaded airplane. The other options are not deficiencies but desirable performance characteristics.

15. **The correct answer is (C).** During takeoff, a headwind will shorten the takeoff run and increase the angle of climb. A tailwind during takeoff will increase the takeoff run and decrease the angle of climb.

16. **The correct answer is (C).** The outer walls of a ship form the hull, the main body of the ship below the main outside deck.

17. **The correct answer is (C).** A ship's windlass is designed primarily for handling anchor chain.

18. **The correct answer is (B).** A nautical mile is equal to 1,852 meters, just a little more than 6,076 feet.

19. **The correct answer is (C).** Position is generally expressed in terms of the coordinates latitude and longitude.

20. **The correct answer is (E).** The 24-hour clock uses four digits. Hours and minutes less than 10 are preceded by a zero. 9:05 p.m. would be written as 2105.

21. **The correct answer is (B).** They are generally 15° in width. $\frac{360}{15} = 24$ time zones.

22. **The correct answer is (C).** The coordinates given indicate a position in the Gulf of Mexico.

23. **The correct answer is (A).** A line drawn from the fix in the direction in which a ship is moving is called a course line, showing direction or course.

24. **The correct answer is (A).** Soundings are used to measure depth of water by using a lead line or other means.

25. **The correct answer is (D).** Increasing the weight of the load raises the waterline, decreasing the freeboard and increasing the draft.

26. **The correct answer is (E).** Objects not established for the sole purpose of assisting a navigator in fixing a

position are not considered to be an "aid to navigation."

27. The correct answer is (E). Fog generally forms at night when warmer air moves over colder water.

28. The correct answer is (A). Red is for port; green is starboard; white indicates in which direction a vessel is going; yellow is for special circumstances.

29. The correct answer is (D). The nun buoy is a conical-shaped buoy

used to mark the right-hand side of a channel.

30. The correct answer is (A). The heading of the ship causes water to push against the side of the rudder, creating a force that swings the stern of the ship to the opposite side. The faster the vessel is moving, the greater the pressure against the rudder and the quicker the turning effect.

Test 6: Aviation Supplemental Test

1. A	8. A	15. B	22. B	29. E
2. B	9. B	16. C	23. C	30. C
3. A	10. C	17. C	24. B	31. B
4. B	11. A	18. D	25. C	32. D
5. A	12. C	19. A	26. D	33. E
6. D	13. D	20. B	27. D	34. A
7. C	14. C	21. A	28. E	

1. The correct answer is (A). $0.1 \times 0.1 = 0.01$. Since $1 \times 1 = 1$, for 0.1×0.1, just move the decimal point two places to the left and you have 0.01.

2. The correct answer is (B). You use $2\frac{1}{4}$ quarts of ginger ale to make the whole recipe, so to get $\frac{1}{3}$ of that, you multiply $2\frac{1}{4}$ by $\frac{1}{3}$. (The word "of" is your hint that you need to multiply.) You can change the mixed number to an improper fraction: $2\frac{1}{4} = \frac{9}{4} \cdot \frac{9}{4} \times \frac{1}{3} = \frac{9}{12} = \frac{3}{4}$.

3. The correct answer is (A). Multiply 93 and 4 to get the total number of points: 372. Add the total

of the 3 targets $(92 + 98 + 96 = 286)$, and subtract from 372: $372 - 286 = 86$.

4. The correct answer is (B). Vertical angles are congruent, so across from the y, between x and z, you can place y. Supplementary angles are a group of two or more angles that form a straight line and whose measurements equal 180 degrees. The sum of $x + y + z = 180$ degrees because they form a straight line.

5. The correct answer is (A). The word "exceeds" signals "more than," so $2r = \frac{1}{2}t + 5$. Multiply each side by 2 to clear the fraction: $4r = t + 10$. The t must be on the same side as the r to make a relationship between r and t. The correct answer is $4r - t = 10$.

6. **The correct answer is (D).** Notice that the distance covered by Sam is equal to that of Jenna—that is, the distance is constant. Letting x equal Sam's time, you can express Jenna's time as $x - 2$. Substitute these values for time and the values for rate given in the problem into the speed formula for Jenna and Sam.

Formula: rate × time = distance
Sam: $(30)(x) = 30x$
Jenna: $(45)(x - 2) = 45x - 90$

Because the distance is constant, you can equate Sam's distance to Jenna's, and then solve for x:

$30x = 45x - 90$
$15x = 90$
$x = 6$

Sam had traveled 6 hours when Jenna caught up with him. Because Sam left at 11:00 a.m., Jenna caught up with him at 5:00 p.m.

7. **The correct answer is (C).** The ratio of length to width is 3:1. The ratio 6:2 is equivalent, and $6 \times 2 = 12$ (the area). Thus, the perimeter = $(2)(6) + (2)(2) = 16$.

8. **The correct answer is (A).** Pressure is defined as $\dfrac{\text{Force}}{\text{Area}}$. For a given force, 20 lbs, the smaller the area, the greater the pressure produced. The smallest area is at position A and therefore would require the least force to lift the weight.

9. **The correct answer is (B).** There are 8 holes in the circular cross-section of the flanged pipe. All circles

have 360°. Thus, each hole is separated by $\dfrac{360°}{8}$ or 45°.

10. **The correct answer is (C).** To tighten the bolt, you would turn it counterclockwise. To tighten the nut on the bolt, the reverse is true—so you would turn it clockwise.

11. **The correct answer is (A).** A fixed single pulley is actually a first-class level with equal arms. The mechanical advantage, neglecting friction, is 1.

12. **The correct answer is (C).** If the block is moved toward the brick, the moment for a given force exerted will increase (being farther from the force), making it easier to lift; the height will be made smaller, hardly raising the brick when moved to the limit (directly underneath it).

13. **The correct answer is (D).** The passage states that cyclonic air begins in the onset of the process and forms the eye of the storm. Therefore, it can be inferred that cyclonic air movement plays a large role in the creation of a hurricane, choice (D). Choices (A) and (B) may or may not be true. The passage doesn't indicate that winds in a tropical system move in a clockwise direction (choice A), nor does it provide any indication that hurricanes are the most violent natural phenomena (choice B). Choice C is not true for several reasons: Tropical storms often contain eyes, and the passage states that tropical systems develop from low pressure air systems.

14. **The correct answer is (C).** The passage states that "Some metal

clips are covered in rubber to prevent damage to documents caused by rust."

15. The correct answer is (B). The passage states that the dangling string "occupied his mind for the better part of the morning" and that he later got the large ketchup stain on his chest.

16. The correct answer is (C). The passage states that the CNO "will determine the venue for each meeting" and that the meetings "may use video teleconferencing or formal meeting techniques."

17. The correct answer is (C). The passage states that each of the approximately 3 billion DNA components "is arranged in a unique and specific order, dictating each human's physical development," so a different arrangement of a person's DNA would change his or her physical makeup.

18. The correct answer is (D). John Paul Jones is known as the Father of the U.S. Navy.

19. The correct answer is (A). The starboard running light is green.

20. The correct answer is (B). Dumping fuel during an emergency landing helps increase maneuverability by reducing landing weight.

21. The correct answer is (A). Latitude is measured from the equator. It is defined as the angular distance north or south from the equator of a point on the earth's surface, measured on the meridian of the point.

22. The correct answer is (B). Runways are numbered according to their compass direction. A runway number is its heading, rounded off to the nearest 10 degrees, with the last digit dropped from the designation. For example, a runway heading of 143 degrees (southeastward) would be rounded down to 140, and with the last digit dropped, it becomes Runway 14. A runway heading 317 degrees (northwestward) would be rounded up to 320, and with the last digit dropped, it becomes Runway 32. If two runways operate parallel to one another, they are known as left and right (for example, 32L and 32R).

23. The correct answer is (C). The Korean War was the first in which helicopters were widely used.

24. The correct answer is (B). Chuck Yeager was the first person to break the sound barrier; he did so on October 14, 1947. Alan Shepard was the first American in space. Yuri Gagarin was the first Russian cosmonaut in space, and Ed White was the first American to walk in space.

25. The correct answer is (C).

Straight-and-level; heading 45° left of coastline.

26. The correct answer is (D).

Level flight; left bank; flying up the coastline.

27. The correct answer is (D).

Diving and banking left; flying out to sea.

28. The correct answer is (E).

Straight-and-level; heading 45° right of coastline.

29. The correct answer is (E).

Diving and banking right; flying out to sea.

30. The correct answer is (C).

Level flight; right bank; flying out to sea.

31. The correct answer is (B).

Level flight; left bank; flying up the coastline.

32. The correct answer is (D).

Diving; no bank; flying out to sea.

33. The correct answer is (E).

Straight-and-level; flying out to sea.

34. The correct answer is (A).

Level flight; left bank; flying out to sea.

answers practice test 3

NOTES

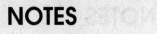

NOTES

NOTES

NOTES

NOTES

Peterson's
Book Satisfaction Survey

Give Us Your Feedback

Thank you for choosing Peterson's as your source for personalized solutions for your education and career achievement. Please take a few minutes to answer the following questions. Your answers will go a long way in helping us to produce the most user-friendly and comprehensive resources to meet your individual needs.

When completed, please tear out this page and mail it to us at:

Publishing Department
Peterson's, a Nelnet company
2000 Lenox Drive
Lawrenceville, NJ 08648

You can also complete this survey online at **www.petersons.com/booksurvey.**

1. **What is the ISBN of the book you have purchased? (The ISBN can be found on the book's back cover in the lower right-hand corner.)** _____

2. **Where did you purchase this book?**
   ❑ Retailer, such as Barnes & Noble
   ❑ Online reseller, such as Amazon.com
   ❑ Petersons.com
   ❑ Other (please specify) _____

3. **If you purchased this book on Petersons.com, please rate the following aspects of your online purchasing experience on a scale of 4 to 1 (4 = Excellent and 1 = Poor).**

	4	3	2	1
Comprehensiveness of Peterson's Online Bookstore page	❑	❑	❑	❑
Overall online customer experience	❑	❑	❑	❑

4. **Which category best describes you?**

   ❑ High school student
   ❑ Parent of high school student
   ❑ College student
   ❑ Graduate/professional student
   ❑ Returning adult student

   ❑ Teacher
   ❑ Counselor
   ❑ Working professional/military
   ❑ Other (please specify) _____

5. **Rate your overall satisfaction with this book.**

Extremely Satisfied	Satisfied	Not Satisfied
❑	❑	❑

6. Rate each of the following aspects of this book on a scale of 4 to 1 (4 = Excellent and 1 = Poor).

	4	3	2	1
Comprehensiveness of the information	❏	❏	❏	❏
Accuracy of the information	❏	❏	❏	❏
Usability	❏	❏	❏	❏
Cover design	❏	❏	❏	❏
Book layout	❏	❏	❏	❏
Special features (e.g., CD, flashcards, charts, etc.)	❏	❏	❏	❏
Value for the money	❏	❏	❏	❏

7. This book was recommended by:
- ❏ Guidance counselor
- ❏ Parent/guardian
- ❏ Family member/relative
- ❏ Friend
- ❏ Teacher
- ❏ Not recommended by anyone—I found the book on my own
- ❏ Other (please specify) _____

8. Would you recommend this book to others?

Yes	Not Sure	No
❏	❏	❏

9. Please provide any additional comments.

_____

_____

_____

_____

_____

Remember, you can tear out this page and mail it to us at:

Publishing Department
Peterson's, a Nelnet company
2000 Lenox Drive
Lawrenceville, NJ 08648

or you can complete the survey online at **www.petersons.com/booksurvey.**

Your feedback is important to us at Peterson's, and we thank you for your time!

If you would like us to keep in touch with you about new products and services, please include your e-mail address here: _____